NIGHT FIGHTER

by

WING COMMANDER

J. R. D. BRAHAM

D.S.O., D.F.C., A.F.C., C.D.

*Belgian Order of the Crown
and Croix de Guerre*

W · W · NORTON & COMPANY · INC · New York

DEDICATION

To "Sticks" and "Jacko" and the other brave men who during the war and since have entrusted their lives in the air to my care

ILLUSTRATIONS
Between pages 128 and 129

The author's P.O.W. card

Robert Spreckels, the man who shot Braham down

Spreckels flying his Focke-Wulf

Reunion with Spreckels

A.O.C. 432 All-Weather Fighter Squadron at Bagotville, Canada

The author and members of 432 R.C.A.F. Squadron

FOREWORD

by

Air Chief Marshal Sir Basil Embry,
G.C.B., K.B.E., D.S.O., D.F.C., A.F.C.,
R.A.F. *(Retd.)*

How right Bob Braham is when he says that his and Johnnie Johnson's combat records cannot be compared. The one fought mostly by night and was a great individualist; the other mainly by day and was a born Wing Leader. Whereas the number of victories in combat was undoubtedly a measure of individual success, both would agree that it was their personal overall contributions to the war in the air which was the most important factor of all.

Of Braham, about whom these few lines are written, I have never met anyone to surpass his sheer aggressive fighting spirit and one who was more determined to come to grips with the enemy in the air. He dedicated himself body and soul to this mission from the first day of the war to the moment he was shot down in June, 1944. Nothing was allowed to stand in the way of the fulfilment of this duty. Fatigue and operational strain were brushed aside and even the attractions of family life were subordinated to the grim business of war.

The relentless determination to get at the enemy, coupled with tremendous courage, vitality, skill and operational experience made him a dangerous and formidable opponent to meet in the air by the end of 1943. How fortunate for us, and Bomber Command in particular, that he was born of British and not Teutonic stock.

9

By the end of 1943, he showed all the signs of operational fatigue and should not really have been allowed to fly any more against the enemy. But his experience was wanted to help devise the tactics for night interdiction in support of land forces and this entailed a certain amount of operational flying. What he could give to the Allied cause in this field had to be weighed against the unfairness and effect of over-flying this willing and very gallant young officer. I must take responsibility for the decision. It must also be remembered that operational flying had been his occupation since the age of nineteen and it was so much in his system that it acted on him like a drug. To deny him of it at a time when victory was in sight might have damaged his spirit irrevocably. His natural ambition was to be in at the kill.

This book is an honest story, simply told, of the day-to-day life of one of the greatest fighting airmen of our time. If it reveals some cynicism towards life, manifest in an attitude of "make merry today, because tomorrow we die", who among those who did not share their dangers, dare criticize?

Bob Braham stands out in the forefront of that band of airmen who did so much to preserve the civilization of the world against the forces of evil.

The effect which the strain of war and hazardous operational flying had on his nervous system is revealed in his post-war difficulties of settling down to peace routine. That is the price of war no government or country can repay. But let those who now live in freedom never forget that it was won by the sacrifice of Bob Braham and men of his kind.

15 May, 1961   BASIL EMBRY

INTRODUCTION

by Robert Spreckels

Ace German fighter-pilot of the Second World War

THAT day, June 25, 1944, when I shot down Wing Commander Bob Braham in air combat over Denmark, was to change my life profoundly and particularly my attitude to war.

I was then a keen young German fighter-pilot who, like Braham at the time, had only one consuming aim in life—to destroy the enemy.

Today I am proud to call Bob Braham my friend and I was delighted and honoured when he asked me to write a brief foreword to his book.

How this transition from enemy to friend took place makes a strange story. During the evening of that June day nearly seventeen years ago, I was celebrating my victory with my comrades. Braham's was the third Mosquito I had shot down and he had given me a hard fight. Mosquitoes were seldom destroyed by our day-fighters because of their speed and their clever manœuvres. I was surprised in the midst of the celebration to be called to the phone and to be told that our General wished to congratulate me. The reason for this unusual jubilation, I was told, was that I had shot down one of the most famous of all British night-fighter aces. Of course we had all heard of the exploits of Bob Braham. I suddenly had a strong impulse to meet my formidable opponent face to face and I asked if it was possible. The result was that we met a few days later at the interrogation camp at Oberursel, near Frankfurt. A disturbing turmoil of feelings possessed my mind—

and no doubt his—as we first shook hands. The cruelty and horror of war faded away and I seemed to be looking at an old friend. I instinctively admired a man who was obviously what we should call "a devil of a fellow". He had just escaped death as if by a miracle and I found myself deeply thankful that he had survived.

At that time, of course, he could not speak frankly. But as we sat opposite to each other at a table I felt the comradeship of an old friend rather than a foe. What he said to me about the course of the war which was then beginning its last and most terrible phase for us made a deep impression on me.

I had grown up under Hitler and, like all my generation, my mind was completely imprisoned by the propaganda to which we had been subjected. For the first time Braham opened my eyes to a different world from that which I had hitherto believed to be the only right and good one.

Braham knew that Germany could not win the war. I was only just beginning to realize what a hopeless position my country was in. At the end of the conversation he said he hoped I would survive and I was sure the wish came from his heart. Then he said he would buy me a glass of whisky when first we met after it was over. Neither of us could have believed then that this meeting was likely.

My meetings with Braham in 1944 set me thinking that, perhaps, if comradeship such as ours could suddenly blossom between foes in wartime, war itself could be averted for ever if such human relationships could be developed between nations. I survived the war only by a succession of almost incredible escapes. I was shot down four times and if the last crash near Aachen on January 1, 1945, had not kept me in hospital for a long time, I doubt if I should ever have seen Bob Braham again. This was the worst time of all for our fighter pilots.

We know now how the war went on until German towns and industries were almost totally destroyed. Then came the dreadfully hard times of transition from dictatorship to democracy. My flying career ended for ever and I returned to my old firm of ship-owners in Hamburg. Of their fleet of fifty seagoing vessels not one was left.

I tried at once to trace Bob Braham but I received no reply to letters and had to give up the attempt. It was not until 1956, when I went on a business trip to England, that I heard he had survived the war. I resumed my efforts to trace him and at last came the great moment when I had a letter from him in Canada. After that we wrote regularly. We both remembered the glass of whisky Braham owed me and finally a meeting was arranged after he had been posted to Paris by the Royal Canadian Air Force to the staff of S.H.A.P.E.

It was a wonderful and moving experience to meet again—this time in civilian clothes, and both of us with our families around us. Our rendezvous was at a rest-house on the autobahn near Hamburg. Braham had not changed much. He looked the same fine fellow I had first met as a prisoner of war. It seemed incredible that we had once been dedicated to killing each other.

Yes, we enjoyed that whisky—and plenty more to follow. We know now that we are friends for life and that our wives and children will be friends too. I hope this story of comradeship which survived so many dangers and difficulties will be an example to young people in every land.

Hamburg, Germany   ROBERT SPRECKELS
1961

I

THIS is a story of war in the air, of ruthless personal combat, man against man, machine against machine and man against death; the most exciting, dangerous and highly skilled form of duelling ever devised.

It is also the story of a whole generation of young men of many nationalities, most of them fresh from school or university, who fought it out in the sky over Britain and Europe between September, 1939, and the Allied victory in 1945. There is gallantry in this story by friend and foe. There is sacrifice, too, of the many young men who died for what they believed to be right. Those of us who then defended Britain lived a strange, unnatural life in a besieged fortress. We were front-line fighters, out day after day or night after night to destroy the enemy. Yet when we came back hot from battle for a few hours of rest we tried to live a near-normal, social, civilized life among a civilian population, often in quiet villages and small towns, which war had not hit and where life remained calm. Many of us came back to wife and children and our own home as, for long periods, I did. We drank with the locals in English pubs an hour, perhaps, after a fantastic escape or a hazardous victory. Who will blame us if we often drank too much to release our tension?

Above all, this is the story of wonderful comradeship, loyalty and devotion. These were the things that gave us the heart and the will to go on fighting until we won.

★　　★　　★

June 25, 1944, was a fine day and the invasion of Europe had been in progress for nearly three weeks. The Allies were consolidating their initial gains, but not making much progress because of bitter resistance by the Germans, particularly against the British and Canadians where the bulk of the powerful Panzer divisions were massed. However, for Don Walsh, my new Aussie navigator, and me, this day will be remembered as long as we live. We set out to destroy my thirtieth enemy aircraft. Instead we became "guests" of the Germans for nearly a year.

We took off from Gravesend in a Mosquito fighter-bomber, borrowed from the obliging "Daddy" Dale, Commander of 21 Squadron, and landed at West Raynham, Norfolk, to re-fuel for a long-range intruder mission to the area of Barth on the Baltic German coast. The object of this freelance flight was to destroy German aircraft in the air or on the ground and to shoot up any transport movements we might see on the roads or railways.

To operate inside enemy territory in daylight surprise was essential. The route would have to be well planned to dodge enemy radar, flak and airfields, from which we might encounter his single-seat Messerschmitt 109s and Focke-Wulf 190s. A single Mosquito, despite its excellent qualities, was no match for determined formations of these highly-manœuvrable fighters. The most important requisite for such a mission as ours was cloud cover over enemy territory and the sea approaches.

While at West Raynham, ground personnel topped up our fuel and checked the formidable fixed forward-firing armament of four 20-mm. cannons and four 303 machine guns. Don and I went to the office of the Station Intelligence Officer, Buster Reynolds, an old friend, about whom there is more later in this book. Buster briefed us on the enemy radar network, flak and fighter dispositions in Denmark and Northern Germany. We planned to cross the Jutland coast just north of

16

Esbjerg, where a lighthouse provided a landmark; then, by a series of changes of course, to confuse the enemy, to another point about ten miles south of Copenhagen, and from there over the Baltic Sea to Barth in Northern Germany. Our enterprise required very low flying over sea and land to make it as difficult as possible for the German radar chain and observer corps to follow us.

This was not the first time I had flown over Denmark on similar missions, but the very latest information was essential if our mission was to be successful. Our main worry was the two enemy fighter fields at Alborg near the northern tip of Jutland and at Husum just below the German-Danish border. Indications were that there were several Messerschmitts and Focke-Wulfs at these bases. If they were alerted to our presence over Denmark things would be difficult. So we changed our route to the target area slightly and worked out a completely different route for the trip back. The Met Officer wasn't optimistic that we would have the sort of cloud conditions we wanted over the whole of our route, but we felt that there was just a chance. Perhaps his uncertainty should have been a warning to us, but our eagerness to have a go overcame any qualms.

We little realized that the uncertain weather, coupled with a number of mistakes I was to make, was to cost us our freedom and almost our lives. Cheerfully we ate lunch in the officers' mess with comrades from 141 Squadron, which I had commanded a year before. In the early afternoon Don and I clambered up the ladder into the chummy side-by-side seats of our fully-loaded aircraft and waved farewell. We were full of confidence. A minute or so later, with the engines roaring evenly, we were on our way to our landfall on the Danish coast. At 240 m.p.h. I flew the Mosquito at nought feet over the rich green Norfolk countryside. In less than fifteen minutes we crossed the coast near Cromer and dropped to within twenty-five feet or so of the North Sea, our props at times throwing

17

up a light spray. All this was no bravado, for the lower we stayed the less chance the German radar would have of picking us up. If we were as lucky as on previous occasions we might achieve complete surprise. This sort of flying was very tiring and required complete concentration. A slight error would put us down with King Neptune.

Don was checking his charts and instruments to ensure that we should fly over the enemy coast at the right place. As we had some 300 miles of North Sea to cross this was no easy task. It would be over an hour before we saw the Danish coastline, so he had time to concentrate.

This part of the flight was always the worst. One had time to think—too much time. I knew from experience that I was afraid and that I wouldn't regain my confidence until we reached enemy territory. It had always been that way; somehow my worries invariably disappeared once we were over the enemy's coast.

The engines sounded sweet and, at the moment at any rate, it looked as if the weather was just what the doctor ordered. Cloud completely covered the sky at about 2,000 to 3,000 feet and visibility was excellent. Soon we became more alert, searching ahead for a glimpse of the coastline and scanning the sky for lurking enemy fighters. Don's navigation was perfect. We should be there in about ten minutes. Now I was leaning forward, straining to pick up the distant coastline. "There it is, a thin pencil-line on the horizon. That tower must be the lighthouse. Bang on." Don checked the position of the landmark on his maps and we changed course slightly to make an exact landfall. At that moment, with the coast still some miles ahead, I saw two ships, German destroyers or torpedo boats. "Damn it." They couldn't help but see us, and would pass warnings to the coast defence units and the Luftwaffe. I changed course to the right in the hope that they might not see us, but we were out of luck. Both ships started to zigzag and increase speed as we could easily see by their wake. So instead of going in north of Esbjerg, we went in some miles south. We could both detect a slight whine over our radio receivers which we knew was interference from some German ground radar unit searching the ether to pick us up. Momentarily I thought about attacking the two ships, but as we had no bombs it seemed pointless. So we continued on over the coast, climbing slightly to cross the sand-dunes.

Ahead of us lay the fertile, flat, Danish countryside, and as we weaved our way low over the fields and hedgerows, Don and I rapidly debated whether to call the mission off. There was now no doubt that we had lost the vital element of surprise, so the cards were stacked heavily against us. Then we noted that the whine in the radios had ceased. "They've lost us. All they know is that we are somewhere inland, and it will be like looking for a needle in a haystack to find us now. What do you say, Don? Shall we carry on?"

"O.K., let's keep going." Unfortunately we hadn't allowed for the enemy's efficient ground observer service which was at that moment phoning in our progress to the Luftwaffe air defence headquarters in Denmark.

We were now committed and there was no turning back. If I had been worried, this state of mind soon left me. In spite of the ill-omens we both still felt confident of success. It didn't perturb us even when, as we crossed eastwards out over Jutland skirting the northern edge of Fyn Island, we were fired on by several small ships. This should have been an indication to both of us that the enemy was very much on the alert. Further, the weather to the east and south seemed to be clearing and our cloud sanctuary was disappearing. Just then Don spotted the radio masts of Kalundborg on the western edge of Sjaeland, the largest of the Danish islands on which lies the capital city of Copenhagen. Many was the time at home before the war that I had tuned my parents' radio to Radio Kalundborg, little thinking that one day I would be seeing it from an aircraft on a warlike mission. We were still on course, hoping that our periodic change of heading by thirty or so degrees (doglegging) would throw the Germans off our scent.

At last, in the distance we could make out the green towers of Roskilde Cathedral, at which point we turned south across Moen Island and so over the Baltic Sea. By now there wasn't a cloud in the sky and again we detected the whine over our wireless. There was little doubt that the Huns again knew just where we were, and at this late stage apprehension hit us both. With the north German coast looming up menacingly in the distance we decided to call it a day and turned to start heading back home.

As we skimmed over the waters of the Baltic, Don quickly gave me a rough course to take us back over Fyn Island and so home. There was cloud to the north and west and although the base appeared to be considerably higher than 2,000 feet, conditions there looked the most favourable. We decided that it would be wisest to fly out over the coast of Jutland at just about the spot where we entered. The faint whine over our receivers was now nearly continuous, so I kept reminding Don to look to the rear and watch for German fighters. I scanned the country ahead, keeping close to the hedges and fields and unintentionally frightening Danish civilians and their cattle. This was the only way to keep out of sight of, or at least make it difficult for, enemy fighters. Don was constantly giving me small corrections of course.

We were about half-way across Fyn Island when we saw a large house which had once been a private mansion. It was now flying a large Swastika flag from its roof. Just turning out of the driveway on to a secondary road was a car. By the time we had taken all this in we had roared over it at 240 m.p.h. I was convinced that it must be a staff car so I pulled the Mossie up and around in a screaming turn till we were at about 500 feet. At least we would stop whoever was driving in this vehicle. It might even be some important Nazi official, or, better still, some Gestapo swine. Quickly switching on the electric gun-sight, I eased the stick slightly forward, putting the aircraft into a shallow 260-m.p.h. dive. Ahead at about 800 yards was the car. Maybe the occupants thought we were German flyers making a friendly low pass. At 500 yards with the car now in my reflector sight I pressed the trigger on the control column. The Mossie bucked a little and the cockpit filled with cordite fumes as streams of shells and bullets poured from our guns. At first the shots threw up dirt from the ditch at the side of the road alongside the car and then the vehicle was smothered with armour-piercing and explosive shells and bullets. I nearly flew into the ground in my concentration at firing, but Don yelled "Pull up" over the intercom, and I yanked back on the stick just in time to clear some small trees. Out of the corner of my eye I saw the car crash into the ditch belching smoke. "That fixed the bastard," was Don's remark. In our excitement we had nearly forgotten our own position, but almost immediately we realized that this little bit of violence would certainly pinpoint us. So we didn't tarry to gloat over our work, but continued on, more alert than ever.

"We shall be at Ringköbing Fiord in twenty minutes." Don's information was encouraging, as this was the place on the West Jutland coast over which we wished to cross out. Once over the North Sea we could relax. German fighters would not have the range to follow us far.

Perhaps our minor, one-sided action had made me over-confident. The cloud cover looked good though it was a little higher than desirable, nobody was shooting at us now and no unfriendly aircraft were in sight. In fact everything was too easy and we were nearly clear of enemy-occupied territory. On we flew over the lovely, peaceful, Danish countryside until at last I could make out the narrow fiord with a thin strip of sand-dunes separating it from the greyness of the North Sea.

It was passing through my mind what an uneventful trip it had been. Next time we would plan a similar one to Norway, where the pickings should be good. My daydream was quickly ended by an urgent, "Two fighters coming in astern." "Damn it. How far off, Don?" Before he answered I saw by a quick look over my shoulder that they were about a mile away, and coming in fast. I was so close to the ground that I couldn't dive to pick up speed rapidly, so I rammed the throttles right forward and we had to wait a few precious seconds for the aircraft to accelerate. Why I was only cruising out at 240 m.p.h. I don't know. We should have been leaving hostile territory flat out at nearly 300 m.p.h., and as our top speed was similar to that of the FW 190 and the Me 109, it is doubtful whether either could have caught us. Don was now on his knees facing aft having loosened his safety-straps. In this way he could keep me exactly informed of the range and relative position of the enemy, which we confirmed as two FW 190s. As soon as we reached 280 m.p.h. I hauled hard back on the stick, pointing the Mossie nearly vertically towards the clouds, knowing well that unless I could escape into this wispy cover our chances would be slim. It would have been a different story if there had been only one fighter; we could probably have held our own as I had managed to do in the past. Two were a different matter. It was only a matter of time before one of them set us up in position for the second fighter to get in a killing burst.

The two FWs had now spread out, one being about 400-yards ahead of the other. "Look out, Bob, the bastard is just about in range." The Mossie was gradually losing speed in its near vertical climb, and still our cloud sanctuary was a good 2,000 feet above us, much higher than I had thought. Quickly I straightened out of the climb and at the same time put on hard left bank, pulling the control column into my stomach.

Things started to go grey as the forces of gravity forced the blood from my head down into my legs. Momentarily I had saved us because the Hun couldn't follow us in the tight turn. As soon as he broke I switched into a turn in the opposite direction, by which time this particular FW had pulled up into a stalled turn and was coming at me head on. We were now at 2,000 feet above the Jutland coast, but in my concentration I had forgotten about the second fighter. This was the sort of error that one was always warning new pilots about, and yet here I was, with four years' combat experience, making the same mistake. The first FW was closing fast and suddenly I saw the wicked winking flashes from his nose and wings as he opened up with his cannons and machine guns. It looked as though he couldn't miss, but in my amazement at not being hit I forgot to press my own trigger, even when for a brief moment he filled my sights. It was too late now. I knew then, I believe, that we had had it because of the urgency in Don's voice and the sight out of the corner of my eye of the rapidly closing second Focke-Wulf coming in from below on my right. Desperately I turned in to him, pulling up at the same time to make his shooting more difficult, but it was too late. In my violent manœuvring I had stalled the Mossie, and as my starboard wing dropped, the aircraft shuddered under the impact of his large 30-mm. shells and bullets. He was so close that the whole nose of the FW seemed to be afire as his guns blasted away. My mouth went dry. The port engine and wing caught fire, and at any minute I expected to be blasted to oblivion. As the nose dropped we seemed to be diving vertically towards the North Sea, and at that moment the instrument and glass side panels of the cockpit disintegrated under another burst of fire. I shall never know why his bullets didn't find a billet in Don or me.

I remember saying to Don, "Well, we've had it." I couldn't see how we could possibly pull out of the dive in time before we crashed. Even though I thought we were going to die I was no longer afraid. I just felt worried as to what would happen to my family, for at that fleeting moment they were uppermost in my thoughts. Perhaps this galvanized me into trying to save us, so I pulled back hard on the control column, and by some miracle the aircraft responded and started to come out of its death-dive. But only just. We levelled out just above the water, flying parallel to the coast and only about 200 yards from the shore. As I switched off the port engine I told Don to feather the propeller to cut down the amount of drag from slowly revolving unstreamlined blades. In his excitement he started to press the wrong feathering button and nearly stopped our good engine. Luckily I saw it in time and knocked his hand away and feathered the correct one. At the same time I operated the built-in fire extinguisher to the port engine in the hope of putting the fire out. But it had got too good a hold. In these few seconds I found that we still had some control and were keeping about 100 feet above the shore. Then Don called, "Here they come again," and over my shoulder I saw the enemy closing in from above and behind for the kill. Again there was the rending noise as more shells crashed into the good old Mossie. "Jettison the top hatch. I am going to crash-land on the beach," I shouted. I knew there was no escape in the air and our only chance of survival was to pancake on the sandy shore, with the hope that our badly-crippled aircraft wouldn't explode when we hit.

I throttled back the good engine as Don let go the top hatch which whipped back in the slipstream over our tail. I even half-heartedly hoped it would clobber one of our pursuers, but no such luck. Our speed gradually fell as we held off for a belly-landing and at about twenty-five feet up both fighters flew over the top of us. For a second I had the chance of getting in one quick shot in revenge. I only had to ease the stick back ever so slightly and press the firing button, but I was so engrossed in landing on the rough, sandy shore that this slipped my mind. It was a forlorn hope anyway. With a crash which threw both of us violently against our safety-straps we hit, bounced up into the air, then hit again at 150 m.p.h. I hadn't dared lower the wheels as the aircraft would most certainly have flipped over on to its back when the wheels sank into the soft sand. But with them still tucked up we slid rapidly to a stop. One wing was just in the water and the rest of the plane was on the beach. Regardless of the cuts and bruises we had suffered Don kicked his way through the side entrance while I went out through the top hatch.

I think we broke all records vacating our fiercely-burning aeroplane. At any moment I expected it to explode, so we both started to run up the beach to the shelter of the dunes. This was hard going as the sand was soft. After about twenty paces we gave up and stopped for a breather. Looking up we saw both Focke-Wulfs peel off and start to dive towards us. This was it. I was convinced they were going to strafe us. There was no shelter and we couldn't run. We just stood still and hoped. As they roared over us at twenty or so feet the leader, whose helmeted head I could clearly see, waved. I waved back, and as they winged away to their base I thought what chivalrous foes they had been. The drone of their engines receded and everything became quiet except for the crackling of flames as the wreckage of our plane was consumed. "God, it's a hell of a long way home." I don't know what I expected Don to reply to this obvious statement, but suddenly as shock set in I felt terribly lonely. It would be a long time, whatever happened, before I saw my family again, and, of course, there was always the grim possibility that I wouldn't. Don was silent and, like myself, dazed by the crash and our escape from death, but I am sure similar thoughts were running through his mind. Poor old Don. This was only his second trip with me, although he had completed a very successful tour as a navigator in Mitchells. He had only been married a few months and as he was older than me—a ripe old thirty-eight—this probably hit him harder.

We saw that we had landed on the sandstrip separating Ringköbing Fiord from the North Sea. Our immediate problem was to try to hide until dark. We had been in the air for nearly four hours. It was now late afternoon. As we climbed up into the sand-dunes I remember thinking that it was tea-time at home.

If we could hang on till dark perhaps we could get help from some friendly Dane and with his aid make our way to Sweden and then home. We reached a point high enough in the dunes to get a good view and to afford some cover. We had some maps with us which for some reason we had grabbed when we crashed, and as they mustn't fall into German hands we buried them. We also buried our Mae Wests, but I decided to keep my Luger pistol which was a trophy an intelligence officer had obtained for me from a German prisoner shot down over England. I felt it might be useful as a persuader, in case some Dane decided to be awkward.

Taking in our surroundings we became calmer and even a little confident of escaping. We noticed a house on a narrow road close to the inland edge of the fiord. It seemed deserted. Perhaps we could hide there till nightfall. Suddenly, about a mile away, I noticed a large camouflaged edifice which we at once recognized as a German radar station. I had flown over this area several times before but had never seen it because of its excellent camouflage. Troops from this site were probably on their way to round us up, I thought, and in fact they were, moving towards us in a ragged, open formation. When we saw them they were only 400 yards or so away. Now we could hear guttural commands and then they must have spotted us. Before we could duck out of sight they opened fire with tommy-guns and for the first time in my life I heard bullets whistle, they were so close. Don and I fell back into the bottom of the dune. There was no future in trying to fight it out with one pistol against such odds, so we sat huddled up looking rather undignified and waited as they blundered forward. The first two or three arrived led by an N.C.O. They were Luftwaffe ground personnel. Neither Don nor I could speak German. The N.C.O. started to search us. He soon found my pistol and it was apparent that he wasn't pleased about it. We were shoved along and marched back towards our still burning aircraft. At first I was convinced they were going to shoot us and then push us into the blaze. But the N.C.O. asked, "*Bomben?*" I didn't fully understand but I nodded. I suppose he wanted to know if there were any bombs aboard. He grunted and hurriedly started off with us and the rest of his troop to an observation post close to the radar station. There he pushed us into a smallish room. One of the Germans went out and returned with two cups of their equivalent of coffee. Whatever it was we were grateful. My mouth was still as dry as a bone. As I sipped the hot drink the fact slowly sank into my mind that the war was over for both of us. I felt numb with shock and could hardly face Don because I knew it need not have happened. Experience should have told me to turn back at the start when we were sighted by the German ships. Then later, after I had committed us to the mission, there were the many other mistakes; not staying alert when it was obvious that the whole German air defence system in Denmark was aware of our presence; not flying at top speed on our way out; and lastly my basic error in combat—forgetting the deadly second fighter in my concentration on the first. These were the main mistakes, and there were other minor ones.

Why did a very experienced pilot make these mistakes? I know now, but it took time for it to sink in. Combat fatigue. This became clear to me in my P.O.W. camp as I thought in moments of loneliness and boredom about my varied career in the R.A.F. It included fighting over England in the early days of the war, train strafing over the Brest peninsula, shipping attacks in the Bay of Biscay, flying night-fighters over Europe and Germany to help protect our bombers, night attacks against German troop movements behind the beachhead just after D-Day in Normandy; and day intruding over Denmark, Germany and France. In ten months as a P.O.W. I had plenty of time to think over these things.

2

M Y parents, after spending large sums of money on my
education, hoped that I should adopt one of the more
serious professions, such as the Ministry (father was a
Church of England vicar) or perhaps medicine. Neither of
these callings interested me, so soon after getting the School
Certificate at Taunton, I left school in late 1936 and took a job
as a boy clerk in the Lancashire County Police offices at Wigan.

My object at this stage was to obtain a background of police
work and later to apply for a job in the colonial police force.

After a year or so as a police clerk I became bored and friends
convinced me that the Merchant Navy was the answer. My
father was strongly opposed to this and I believe that it was as a
result of our disagreement that I decided in December, 1937,
"for the hell of it", to apply for a Short Service Commission in
the R.A.F.

Eventually, to my amazement after noting the large number
of keen, fit applicants, I learnt that I was among the relatively
few accepted. A few weeks later I set out for the Elementary
Flying Training School at Desford, near Leicester. This was
one of several such schools, civilian staffed, but sponsored by
the Air Ministry.

Typical of a number of clubs which sprang up at that time,
it was a small grass aerodrome with two or three hangars,
some office buildings, a club-house which served as a mess
for students and staff, and a number of buildings as bachelor
quarters for us students.

My comrades on this initial flying course came from all parts of the Commonwealth, and a happy, carefree bunch we were. I palled up with a boy named David Blomeley and we were allocated quarters together. On March 9 the students were taken down to the flight-line and introduced to our aeroplanes, the delightful little Tiger Moth. There were rows of these aircraft drawn up and waiting to be taken aloft by instructors and pupils. At that moment I was excited and eager to get going. It was a different story thirty minutes later when we landed. After having been subjected to every form of aerobatic manœuvre in the book, it was a very green Braham who lurched out of Tiger Moth G-ADPH. But recovery was rapid, and within a few hours we were up in the blue again. This time things were much more straightforward and gentle. Braham was learning the rudiments of flying.

Just when I thought I was ready to solo my instructor was changed, probably because of my rather slow progress, which I must admit was beginning to worry me. Most of the students had soloed after about eight hours of dual instruction. We were informed that unless we went solo within fifteen hours our training would cease. I drew consolation from the fact that Blomeley was having similar troubles. He had fifteen hours' dual before being considered fit to make a solo flight, but he passed it successfully.

At last, after a flight of half an hour, my instructor climbed out of the back seat and told me, "You've got her. I want you to take off, fly round the circuit and land—any questions?" "No, sir." I was on my own at last after fourteen hours of dual. It was a beautiful day and I felt like flying round for a long time, but at this stage I did not want to blot my copy-book, so I completed the circuit and made a gentle gliding turn for my first landing. Now was the test. The ground was coming up rapidly. My speed and my tail were a little too high, so that I bounced in an alarming fashion. I remembered what my instructors had told me, opened up full throttle and climbed away for another landing. Round I went again, repeating out loud to myself all the things I must remember to do. In this way I quickly regained confidence and on the second attempt made a perfect landing. I taxied slowly up to where my instructor was standing, expecting to get a blast for mucking up my first attempt. Instead he was most pleasant and congratulated me.

The time at Desford now went very rapidly. In the evenings we young bloods became the bane of the pubs in Desford with our ribald sing-songs and wild games. We were not yet in the R.A.F. We wore no uniform and held no rank. Our pay, however, was about on a par with a Pilot Officer in the R.A.F., 11s. 10d. a day. We managed to get rid of it in an alarmingly short time.

Hitler was beginning to put the pressure on at this stage, and we all felt that unless we were lucky the war would start before we were ready to join a squadron, for it would be many months yet before we could complete our training.

At last the day arrived for the final air check at Desford. I was introduced to my instructor for this ordeal, Flight Lieutenant Whitley. He explained what he wanted me to do and off we went together. I was fairly confident of everything except instrument flying, so when he told me to pull the hood over my cockpit I wasn't happy. I soon realized I wasn't doing too well. Then, because I was nervous, I started to make major mistakes. So when Whitley said, "All right, Braham, you can come out from under the hood now," I was certain I had failed, particularly as he said nothing more until we landed. He then took me aside and went over the mistakes I had made. But at last he said, "Well, that's all, but watch your instrument flying. Good luck." I had passed the first step.

Next, after a short leave, we had to report to R.A.F. Uxbridge for two weeks of "square-bashing". At Uxbridge, Blomeley and I were again allotted quarters together, and we

wondered why it was necessary for flyboys to concern themselves with such things as drill. However, we were now in the
R.A.F. and it was our duty during these two weeks to get ourselves fitted out with uniforms. The drill and service lectures
smartened us up and eventually our uniforms arrived and we
were paraded for a final inspection. We thought ourselves the
pride of the R.A.F., but none of us yet had the coveted wings.
Towards the end of May, 1938, we were told to report to an
R.A.F. flying training school. Dave Blomeley and I were to go
to No. 11 F.T.S. which had just opened at Shawbury, near
Shrewsbury.

3

I went home for a short leave and took Dave along. My parents seemed to have got used to the idea that flying was to be my career, so my leave passed pleasantly. Dave showed considerable interest in my sister, which left me free to indulge in my own affairs. Eventually Dave became my brother-in-law.

For the next three months we were to fly Hawker Hart and Audax two-seat, single-engine biplanes. Our instructors would assess us to see if we were suited for fighter, bomber or other types of air force operations. If we passed this course we should win our wings. It was apparent to us all that our careers were now being directed more along military lines, and that we should have to put more effort into our air and ground work if we wished to succeed.

Except for the Flight Commanders, most of our instructors were N.C.O.s. A fine bunch of chaps they were. Most of them had been in the service for many years, having joined as technicians and later remustered as Sergeant Pilots. Again I was a little slow at first. These aeroplanes seemed to be a handful after the Tiger Moth. Dave and I seemed to have the same problems, but once started we progressed well. One effective punishment for bad flying was to be told to wash one of the aircraft with soap and water, a lengthy and tiring job. I had my fair share of this chore.

One day the Flight Commander, Flight Lieutenant Bax, called us together and told us we could elect which arm of the R.A.F. we would prefer to serve in. He pointed out that he couldn't guarantee that we would get what we chose, but our choice would be borne in mind. Most of the students, David included, elected for heavy aircraft—bombers or coastal. The reason for this was a wish to get as much multi-engine aircraft experience as possible during their short-service term in the R.A.F. This experience would be of value to them if they wished to join one of the civil airlines or charter companies at the end of their service. Fighter boys were generally considered too "split" for civil passenger flying. I had no desire to be a civil pilot and still had ideas of joining the colonial police at the end of my term in the R.A.F. Also, I liked aerobatics and the glamour of the single-seat fighter appealed to me, so I elected fighters.

Towards the end of the junior term the students were given some night-flying training. We all thought this was rather hazardous and a little unnecessary because of the very limited aids we had in those days for night flying. Before our night flights a caravan was towed into position at the take-off point along with a "chance light" (a low-powered searchlight to illuminate the touch-down area). This was where the duty instructor for the night was located. In addition, goose-neck flares were laid out along the path to indicate to the pilot the direction for take-off and landing. I soon found I thoroughly enjoyed night flying.

As the junior term approached its end the tempo of work increased. Last-minute studying for our wings examinations tended to limit the number of visits to Shrewsbury. I reckoned I was coping satisfactorily in most subjects, but I should be glad when it was all over. The final drill test stands out in my mind. I was given a squad of student pilots and directed to lead them in arms drill and a march-past in front of the chief ground instructor. Unfortunately, because of wet weather, the test was carried out inside one of the large hangars. In marching my squad into position I suddenly became tongue-tied and forgot to call a halt. My comrades calmly marched into the wall of the hangar. Faithful unto death! I don't believe the drill instructor was impressed with Braham's performance.

I passed my flying test satisfactorily and this time my instrument flying had improved. The test was a short one and the testing officer made no particular comment. Most of us passed successfully and I was awarded my R.A.F. wings, effective from August 20, 1938, four months after my eighteenth birthday. A few days later a full-dress parade was held at which we were formally presented with our wings by the Station Commander, Group Captain Lale. For me it was a turning-point. I felt that now I was in the R.A.F. proper, but I was soon to discover that I still had much to learn.

On return from leave at the end of August, we were gathered together and informed as to our future. Although most of the course had elected bombers or other heavy-type aircraft and only four of us chose fighters, it was decided that our course had to produce fifteen fighter pilots. This was due to the rising tension in Europe and the approaching Munich crisis. The R.A.F. wanted to build up its fighter defence as rapidly as possible. I was pleased by my selection. Some of the others, who had wanted heavy-aircraft training, were disappointed. Each of us was given a refresher dual trip in the Hawker Hart and then, after verbal instruction on the fuel system and the general behaviour of the single-seat Hawker Fury biplane fighter. we were seated in turn in the cockpit of this delightful little aircraft and given a cockpit check before being sent off on our own. At this time the Fury was just about out of service in Fighter Squadrons in the U.K., much to the disappointment of those pilots who had flown and loved it. Now Furys were honourably relegated to the advanced flying schools of the R.A.F., their places in the front line of Fighter Command squadrons being taken by Gladiators, the new Hurricanes and the first of the Spitfires. After the Hart and the Audax, I found the Fury simple to fly, and its 180 to 200 miles an hour straight and level speed was really something after barely 90 miles an hour in the Tiger Moth, and the 140 or so in the Hart and Audax. To me this was real flying.

On occasion my enthusiasm and lack of experience led me into trouble. I was fond of aerobatics, and having heard of flick rolls, decided that the next time I w s up in the Fury I would experiment. Unfortunately nobody had briefed me on how to perform this manœuvre. In any case flick rolls were not encouraged because if they were done at too high a speed it was possible to overstress the aircraft. Off I went on this particular flight, climbing to gain a safe height of about 8,000 feet. I completely forgot the important step of reducing speed to a little above the stall, and at 160 miles an hour I pulled the stick hard back in my stomach and at the same time kicked on full right rudder. The result was most spectacular. What exactly happened I am not sure. However, the Fury eventually righted itself, and a very frightened pilot started to survey the situation. At least the wings and tail surfaces were still present, but movement of the control column laterally caused no rolling motion at all. In fact, all the controls behaved in a peculiar manner. I decided that I had made a major boob and started to undo my shoulder-straps ready to bale out. But after a final check of the controls I found there was enough control left to manœuvre the Fury gently. So I strapped myself in again and gingerly started a descent towards the airfield. At last the aerodrome appeared in view and a very apprehensive Braham made a wide circuit and landed without further incident. What was I to say to my Flight Commander? I decided I had better admit the truth. The result was a considerable blast, plus an aircraft to be soaped and cleaned.

On another occasion I rather carelessly landed across-wind on a very windy day, with the result that the Fury tilted over on one wing-tip. This didn't cause much damage, but unfortunately the chief flying instructor, Squadron Leader Johnson, was watching, so, as I got out of the aircraft, he was there to meet me with, "What the hell do you think you're doing?" I didn't know, so another aircraft got a cleaning.

October, 1938, was spent chiefly in polishing up our practice gunnery attacks before a month's attachment at the armament practice camp at Penrhos on the North Wales coast. All the students were looking forward to this. It was the high point of our training and the nearest thing to air combat. We moved to Penrhos at the end of the month and found we had a very tight schedule of flying exercises which began at dawn and ended at dusk. The fighter flight started with attacks against ground targets, while the bomber boys dropped practice bombs on the range from their new Oxford twin-engined trainers. The Fury was fitted with two Vickers machine guns which fired through the propeller, using a device designed by Constantinescue to ensure that the bullets didn't hit the prop. Ground gunnery was followed by attacks against a banner towed by a Hart or Audax. This was what I enjoyed most. I could imagine how men like Ball, Mannock, Bishop and Richtofen felt as they dived on a foe. After one or two air-to-air firings I began to get quite good scores on the banner, and felt that the long period of training was at last beginning to show something. All too soon the practice camp came to an end, and on December 2 I was detailed to fly one of the Furys back to Shawbury, where our postings at the end of our training would be awaiting us. But before that we each had to pass a final flying and navigation test in the Hart with the Flight Commander, Flight Lieutenant Stubbs. This I managed satisfactorily. Then one day we were assembled in a lecture-room and informed of our postings. The long-awaited day. As the names and units were read off, I became more and more nervous. I wanted to go either to a Gladiator or one of the new Hurricane or Spitfire squadrons. At last my name was read out: "Acting Pilot

Officer Braham, No. 29 Fighter Squadron, Debden, Essex."
As soon as we were dismissed I sought out one of our instructors, Pilot Officer Brooks, and asked him what aircraft this squadron was equipped with. He said he thought Gladiators. I was satisfied. David Blomeley was to join No. 1 Squadron at Tangmere, equipped with Hurricanes. After a glorious farewell party, we all had a few days' leave before joining our units. I now felt I was an experienced pilot. I was soon to learn otherwise.

4

ARLY in December, 1938, I arrived at my first operational station, Debden, a few miles from the country town of Saffron Walden in Essex. I reported to the Station Adjutant full of confidence, an experienced pilot with 136 hours' flying under my belt. He directed me to 29 Squadron Headquarters in one of the three large hangars on the airfield. I immediately noticed that there were no Gladiators. All I saw were Hawker Demons. These were two-seat, single-engine biplane fighters with the first hydraulic armoured turret in which the rear gunner sat. This was a shock. Outside the other hangars I noted the Hurricanes of 85 and 87 Fighter Squadrons. I climbed the stairs in the hangar to the office quarters of my new Squadron, a very deflated and disappointed Acting Pilot Officer. Flying Officer Brett, the Squadron Adjutant, met me and while I was waiting to meet the C.O. told me that the Squadron was in the process of re-equipping with a long-range fighter version of the Blenheim medium bomber, a twin-engined monoplane. This was the end. Things were going from bad to worse. It was bad enough seeing the old, obsolete Demon which was similar in most respects to the Hart and Audax on which I had trained, but to be told that I would now be flying a twin-engined bomber-like aircraft seemed most unjust. More than anything, from the very start I had wanted to fly the speedy and manœuvrable single-seat fighters.

At last I was ushered in to see the C.O., Squadron Leader Gomez, a fine-looking man who, I noted, had only one leg.

39

He welcomed me to the Squadron and told me something of its history and tradition, but I regret that I wasn't a very good listener. I wanted somehow to get into a single-seat squadron. When he had finished I am afraid I shocked him by telling him I wanted to fly single-seaters and could he arrange for me to be transferred to one of the other squadrons on the station. I didn't put it very tactfully and received a somewhat frosty reply. "Braham, we are proud of this Squadron and as a new pilot I expect you to be proud to serve in it." With that I was dismissed. I retired unhappily to the Adjutant's office where Brett told me I was to report to B Flight, commanded by Flying Officer Bill Cambridge. On arrival at his office I walked in and introduced myself. He shook hands with me and said, "I expect you to salute when you enter this office the first time each day, and call me 'Sir'. There will be no formalities other than that." My eyes were being opened gradually to service tradition. I believe he had been warned by the C.O. of my lack of enthusiasm for the Squadron's aircraft, and I could tell by his manner that I was going to have to watch myself. "Twenty-nine" was a very proud outfit in spite of its obsolete aircraft.

There was an excellent spirit of rivalry at Debden between the three squadrons and 29 was always able to hold its own at the various "games" played in the mess. I soon found that this spirit was rubbing off on me, and I began to forget my initial disappointment. Most of the Officer Pilots at Debden were young chaps of about my age or a little older. Only the Flight Commanders and C.O.s of the squadrons were some years older. There was also a high percentage of N.C.O. pilots in all three squadrons, and a fine bunch they were.

After I had been in the Squadron for about three months I was at last checked out on the new Blenheims with which 29 was being re-equipped. Previously I had to be content with flying the Demons or going up as a passenger in a Blenheim with one of the older members of the unit. We had heard a lot of nasty stories about the Blenheim from visiting bomber boys. One such story was that if you couldn't get the undercarriage down and had to belly-land, the aircraft would go up in flames. Nevertheless, I had no trouble with my check-out. From then on I got my fair share of Squadron flying and was an accepted member of the 29th.

One day a Gladiator came in from Hornchurch with Pilot Officer Mackenzie on board. Mac was a New Zealander who had been with me at Shawbury. I talked him into letting me have a ride in his aircraft, the one I had always wanted to fly. He agreed after a bit of coaxing. I strapped myself into the cockpit with Mac pointing out the various tits and switches. With a final "For Christ's sake don't break it", he waved me away. I taxied out, turned into the wind, opened the throttle and thundered off down the grass strip. In a moment I was airborne and climbing fast. I gingerly practised some of my rather rusty aerobatics, and again the yearning to fly the single-seater came back. After a while I turned towards the aerodrome and came in to land. Mac was waiting, biting his nails, as he realized that if I broke his aircraft, he would have to answer for letting me check out without authority from the C.O. of his squadron. I thanked him and made it clear that I was exceedingly jealous of his luck. Unfortunately this trip unsettled me for some time and it was with difficulty that I restrained myself from having another go at my C.O. about a posting. By this time, however, the fact that I was a member of 29 Squadron meant something, and my sense of loyalty to the unit was uppermost.

It was during these early days that I acquired a nickname that has stuck with me in the Service ever since—Bob. It has also on occasion caused much confusion, as my parents and later my wife rather naturally knew me as John, the name with which I was christened. It was habitual in the Squadron in those days for the pilots to refer to themselves on the radio by their Christian names. 29 Squadron had a spate of Johns, so it was decided that to overcome possible misunderstanding we Johns should draw a name out of a hat. I drew Bob. So Bob it was and Bob it has remained.

News and radio reports at this time indicated very clearly that war with Germany was only a matter of time and that time was running out fast. Most of us wished the talking would end so that we could pit our skill against our German counterparts. I think many of us still thought in terms of chivalrous air combats similar to those fought by our fathers in World War I. The new C.O. of 87 Squadron was soon to sober us up. Before his posting to Debden he had been Air Attaché in Berlin, where he had had ample opportunity to see the rapid build-up of the Luftwaffe. One day this officer lectured all the officers on the station and made it very clear that the new German air force was indeed a force to be reckoned with. It appeared that their new Messerschmitt fighters were on a par with, if not slightly superior to, our Hurricanes, and were far superior to the Blenheims of our Squadron. With the Spitfire we had an edge on him, but these aircraft were only just entering service and we then had exceedingly few of them. Nevertheless we were a carefree lot and didn't let this sobering talk get us down.

Early in August, the Air Forces of the U.K. and France were involved in air exercises to test the defences. This was the nearest thing to realism we could hope for in peacetime and for the period of the exercise we were on a war footing. The exercises lasted a week and we were scrambled at all times of the day in an attempt to intercept the "aggressor" of Bomber Command and the French Bomber Force. Sometimes we were successful, but more often we were not. There was no ground-control radar to direct us to the target aircraft and we relied almost entirely on information from ground observer posts. Delays in transmission of information resulted in many missed interceptions. We also found that the attacks laid down in the tactics manual were of little value, as most of the time we were sitting ducks for the rear gunners of the Wellingtons, Hampdens and Whitleys. The exercise did much to sharpen up our air-defence system for the war which was now so imminent.

It was with great excitement that one day in August we received news that we were to be re-equipped with the latest Hurricanes with variable-pitch propellers. We were the first squadron to have this mark of Hurricane so our morale hit the bell. We collected our new aircraft from Hawker's little airport at Brooklands and it was a very excited Braham who arrived there in a Blenheim. I had previously flown a Hurricane with the fixed-pitch prop once, so after a quick explanation of the workings of the variable-pitch control by Hawker's personnel I was sent on my way back to Debden. Now we would no longer be chided by our single-seat friends about the poor performance of our Blenheims.

Near the end of August all leave was cancelled because of the worsening situation in Europe. A twenty-four-hour watch was maintained by two officers at a time. It was their duty to receive and decode incoming signals. Pilot Officer Winn and I were on duty during the night of September 2 and we received the information that Britain intended to declare war on Germany. All squadrons were brought to a high state of readiness. Squadrons 85 and 87 had gone to France a week or so before. They had been replaced at Debden by 17 Squadron, also equipped with Hurricanes—the older, fixed-pitch prop variety.

5

Most of us thought that England would be immediately attacked by hordes of German bombers and many of us were looking forward to getting in among them. Before lunch on the day war began the whole Squadron was scrambled to intercept "Bogeys" (unknown aircraft) approaching the east coast. Off we took. What we lacked in training in our new aircraft we certainly made up for in spirit. As soon as we were airborne the controller came in over the wireless telling us to climb as fast as possible to 15,000 feet on a heading of 090 degrees. I remember thinking, "This is it", and switched on my electric reflector gun sight, ready for the moment when the Luftwaffe came in view. But we soon received the recall signal and disappointedly wheeled for home. It was a false alarm.

A few days later 11 Group came through with orders for 29 Squadron to maintain one flight daily at our forward base at Wattisham in Suffolk. This was a 2 Group Blenheim Bomber field. Each day throughout September one of our flights took off at dawn for this forward base, the remaining flight looking after the readiness state at Debden. On landing at Wattisham we dispersed our six or nine Hurricanes round the control tower and sat on the grass if it were dry, or in a wooden hut when wet, and waited for the expected call to scramble. At first we viewed our bomber hosts as rather staid gentlemen, but they were to see action long before us, performing very gallantly against German shipping off the Frisian Islands and against military targets on the North German coast. During this time we had many false alarms. They gave us an opportunity to become proficient in our new machines and we soon felt we were a match for anyone.

One day towards the end of September, 1940, Squadron Leader Gomez received news that 29 Squadron was to change its role to that of a night-fighter squadron, four of which were being formed immediately. This didn't sound promising, even less so when we found we were to hand our beloved Hurricanes over to another squadron and were to receive in exchange our old short-nosed Blenheims. The Blenheims were only fitted with one forward-firing machine gun in the port wing and a gas-operated Vickers gun in the rear turret. Some bright boy at headquarters had appreciated that to use these aircraft in a fighter role more armament would be required. So we took delivery of a belly-pack fitted with four more Browning 303 forward-firing machine guns, and it was our job to fit these packs to our aircraft. Ground and aircrew personnel toiled day and night until the job was complete, and a very tough job it was.

The next few months were taken up in retraining for our new role, and as none of us had much idea what night-fighting entailed, our training was rather varied. We had no airborne radar and there was then only the most primitive form of ground control. Our night patrols consisted chiefly of flying over groups of flares set out in various patterns on the ground. Flares were laid out in a particular pattern and repeated every few miles over a distance of twenty to thirty miles to form a patrol line. From these lines we were directed to some point in space in an attempt to intercept one of our own aircraft simulating the enemy. It was a hit-and-miss affair, dependent on there being little or no cloud so that the fighter crew could see the flares from 10,000 feet or more. At other times we worked in conjunction with the searchlights. There were many times when an aircraft could be seen coned in these lights. But by

45

the time the fighter had turned towards the target, the search-lights would lose their quarry and wave aimlessly over the sky. Invariably as the fighter closed the range it would be coned so that the pilot was temporarily blinded, or at least had his night vision temporarily impaired, making any further chances of finding the elusive "enemy" impossible. Yet this training, which at times seemed so futile, was to help us in the future. The night-fighters were feeling their way. Although our combat casualties at this stage were nil, we lost some fine crews in our efforts to overcome the weather. Everyone realized that it was possible for the enemy to take off in the clear, bomb a target in the U.K. blind, and return and land in good weather. The night-fighter would have to take off in the foulest of weather to intercept the intruder and then return in similar weather. The losses we suffered would not have been acceptable in peacetime but pioneering was urgent if the enemy was to be defeated in the night sky.

It was while returning to Debden from our new forward base at Martlesham Heath, near Ipswich, with my gunner, L.A.C. Harris, that I was involved in my first aircraft accident. On the night before it had snowed fairly heavily, and the grass surface of Martlesham was covered with four to six inches of it. I didn't take this very seriously and Harris and I taxied out in our Blenheim and turned into the wind. The take-off run in this direction was short and the pilot was confronted with trees just beyond the end of the run. After checking the engine I opened up to full power and the old Blenheim started to gain momentum. Soon it was clear that, although the engines were giving their best, the aircraft wasn't gaining speed fast enough. But I had passed the point of no return. I was too far down the runway to throttle off and pull up on the slippery ground without crashing into the now menacing trees. I remember telling Harris to hang on as I heaved the control column back to pull the Blenheim into the air. She just lifted off the ground and, as quickly as I could, I retracted the landing gear to reduce the drag. But the aircraft had barely attained flying speed and it sank back on to the ground with sufficient force to break one of the main wheel hydraulic jacks. We heard the snap of metal and both guessed what had happened, but our immediate concern was to clear the trees. This we just did. I contacted the ground control at Martlesham and told them that I had damaged the undercarriage, but would return to my main base at Debden where the aircraft could be more easily repaired. On the thirty-minute trip I had plenty of time to think. The old stories that Blenheims were fire-traps in the event of a belly-landing came back to mind. As I neared base I was told to fly around and burn off as much fuel as possible.

Gomez took off in an aircraft to look at the damage to my Blenheim. He was soon alongside and confirmed that one undercarriage leg was hanging down with a broken jack. This meant one of three things: belly-landing with the gear in the up position so that the hanging leg would collapse as soon as we touched down; a landing on one wheel, and again the hanging leg would collapse; or we could bale out. Gomez told me, "It's up to you." When I asked Harris if he wanted to jump or stay with me while I attempted a belly-landing, his comment was, "I'm sticking with you and the kite." I appreciated his trust. I told ground control what I had decided to do, and as I circled the airfield at about 1,500 feet I could see crowds of aircrew and groundcrew standing on the tarmac looking up like a crowd at a car race waiting for someone to prang. Also there was the ominous fire engine and ambulance. I swallowed hard and turned downwind, then across-wind and so to my final approach holding the speed back as far as I dared. The snow-covered ground came up rapidly as the aircraft gradually settled. At the last minute I hauled the control column hard back into my stomach. The first impact was slight but was followed immediately by a much harder impact and, with

47

much scraping and grinding, the good old Blenheim slid grace-fully along on her belly at ninety miles an hour for a hundred yards or so in a flurry of snow. After checking that all essential switches were off, Harris and I made a rapid exit through the top hatch, right into the arms of the Station Commander, and a crowd of my comrades. The Station Commander, a Cana-dian, congratulated me on a good show. Later I was to receive a blast from him for not checking the conditions at Martlesham before take-off. It was well deserved and I had learned another expensive lesson.

The Blenheim wasn't too badly damaged. This accident had one good effect on the Squadron. We all knew now that it was possible to belly-land a Blenheim without going up in a cloud of smoke.

Soon afterwards Gomez was posted to a staff job and replaced by Squadron Leader MacLean, a New Zealander. Mac continued to ensure that the morale and spirit of the 29th stayed high. This was a trying time for any C.O. of a Blen-heim night-fighter unit, as our comrades in their Hurricanes and Spits were now in continuous combat with the enemy in the day skies over France covering the retreat of the Allied Armies, and in sporadic fights over the east coast and the ship-ping convoys. I am afraid that as soon as Mac arrived a deputa-tion of officers appeared at his office door requesting transfers to day-fighter units. His reply was, "If I can put up with it so can you. We shall have our turn yet, so let's really make an effort to get the Squadron in top shape for that time."

Throughout early 1940 we continued to develop night-fighting tactics, although we still had no airborne radar. But by continual practice we improved our "cat's-eye" techniques, working over the flare patrol lines and with the A.A. search-lights. Our dusk and dawn patrols at Martlesham were also stepped up because of the cowardly and pointless bombing and machine-gunning of some of our defenceless coastal lightships.

I was leading one of these dawn patrols of two Blenheims with a relatively new pilot named Sisman in the other aircraft. We had been patrolling for some time when he shouted over the R.T., "Aircraft to port about five miles away." We swung round with throttles wide open, just skimming the wave-tops, and I also saw in the distance what seemed to be a JU88 flying parallel to some of our coastal shipping. It had become a race between Sisman and me to see who could get at the enemy first. The poor old Blenheims were groaning in every rivet as we pushed the throttles wide open. My gunner, Harris, was manœuvring his turret and firing short test bursts from his Vickers machine gun, and as I tested my front armament I could see streaks of smoke from Sisman's fuselage machine gun pack as he did the same. We were still two or three miles away and gradually closing the range when the JU88 must have seen us. He turned away, heading back towards the coast of Belgium or Holland. Black smoke belched from his exhausts as he poured on the coals, and it was soon apparent that he was drawing away from us. There was much cursing between Sisman and myself as we vainly tried to catch him. How we wished we had had our Hurricanes, for we would have then most certainly caught him.

Early in April, 1940, the Squadron was given urgent instructions to proceed to Drem, near Edinburgh, to cover troop convoys on their way to Norway. Once again the spirit of 29 rose. We felt sure that we would encounter German air opposition. We were informed that we were to provide dawn, dusk and night patrols for the shipping in and out of the Firth of Forth. We shared Drem airfield with a couple of Spitfire-equipped Auxiliary Fighter Squadrons. They had already been in action during a raid by a Heinkel III formation in October, 1939 and had dealt severely with the enemy. So again we tended to feel something of an inferiority complex. Still they were a grand bunch and included men like Ras Berry, who was to become one of the ace Wing Leaders during the North African campaign.

In May, the Squadron returned to Debden to carry on with night training and to maintain the forward detachment at Martlesham. Meanwhile the war was looking black for the Allies. Everywhere we were facing serious setbacks and it seemed as if 29 was fated not to see action. MacLean was probably more disappointed than anyone, for he had constantly badgered Group Headquarters to send us somewhere where we could get at the enemy. Mac set a wonderful example to us all during many disappointments and to support him we put our backs into our night training. We tried to develop tactics for the day when we should at last meet the enemy. Many of the things we tried seem foolish now. We experimented with night formation flights as it was thought that the more fighters we could bring to bear against a single enemy aircraft the better chance there would be of shooting him down. While this may have been good policy in daytime, it was no good at night, particularly as we had no airborne radar equipment. To fly formation at night without navigation lights required really close precision flying, but only the crew of the lead aircraft could use their eyes to search for an enemy. The pilot of the formating aircraft had to keep his eyes firmly fixed on the leader to keep in formation. This tactic was soon dropped, and we reverted to single aircraft interceptions. An exercise to improve our night vision was to send two aircraft up together, one acting as target, the other as fighter. The target would be told to pull ahead slowly with his lights out while the fighter tried to keep a visual sighting of him. The fighter would then open his throttles and gradually close to simulate an attack. We called this stalking and it taught us how to search the sky at night for another aircraft.

For some time we had heard of work being done by our scientists to develop an airborne radar set known as AI which

50

would enable the fighter crew to pick up a target some miles away from the information being displayed to the AI operator on cathode-ray-type scopes. Some of this work was at Martlesham Heath, with early equipments in Blenheims. On our regular visits there we noticed aircraft of this type belonging to the Fighter Interception Unit, fitted with peculiar aerials on the leading edges of the wings and nose. One day we received a few of these aircraft at Debden for the Squadron to try out. The briefing on the equipment was short and we had few people who knew anything about it. These aircraft had the turret removed and now our gunners were to be trained, or train themselves, on how to work this magic gear located in the bowels of the old Blenheim. The early equipment was very temperamental. This, coupled with the lack of training of the gunners, and, I am afraid, the scepticism of the pilots, didn't give the AI equipment much of a chance. Usually after take-off on a night sortie the pilot would be told that the AI was unserviceable. There would be sighs of relief and the gunner would clamber forward to sit beside his pilot and add another pair of eyes to the business of searching the skies.

In June, 1940, the Squadron had its first kill. It was both a happy and a sad occasion. Pilot Officer Barnwell, the pilot of the Blenheim, was one of the sons of the designer of the aircraft, who had been killed a few years previously in a flying accident. On this occasion Barnwell was operating out of Martlesham and was scrambled on to a hostile raid approaching Ipswich. A few minutes later we heard machine-gun fire in the air and a plane was seen to come down in flames not far from the airfield. Barnwell had shot down the Squadron's first enemy aircraft, a Heinkel III. Shortly afterwards we heard more combat in the sky and another aircraft was seen to be on fire. John didn't return and we were to learn that he had been shot down in combat with another enemy and had crashed in the sea just off the coast. Both he and his gunner were killed.

The Squadron lost one of its most popular members in the moment of victory. Barnwell was flying an aircraft which was not fitted with any AI. He had been aided solely by the searchlights and flak in picking up his foes and although he had paid the extreme penalty he had proved to all of us that our seemingly aimless "cat's-eye" night training could pay off.

6

Towards the end of June the Squadron was transferred from Debden to Digby, Lincolnshire. This was a hard blow. It seemed that Headquarters were determined to keep our Squadron as far away as possible from the enemy. Most day-fighter squadrons had been thoroughly blooded in fighting in France and the withdrawal of our troops from Dunkirk. Even one or two of the night-fighter squadrons on the south coast and around London were getting regular kills, but not us.

We soon settled down at our new base, however, and spirits were kept alive by Mac and his newly-arrived Adjutant, our father confessor, Sammy France. He was a pilot of the First World War who, like many of his generation, had chucked up his civvy job for the second time to do his bit.

Our routine at Digby was much the same as at Debden—mostly night co-operation with the searchlights. There was still no ground radar control for interceptions in this part of the country. The searchlights and flak were our only true guide. Where flak burst or searchlights were coning there was probably an aircraft, so in we went to have a look. We frequently caught fleeting glimpses of an aircraft only to lose visual contact again.

One night I was on readiness with B Flight under Sandy Campbell. Nothing was doing so a number of us started horsing around in the dispersal hut. Peter Sisman and I thought it was time to flatten Sandy—all in fun of course. But Sandy was an exceedingly large man and he gave us both a rough time. In the middle of this friendly mêlée the phone rang. Breathlessly we got to our feet. Sandy grabbed the phone and shouted to Sisman and myself to scramble. He followed shortly after. The three of us with our gunners rushed out into the darkness to our planes and roared off into the sky, still a little breathless from our mock battle. I was vectored on to one of the flare patrol lines near the coast and told to maintain a standing patrol at 8,000 feet. Sandy and Sisman were sent to other patrol lines. My air gunner brought my attention to some flak in the distance and a few seconds later I heard Sisman's voice on the R.T. saying he was firing on a Heinkel. I banked my Blenheim hard over and headed for him. We heard Peter's voice again but this time it sounded very excited and it was difficult to hear what he said. Apparently he was telling his gunner to put out a light. Then there was silence. A moment later we saw a huge flash on the ground ahead of us. Was it a bomb-burst or was it the Heinkel Sisman had been shooting at? Ground control could tell us nothing and half an hour later we were ordered back to base. In the dispersal hut I was greeted by Sandy who, although happy to see us back, was troubled. He was certain one of our aircraft had been in difficulties.

As I was back and Sisman wasn't we had to conclude that something must have happened to him. Sandy had heard the same chatter I had heard over the radios and had actually seen an aircraft burning an identification light being fired on by another aircraft. It had caught fire and crashed. It looked as if poor old Sisman had somehow left his identification light on when he was in combat with Jerry, whose rear gunners must have used it as an aiming point. Next day our fears were confirmed. The crash was found and Sisman and his gunner were dead. They were buried with military honours. I was one of the pallbearers and although one tends to be callous towards death in wartime, this funeral of a very good friend, whom we teased because of his schoolboyish appearance, affected me deeply. His parents and sister attended the funeral and afterwards we, his comrades, tried our embarrassed best to cheer them up. They were very brave and I think they accepted their tragedy more stoically than many of his airman friends.

During my early days at Digby a girl-friend in the W.A.A.F. presented me with a beautiful little English setter pup. He was a most affectionate animal and I decided to try him out in the Blenheim. At first I thought the noise would frighten him, but soon found that he just curled up on the floor of the cockpit beside me as though nothing was happening. I wasn't to have him for long. Charles Winn came up to me in the mess and told me that my dog had been killed while running across the road. He had escaped from my room and been hit by an army truck. I retired to my quarters and wept. I had grown very fond of that delightful little dog, and I swore that I would never own another, a promise I kept for a long time.

Soon after the Battle of Britain began in late July, 1940, our popular Squadron Commander, MacLean, was moved to a staff post, and his place was taken by Squadron Leader Charles Widdows. The Squadron had become awfully attached to "Kiwi Mac". The farewell we gave him was the usual hectic affair, with 29 offering *en bloc* to follow him anywhere if he got himself another squadron. Like all good C.O.s he sobered us up a little towards the end of the session by asking us to give the new Squadron Commander the same sort of support that he had been given. At first Charles Widdows seemed a little sticky but we soon got used to him and during his lengthy tour in command he was to prove that he was not only meticulously fair, but also a very brave man.

Not long after Widdows arrived, Dave Humphries attacked

55

and probably destroyed a Heinkel III over the east coast. This had an excellent effect on the Squadron. The rest of us were getting pretty jealous and wondering why the elusive enemy wouldn't come our way. Some night-fighter crews on the south coast and near London were building up quite substantial scores, and the names of John Cunningham and Rawnsley, his AI operator, were soon to be on everyone's lips.

The Squadron now had so many gunner/AI operators that we were continually switching crew members. Like all the other pilots, however, I preferred to fly with a select few. Pilot Officers Wilson and Watson, Sgts. Wilsden, Waller, Wingfield and Moss were among those with whom I worked well. It was quite clear that success was most likely to come to the crews who regularly flew together and fully understood one another.

August 24, 1940, was one of the more successful dates for the day boys and also for myself. That night Sgt. Wilsden and I got our first kill. There was a lot of activity over the Humber area in the early hours of the night and it wasn't long before B Flight received orders to scramble towards our patrol lines. It was a dark night, but clear of any cloud, and I was patrolling backwards and forwards over the area at 10,000 feet watching the flak and searchlights far to the north. Suddenly I felt a tap on the shoulder and the shock nearly made me jump out of the aircraft. Wilsden, as large as life, had clambered out of his turret, crawled through the bowels of the aircraft to shout in my ear, "Want a bottle of beer and a sandwich?" This was so unexpected that it put me into tucks of laughter. I accepted, gave him a friendly clout and ordered him back to his turret. I enjoyed the beer regardless of the fact that such beverages were strictly forbidden in aircraft.

I kept badgering the Sector Controller on the R.T. to see if there were any trade for me. At last he said "Yes" and vectored me towards searchlights which were coning some miles ahead. With throttles wide open we made for the area, and suddenly, in a distant cone, I could distinguish an aircraft, which at that range looked like a moth flying round in a light beam. Excitement had now reached a peak in our Blenheim. I pulled the ring and bead sight down into firing position and fired a short warming-up burst from my guns. As Wilsden in the rear turret couldn't see ahead very well I gave him a running commentary of what I saw in the searchlights and heard him fire test bursts from his single Vickers gun.

It seemed to take an age for the range to close but it must have been only a few minutes. Not only was I excited but I opened fire at too great a range, and unpardonably without identifying the aircraft. My tracers showed that I was too far out, so I continued to close more coolly. Now I recognized it as a Dornier twin-engined bomber. Other searchlights were sweeping the sky near us and, as I continued to close the range, I caught a brief glimpse of a Hurricane diving through a searchlight beam. He was above me and suddenly I heard Wilsden's gun rattling away in the back. I realized that he must be shooting at the Hurricane in error, as the Dornier was still ahead of us. I shouted over the intercom to him to cease fire, but too late as I could see in the light of the searchlights that the Hurricane was streaming what looked like glycol from its engine. I didn't tell Wilsden at the time as I knew it would worry him. Besides, I wasn't sure it was his fire that had caused it or whether the Hurricane had been hit by our own flak which was coming up thick and fast. By this time I was well within range of the Dornier which the searchlights were still industriously illuminating for us, but unfortunately my closing speed was now so fast that I only had time for a very short burst as I vainly tried to slow my aircraft down to stay behind him. However, I had the satisfaction of seeing him blossom smoke and could see sparks as my bullets bit into him. As I couldn't keep behind him, I gradually overtook him on his starboard side as closely as possible to give Wilsden a crack with his gun. This would enable him to fire bursts into the enemy's most vulnerable area, the cockpit. The German gunners must either have been blind or injured for I received no return fire as we slowly flew past. Wilsden was firing long bursts from his gun. I saw the flames at the same time as I heard him whoop with joy "Got him." The Dornier slowly peeled off to port, its dive steepening as it headed for the ground with flames trailing astern. We circled, waiting for the crash on the ground, and in a highly elated mood headed back for base, shouting our success over the radio to the Sector and anybody else who wished to listen. On my way back my excitement cooled as I had time to think about the Hurricane. I hoped and prayed the pilot was safe for I could not help feeling he might have been hit by our fire.

At last we circled the dimly lit strip and landed. Everyone on the airfield had heard of our luck, as Sector had phoned through. We crawled out of the aircraft and were overwhelmed with congratulations from the groundcrew. When the back-slapping ended, the intelligence officer took down our statements and completed a combat report. I told him of the incident with the Hurricane and Charles Widdows, who was listening in to our report, put a call through to Sector requesting them to find out which Hurricane squadron had been flying that night and if they had all got back safely. He was informed that the pilot of a Hurricane who said he had been hit by our own flak had baled out but was safe and uninjured. The main thing was that he was safe. Now our victory was complete, so Wilsden and I thought. But we heard that the A.A. gunners in the Humber area were also claiming a Dornier destroyed and as there was only one wreck on land an argument followed between the Army and the Air Force as to which should be credited with the claim. According to our intelligence officer, the Army needed the victory from a morale point of view to inspire their gunners to even greater efforts. I was slightly hurt by this attitude as I felt that if anyone needed a shot in the arm it was 29 Squadron, who had seen so little action to date. The matter was eventually settled amicably and we were credited with our victory. My first combat convinced me that I must see action again. The excitement of the chase had got me.

7

SHORTLY after our first victory, I was standing outside the maintenance hangar at Digby talking to some of the pilots and gunners of the Squadron. The day was overcast with stratus cloud at about 1,000 feet but with excellent visibility beneath. Some of the Canadian Hurricanes were airborne and we watched them as they came in to land after a scramble. All but two had landed when out of the cloud right over the airfield appeared a JU88, manœuvring for an attack. We were shouting ourselves hoarse in a useless attempt to attract the attention of the two Hurricanes still in the air. They appeared to be oblivious of the enemy's presence. Suddenly it dawned on us that the brute was going to bomb or strafe our abode. The JU88 was in a shallow dive heading for the hangars with his forward machine guns firing long bursts, all of which seemed to be addressed to each one of us personally. We dived for a near-by bomb shelter. In my haste I collided with Charles Widdows. Down we crashed in a heap, both apologizing profusely, as a stick of bombs burst harmlessly on the airfield. With this and a parting burst of machine-gun fire the enemy disappeared into cloud. Two red-faced Hurricane pilots landed shortly after, having failed to see the elusive enemy. In fairness to them, the German didn't give them much chance as he sought cloud cover as soon as he had made his attack. Probably he saw the Hurricanes and wanted to get the hell out of it as soon as possible.

With the arrival of another Hurricane squadron at Digby it was decided that 29 Squadron should move to Wellingore. At first we didn't like leaving the comforts of the mess and our Canadian friends, but soon found that our quarters at Wellingore were excellent. Also the fact that the Squadron was on its own did much to develop an excellent spirit in the late summer and autumn of 1940.

In September we began to receive a variety of types of aircraft with which to practise and improve our night-fighting techniques. At one stage we had, in addition to our Blenheims, some Hurricanes and one or two Fairey Battles which had been used as light bombers in France earlier in the year. In their brave attacks they had suffered very heavy casualties, since they were no match for the German fighters. The Hurricanes we immediately put to use, not only in a night role but also for use in airfield defence in daylight, to defend ourselves against the sort of attack we had at Digby. It was grand to get back in these fine machines even though they were less suited for night-fighting than the Blenheim. Although we had no success with our few Hurricanes either by day or night, Flight Lieutenant Stevens, a pilot in 151 Squadron at Wittering, was building up a fantastic score at night in these aircraft. He had no aids other than searchlights and flak, into which he flew with reckless abandon in search of the enemy. His argument was that the German must be somewhere near the flak bursts. Often he was right and this technique, coupled with his wonderful eyesight, yielded a high score. Later he was killed in an intruder raid over the Continent, after destroying fourteen enemy aircraft at night in his Hurricane. A truly remarkable pilot.

I have briefly mentioned the equipment with which some of our Blenheims were fitted. Because of our lack of understanding of it and the early stage of its development, we rarely bothered with it. But our attitude to AI was to undergo a radical change. Already one or two of the southern night-fighter squadrons had been re-equipped with the powerful Beaufighter. This was a twin-engined, two-seat night-fighter armed with four 20-mm. cannons and six 303 machine guns. All these guns were fixed to fire forward and controlled by the pilot. This aircraft was to remain the most heavily-armed fighter of the war. It was also the first British aircraft with a satisfactory AI set. The equipment and operator were located towards the rear of the fuselage and enclosed by a perspex cockpit dome. From two small cathode-ray tubes, the AI operator could direct the pilot towards any enemy aircraft that appeared within the coverage of the radar set. Its range was equivalent to the height of the fighter above the ground. For instance, if the Beaufighter was flying at 12,000 feet, it could, in theory, pick up target aircraft at ranges up to 12,000 feet. In fact, ground returns on the scope and "noise" made the range less. The equipment, known as AI Mark 4, was also able to detect targets behind the fighter, although backward ranges were limited by the shielding effect of the aircraft structure.

AI-equipped Beaufighters came into service about the same time as the Ground Control Intercept radars, which were now rapidly springing up around the coasts of Britain. From these stations it was now possible for the controller to direct day- or night-fighter aircraft accurately to within one or two miles of an enemy. This was a great advance. The G.C.I. controller could position the AI-equipped night-fighter near enough to a target for the AI operator to get a radar contact on his airborne set. It was then up to the crew of the Beaufighter to complete the interception and destroy the enemy. John Cunningham and his operator, Rawnsley, had already been very successful in night combats in their AI-equipped Beaufighter and were to become one of the leading night-fighter teams of the war.

We heard that 29 was eventually to receive Beaufighters, and in early September one of these fine machines arrived for demonstration. A number of us were permitted to fly it. Although I was still a pilot officer, I was now one of the old hands of the Squadron and so was one of the lucky few who flew the Beaufighter. After the Blenheim it seemed a huge machine, particularly for a fighter, but much thought had gone into its design. The vision out of the aircraft was excellent and the instruments and controls were laid out in a much more satisfactory manner than those in the old Blenheim. After I had flown the Beau around for a few minutes, I landed and taxied back to the remainder of the Squadron aircrew who had gathered to watch the performance. "What do you think of her?" Charles Widdows asked. "The sooner we get them the better. She's marvellous," I replied. The other pilots who flew the machine were unanimous that this was the answer to the enemy night bombers. But the C.O. told us we should have to be patient. It would be at least two months before we could be re-equipped with Beaufighters.

Soon afterwards I was told that I had been promoted to the exalted rank of Flying Officer.

8

MANY new faces now showed up at Wellingore, among them Miles and Davidson, pilot officers straight from training schools, and Flight Lieutenant Guy Gibson transferred from a tour on bombers to try his hand as a night-fighter. During his stay with us Guy was to become a first-class night-fighter pilot, and he destroyed three enemy aircraft. But Bomber Command was his first love and he returned there where eventually he led the famous "Dams Raid" for which he was awarded the V.C. He was later killed over Holland. Flying Officer Don Parker was another Bomber Command type who joined us at about the same time. He had been awarded the G.C. for getting the crew out of a crashed and burning bomber. He, too, was to return to Bomber Command and to a gallant death.

In due course it was my turn to take over the section at Ternhill, yet another of our small detachments away from the main base. On this occasion I led our four Blenheims, taking with me as gunner Pilot Officer Wilson, a new gunnery leader, and also the indomitable F/Sgt. Simms, who was to be in charge of ground personnel. At Ternhill the detachment headquarters was a tent with a telephone to flying control through which scramble instructions were passed to us. I had little to do except make myself known to the Station Commander and to Jack Leather, leader of 611 Squadron flight of Spitfires. The Spits maintained a readiness state from first light to dusk, then we took over.

One day we had just been relieved at dawn and were getting

ready for bed when there was the roar of a low-flying aircraft. I ran to the window and saw below the low cloud, which was at about 600 feet, a JU88 making a turn for a run over the field. In my exasperation I rushed to my wardrobe where I kept a .22 sporting rifle, grabbed it, loaded it, and leaned out of the window, hoping the JU88 would pass close enough for me to have a shot. What I thought I would achieve with this puny weapon I don't know, but it seemed better than helplessly watching and not hitting back.

By this time the JU88 was on his attack run and still there was no sound of engines starting at the Spit dispersal. The enemy made a beautiful pass at one of the large main hangars which was full of training aircraft, Ansons and the like and also one of my Blenheims which was under repair. It was a first-class attack and his stick of bombs hit the hangar fair and square sending up sheets of flame and smoke. He then flashed past our quarters, machine-gunning targets of opportunity as he went. Finally he pulled up into the low cloud and was gone, followed by my .22 bullet fired at about 300 yards range!

I pulled on my clothes and rushed down towards the hangar, where airmen were trying to get aircraft out of the burning building. I met my Flight Sergeant and saw that he had things under control and that our unserviceable aircraft had been pulled out without much damage. But most of the training aircraft were now burning. It appeared that no one had been seriously injured, although someone had been blown through an office window. Having done all I could I started to walk back to the quarters for some sleep when a voice roared at me, "Where's your hat?" It was the Station Admin. Officer, a World War One veteran and rather a "sticky" individual. I apologized and told him that I had rushed out to check on my men and aircraft and had forgotten it. This remark didn't impress him a bit and he continued to dress me down. By this time I began to think the man a clot and remarked rudely that, with his permission, as I had been up all night, I was going to bed. Nothing more was heard of the incident.

This enemy attack and the previous one on the airfield at Digby in very bad weather impressed us with the excellence of German navigation and lent credence to the story that he was using pilots who had lived in England pre-war to lead these raids. In both cases he dropped out of low cloud right on the airfield, attacked and then got away unscathed.

A night or two later Wilson and I were scrambled because of activity over the Liverpool area. It was dark with cloud patches at between 10,000 and 15,000 feet. The ground control vectored us towards a "bandit" at 12,000 feet, and in the distance we could see flak and some searchlights. I tested my guns and told Willy to fire a burst from his. Somehow I felt confident that we should shortly be having a crack at another German, but this time I was going to be cool about it and wait until I got in close before firing.

The Sector Controller gave us changes of course, indicating that we were closing with the enemy. We were sometimes in cloud, which meant a quick transfer from visual flying to instruments. I cursed; we must get out of this cloud if we wanted to see anything. Then we were out in the clear again for a few minutes. The flak and searchlights were closer now. So the enemy must be somewhere close. There wasn't a light on the ground, although between breaks in the cloud I could make out the different shades of darkness, which indicated where the darker land merged with the lighter sea. Occasionally there was a flash on the ground far below, probably A.A. guns, or possibly bombs bursting on Manchester or Liverpool. The Controller's voice became more urgent. "Your tracks have merged. Keep a sharp look-out." Now we were very close. His words could mean that we were anything from a few miles to a few yards apart. Suddenly I caught a glimpse of what appeared to be two stars slightly above me. I saw they were moving—therefore they weren't stars. This must be the glow from the exhausts of a twin-engined plane.

I shouted to Wilson, "Can you see an aircraft above us?" He answered, "I can see exhausts." I eased the Blenheim into a gentle climb and opened the throttles to lessen the gap between us. I couldn't make out what kind of aircraft it was. Then I flew into cloud. "Damn it, now we shall lose him." But a moment later we were in the clear again and there he was close enough for me to see a distinct shape. "A single rudder and fin. Must be a Heinkel or a JU88." But I still wasn't positive. We went through another patch of cloud and it was obvious the cloud was increasing. I should have to do something quickly or lose him. I called control and told them that I was behind an aircraft but couldn't be sure what it was. Sector confirmed that it was hostile. We were the only friendly fighter in the area.

I must fire now or lose him in the cloud. I knew I was out of effective range at 800 feet, but hoped to get in a lucky burst. I aimed between the exhaust glows. A long burst and I saw what appeared to be sparks coming from the enemy. These must be hits. Curse it, he was heading into cloud again. I followed but the cloud was now thick. I desperately held course and height on instruments hoping that the enemy would be in the same relative position when we broke clear. No such luck. He was nowhere to be seen. We flew around aimlessly hoping to pick him up again, but it was hopeless. Sadly we headed back for Ternhill as we were now short of fuel. On landing, Willy and I reported to the Intelligence Officer, but claimed nothing, as we didn't feel we had done much damage.

Our long-promised Beaufighters had now started to arrive. The Germans had also practically given up mass day raiding and were now going over to a full-scale night offensive. London was soon to feel the maniacal anger of Hitler in the indiscriminate attacks of his aircraft by night. If the German attack swung to the Midlands or the east coast ports we should be fully engaged. Immediately on our return from Ternhill we started an intensive day and night training programme with the Beaufighters, at the same time maintaining readiness with our few remaining Blenheims and Hurricanes. These were busy days, yet my friends and I managed without fail to get into trouble of some sort.

The Squadron had on its inventory a little two-seat monoplane, a Magister, which we used for communication. The Squadron Commander let a couple of us take it away sometimes for a week-end furlough. Between serious work we could always find time to go for a spin round the airfield in the Maggie and indulge in aerobatics of a sort. Charles Winn was up one morning circling low when he spotted me. Next thing I remember the Maggie zoomed over my head. I ran to a parked Blenheim and got one of the airmen who was working on the aircraft and laughing his head off at the performance, to hand me the Very signal pistol from the cockpit. As Winn came winging down for another "attack" I fired a red flare at him with my portable flak gun. This game was carried on for ten minutes or so with the Squadron and ground-crew taking a ringside seat to watch the mock battle. A.A. gunner Braham lay flat on his face as the Maggie came over lower and then fired snap-shots with the Very gun. Eventually we both got tired of the game and Winn landed, highly delighted at his success which he judged by the state of my muddy uniform. Widdows was absent on this occasion, or I am sure our dangerous little game would have been brought to an abrupt end.

A few days later it was my turn. I was flying round the airfield in the Maggie with Jackie Page, one of our officer gunners, in the back seat, when I espied what I thought to be friend Winn ambling across the field. This was too good to miss.

Now for revenge. Down we went, and it was with great satisfaction that I saw him dive to the ground. I repeated my swoop and he had to dive again before he reached the sanctuary of our dispersal. I was congratulating myself on this success when Jackie called over the interphone, "You know, I don't think that was Charles." "Well, who was it then?" "I think it was the Old Man." "Oh. . . ." I flew round once more at a more respectful altitude and surveyed the faces looking up. A red flare rose recalling us to land. Down we came. Jackie was right. It was Charles Widdows I had selected as my target, and he was livid. "That was one of the most dangerous exhibitions of low flying I have ever seen. As a punishment you will act as duty pilot for a week and think yourself lucky to get off so lightly." "Yes, sir," I said as I glanced over his shoulder at the faces of my comrades. They were desperately trying not to laugh. The punishment made me responsible, among other things, for laying out the flare paths of portable paraffin lights along which we landed at night, and also the control of night flying from a small caravan at the touchdown end of the landing strip. But, far more serious, I was not allowed to fly for a week. The punishment was well deserved and I got off lightly. It ended a game which was getting out of hand and which might have ended in a fatal or serious accident.

November, 1940, saw the German night attacks spread to cities other than London. On the 14th the Luftwaffe attacked Coventry in strength and virtually destroyed the centre of that old city. For us it was a busy and frustrating time. Each crew was scrambled twice or sometimes three times a night against these heavy attacks. Our Beaufighters were only just operational and many of our sorties had to be flown in the old Blenheims. Even when we were lucky enough to get off at night in the Beaus troubles arose with the AI gear, or the operators lacked sufficient training to use it.

During the hectic period of a few nights including the Coventry raid, the Squadron was unable to shoot down any of the attackers. We were angry and bitter, and our attitude was not mollified when we noted the smoking ruins of the city during our daylight training missions. On the night of November 19, while flying a Beau, I saw three enemy aircraft, but they were either crossing in front of me or coming head on, so that by the time I had turned they had passed out of the range of my vision. The AI was unserviceable, and how I cursed this device, which was later to bring me and other night-fighters so much success. At the time all I could think was, "I've missed another of the bastards."

9

A T the end of the year I was sent on an Instrument
Approach course at Watchfield, near Swindon, to get
up-to-date with the latest bad-weather techniques. I
had been flying in some foul weather and felt confident of
my ability, but there was still much to learn. The first morning I woke up in the wooden quarters and saw there was a
thick fog. I could barely see the next building. This was fine;
back to bed. Not a bit of it. There was a knock on the door
and my instructor told me to hurry up and get down to the
flight line as we should soon be flying. "This is just the sort
of weather we want," he said. By the time the course finished
I for one felt that I had learned a lot about landing with little
or no visibility, using a radio-type beam. This blind approach
equipment was being fitted in our Beaufighters and was to
prove an invaluable aid.

I was given a short Christmas leave and visited my parents
who were now living at Duxford, a village just outside Cambridge, which was the site of one of the more famous day-
fighter airfields. My father was the rector of this quiet little
village. The leave was pleasant but I was glad to get back to
the Squadron. I am afraid my parents found it disturbing that
I should not want to stay at home longer, but they were to
get used to my "flying" visits during the war.

Again there were changes in the Squadron. Old hands were
posted and new faces appeared in the mess. All rapidly became
imbued with the spirit of 29, which, in spite of our lack of
success, had as high a morale as any squadron in the R.A.F.

The new year brought snow in great quantities. Sammy France, the Adjutant, phoned me at the dispersal during this cold spell and asked me to call in at Squadron H.Q. as he had news for me. I learned I had been awarded the D.F.C. and F/Sgt. Munn, one of our pre-war N.C.O. pilots, the D.F.M. This was certainly a surprise. Normally decorations weren't given to fighter pilots unless they had shot down at least three aeroplanes. I had only destroyed one and Munn, at this stage, none. According to the citations, however, the awards were for "Determined operations against the enemy under adverse weather conditions." Charles Widdows congratulated us both, not only for receiving our gongs but for being the first members of the Squadron to be decorated during the war. Naturally this affair was an excellent excuse for a wild party, and in spite of our readiness commitments some of us suffered from thick heads for many days.

A few weeks later Munn and I were ordered to attend an investiture at R.A.F. Waddington. King George VI, in the uniform of a Marshal of the R.A.F., arrived at the 5 Group Bomber Station to present decorations to officers from various commands. It was a proud moment for me. We were drawn up in the middle of a hollow square formed by the station personnel in one of the large hangars. Before the King pinned on my D.F.C. he shook hands and said a few kind words. I was struck by the slightness of his build. Photographs and films always made him look taller. Little did I realize at that time that I was to be ushered before him on several more occasions in the future. King George, by his courage, determination and example, probably did more for the morale of the British people than any one person in the Commonwealth, including the indomitable Prime Minister, Churchill. Rarely has a monarch received and deserved such unanimous respect and affection from his subjects. The people could withstand the German onslaughts more easily in the knowledge that their

King and his family were unflinchingly sharing their dangers and distress. It's a pity there is no way of presenting decorations for bravery to one's monarch. King George VI certainly earned one.

In February, 1941, Sandy Campbell, who had been my Flight Commander, was posted and replaced by Squadron Leader Pat Maxwell. Meanwhile the night-fighter squadrons were being reorganized. The Squadron Commander was now to be Wing Commander, one Flight Commander was to be a Squadron Leader and the other a Flight Lieutenant. This seemed ridiculous to us. We thought both Flight Commanders should have the same rank and a few months later our view was officially accepted. In the interim, however, Widdows was still our boss, Pat was O.C. B Flight and Guy Gibson was Flight Lieutenant in charge of A Flight. I was Pat's deputy as the senior Flying Officer in B Flight. He was a grand chap to work with and practically impossible to keep up with off duty.

New crews began to arrive after courses at the newly-formed night-fighter O.T.U.s. They were indoctrinated in the use of the AI equipment and techniques. The older hands in the Squadron soon picked up the principles of the AI after short courses. It was becoming still more apparent that pilot and AI operator should stick together to develop team work. The most successful night-fighter crews had flown together for long periods, some throughout the war; such as Cunningham and Rawnsley. Our interception chances were further enhanced by the new G.C.I. radar stations on the east coast within our area. We spent all our spare time practising interceptions and giving our AI operators every chance to become familiar with their equipment. On days off we visited the G.C.I. sites and got to know the controllers personally so that our job of night-fighting became a first-class team operation of controller, AI operator and pilot, each knowing the others on a first name basis. Now we were getting somewhere. No longer would there be aimless patrolling or attempting interceptions from scanty information.

By mutual consent I became "wedded" to Sgt. Ross, a Canadian AI operator. He was a wild man off duty, but in the air he was first-class and was getting the hang of the AI gear rapidly. I flew with Ross on as many operational sorties as possible and we built up an excellent understanding. The Germans soon obliged us by giving us more than enough to cope with. The Squadron was actively engaged throughout the early part of 1941 and our successes began to mount. In the first few months of the year Widdows, Guy Gibson and I each scored successes.

We were all elated by Charles Widdows's first kill, because he had always been so keen and in many ways was unlucky until this moment. He destroyed a JU88 one night over the east coast and the enemy crashed not far from our camp. Next day a number of us, including Widdows, decided to visit the scene of the "prang" to see if we could get souvenirs for the mess. The enemy plane had crashed in a ploughed field and was guarded by R.A.F. airmen. When we arrived the bodies of the enemy crew had been removed, but the smouldering wreckage still reeked of death. I wasn't over-keen to ferret around in the wreckage, but one of the squadron members had noticed what appeared to be an interesting, short-barrelled, heavy-calibre machine gun in the tangled metal where the nose of the aircraft had been. It appeared to be in pretty good shape, and we all felt that this weapon would be a fitting item for the officers' mess. After a lot of tugging we got the weapon clear, but not before we had unearthed some gruesome remains—part of the leg of one of the German crew. Up to this stage I hadn't really thought in terms of killing individuals. Air combat to me was an impersonal thing, one machine against another, with none of the un-pleasantness of close combat land warfare. But after seeing the wreck of this German plane, I couldn't help feeling some remorse for the enemy crew who, although enemies, were fighting like us for their country. They would be mourned in their homeland like any of our lads who had fallen.

My second confirmed success occurred on the night of March 13, a beautiful, cold, moonlight night. Ross and I were scrambled and vectored towards the coast near Skegness. As we climbed Ross was checking his radar equipment. We levelled out at 15,000 feet and with throttles wide open headed east. The G.C.I. controller directed us towards the enemy, keeping up a running commentary. "He's four miles dead ahead." . . . "You should get contact in a minute." I asked Ross if he had picked anything up. "Nothing yet." Tension was mounting. On a night like this we should see him nearly half a mile away. To gain surprise we had to plan our approach to make it difficult for him to spot us as we came in for a kill. The controller's voice was now becoming more urgent. "Three miles, a little to port and above." . . . "No contact." Then Ross came through over the intercom. "Contact, 4,000 yards and 20 degrees above. Turn gently port." This was it. I pressed the transmitter and shouted, "Contact" to the G.C.I. controller. "Good luck, Bob, go in and get him."

Now Ross had taken over the commentary where the G.C.I. controller had left off, and was calmly directing me from the information on his scopes to a position from which I should be able to get a visual contact on the enemy. "Where do you want him, Bob?" "Dead ahead about 100 feet above me." This positioning should give us the advantage. His gunners would be searching the sky, but anything coming in from below was a dark, moving object against a dark background, making visual sighting difficult. Ross and I were ensuring that he was above us, a dark object against a lighter background.

I could tell by the tone of Ross's voice exactly how much bank he wanted me to apply as I positioned myself to close the range. "Harder port, ease it, now steady, range 2,000 yards and he is about 200 feet above." From these instructions I had a complete picture in my mind of the enemy's position relative to us. My eyes strained to pick up an aircraft, but not yet. We were still too far away. I adjusted the brilliance of my electric reflector sight, till I could only just see the reticle. If it was too bright my night vision would be impaired and it would take me longer to pick up my enemy. The range closed still further. "Steady, Bob, hold that height. He is just about 100 feet above at 1,000 yards." "I can't see him yet." "O.K.; throttle back a bit. Range now 900 yards, hold that course."

What was that? As I stared, I thought I saw something moving. I blinked. My eyes were watering with the strain. Yes, there he was, a black object moving ahead of me and above, still too far to make out what sort of aircraft he was. "I can see him, but keep up the commentary, he is still some way off." "O.K., 700 yards, a little to port and above." I could now vaguely make out twin rudders. I called G.C.I., "Tally-ho. I think a Dornier, will confirm when I get in closer."

"Good show, he's all yours."

Now I could clearly make out the enemy and identified him as a Dornier. Apparently he still hadn't seen me. I closed the range further. Ross had now taken his head out of the visor over his radar scopes and was looking ahead through his canopy in the rear of the Beaufighter. "Can you see him yet, Ross?" After a second or two, "Yes, I've got him now." I had to get in closer to make certain of him. The Dornier had just crossed the coast near Skegness and might be heading for one of the Midland cities to dump his load of destruction. Now I was within about 400 yards, Ross was urging me to fire and this seemed to be the time. If I closed farther I would probably lose surprise and be spotted by the enemy rear gunners. I half expected to see tracer coming my way any minute because it was such a bright night. I eased gently back on the control column, allowing a little deflection, and pressed the firing button. The four cannons roared for a second then stopped. "Damn it, they've jammed," I shouted. I saw a flash on the fuselage of the Dornier, where at least one of my shells had hit, and the enemy turned gently round to starboard back in the direction from which it had come. I followed. Still no return fire. I pressed the firing button again. Nothing happened. "Oh hell, Ross, see if you can fix the guns." Ross was already out of his seat, removing the heavy sixty-round magazines from the guns and working the firing mechanism back and forth to clear the trouble. He had connected up with a radio intercom plug in the mid-section of the aircraft, as he had to leave his seat to get at the guns. "O.K., have another go, boss. I've changed the ammo drums." I placed the gunsight again on my target. He had crossed out over the coast again, apparently hoping to head home. Still no return fire. Perhaps I had killed or injured the rear gunners with my first short burst. I pressed the button. Nothing happened. "The damn things still won't fire." "O.K., hang on. I'll try the mechanism again.. I think the oil in the guns is frozen."

I had now made up my mind that I couldn't let this aircraft get away. Perhaps we could ram it and survive. If I timed it just right and put my port wing under his starboard rudder, and then put on full right aileron quickly, maybe I could knock his tail off, and he would be out of control. We were only just off our own coast and stood a fair chance of being picked up if we baled out. "O.K., Ross, how are things coming along?" "Not very good." "Right. Get back in your seat. I am going to try and ram him, you may have to bale out." "Hang on a sec. Have another go with the guns. They may be all right."

One more go, and by this time the strain was beginning to tell. I didn't relish the thought of ramming the so-and-so, even though I had reasoned with myself that there was a chance of getting away with it in one piece. There was also a very good chance that we would buy it. Ross's suggestion gave me a few seconds to think.

Again I eased back on the stick and closed the range to about fifty yards as it was apparent there was no opposition from the rear gunners. The enemy didn't appear to be badly hit. There were no signs of fire, and oddly enough he was taking no evasive action. Perhaps since I hadn't fired since the first short burst some minutes before he thought he had lost me. I pressed the button, hoping against hope that the guns would fire. The Beau bucked as they roared away and, in a blinding sheet of flame, the Dornier 17 blew up in my face. I was jubilant but poor old Ross was exhausted as he had disconnected his oxygen tube to get at the guns. Like me he was thankful that we hadn't had to ram. As we turned for home we saw the flaming wreckage crash into the sea.

The G.C.I. operators were as bucked as we were over our success. Back at the airfield the news had gone ahead of us and we stepped out of the aeroplane to be surrounded by air- and groundcrew. My groundcrew had prepared a swastika stencil, and started to paint two of these emblems on the nose of the aeroplane before we had time to walk back into dispersal hut. After we had given the "spy" our combat report, I grabbed an armourer and asked him about the gun problem. He told me that they had been having a lot of trouble in cold weather with oil freezing in the mechanism, which confirmed Ross's opinion. Modifications were being carried out. The guns in later Beaus were much more satisfactory, being adequately heated and also fitted with belt-feed ammunition instead of drums.

It was during this time of increased activity that Charles

Widdows and his AI operator, Flying Officer Wilson, had a narrow escape from death. Wilson owed his life to the courage of his pilot. Charles was scrambled after an incoming raid and was soon in trouble. The engines of his aircraft were acting up and he was losing so much power that he couldn't maintain height. Nor was he close enough to turn round and make a straight-in landing at base. When it was clear that nothing could be done he ordered Wilson to bale out. Willy acknowledged the message over the intercom and clambered out of his seat to open his escape hatch in the floor of the aircraft. In doing so he must have disconnected his wireless lead so that he and the C.O. couldn't talk to each other.

Widdows, suspecting that Wilson's wireless lead was disconnected, gave him what he thought was sufficient time to abandon the aircraft, and then eased himself out of his cockpit to follow. He happened to look back from the darkened fuselage and dimly discerned Wilson still struggling with the rear hatch. The aircraft was now only 1,000 feet up but Widdows could easily have ensured his own safety by jumping out. Without hesitation he clambered back into his cockpit and prepared for a crash-landing in the pitch blackness of the Lincolnshire countryside. Luck was with them as the ground below was flat and not heavily populated. Wilson was unaware of what was going on, and must have assumed that by now Widdows had left the aircraft. His predicament, as he desperately struggled with the rear hatch, must have been terrifying. He knew that the ground was coming up fast. But Widdows was guiding his aircraft down towards the solid blackness beneath him as gently as possible. As his altimeter showed he was approaching contact he put on the aircraft's landing light, hauled the control column back into his stomach and made a wheels-up landing in a field, narrowly missing a pylon carrying high-tension cables. The aircraft came to a grinding halt.

A second or so before the crash-landing Wilson at last got the hatch open. He had no idea of the height of the Beau above the ground, but he decided to get out as there could be no hope in staying in a crashing "pilotless" plane. Wilson had one foot out of the hatch as the aircraft crashed into the plough. He suffered severe injuries to the foot. Charles Widdows was not badly hurt and it was a rejoicing squadron that welcomed him back. Wilson spent some time in hospital, but he eventually rejoined us with a permanently stiff ankle, and I am sure with gratitude in his heart for the bravery of the man who had saved his life. The Squadron was deeply disappointed when Widdows's cool courage went unrewarded. In our opinion his action ranked with the bravest.

10

On our days off, most of the Squadron aircrew spent their time in Lincoln, but after a while we became a little bored with this city, so a number of us who owned cars of a sort began to wander farther afield for our pleasures. It was on such a day off that Don Parker, ex-bomber boy now night-fighter, and I set off for the larger city of Leicester in my old but trusty Wolsey Hornet. That evening in Simon's Bar in the Grand Hotel I espied a beautiful girl sitting at a table with an older woman. To the annoyance of the girl-friend beside me, I couldn't take my eyes off this new attraction. After a while I called a waiter and sent him to ask if the ladies would care for a drink. He returned and said they would, so I rather rudely took leave of my original girl-friend and the rest of the party and went over to join my new friends.

I quickly found they were mother and daughter and that Joan, the daughter, was a nurse in the V.A.D. on leave. I learned that there was a dance at a near-by hall, so I asked them if they would care to go, hoping that Mum would decline, which she did. So away we went to the dance, on the way shepherding Mum on to a tram for home.

I realized as we were dancing that I wanted to see Joan again, and very often, so on the way home I asked her if I could call for her on my next day off and take her to my parents' home in Duxford. At first she seemed to think I had some ulterior motive, but finally said, "We must ask the folks." I dropped her at the door of her home and we arranged to meet three

81

days later at lunch-time in Simon's Bar. From there we planned to go to her home, see her parents and get their O.K. for the trip to Duxford.

Back at the hotel, Don complained bitterly that I had left him with two females on his hands. I am afraid I wasn't very sympathetic. Next morning we returned to Wellingore in my old car, but the love-bug had caught up with me. All I could think of was the coming day off, hoping nothing would happen to spoil my plans.

I wrote to my parents and told them I would be down and that I would bring a girl with me. By the time my two days off arrived, I began to get jumpy about having so glibly said that I was taking her to my home. I had not yet got her parents' permission. I had already met her mother and felt that I could win her consent. But Joan's Dad was a different matter. Perhaps he was a big, tough chap who would mis-interpret my intentions. So I decided to take moral support with me in the form of Sammy France, the Adjutant, a trusty and experienced friend.

When the time arrived Sammy and I set off for Leicester in the Wolsey which was an open sports car. It was a cold drive indeed. Poor old Sammy's face, which was normally of a ruddy hue, was positively blue by the time we pulled up out-side the Grand Hotel. Joan was waiting and, after a drink or two to warm us up and also to give me some Dutch courage, off we set to the other side of the city to meet her parents. As I got out of the car outside her home I thought this was worse than facing a whole army of Germans. Now for it. Square the shoulders, make a bold front and ring the door-bell. The door opened. I was looking for something above my head and there was nothing there! Why, there he was—and smaller than me! "Hullo, I've been expecting you, come in. Mother, here's Joan's young man." This was a friendly and reassuring start. Joan had apparently convinced her parents about our trip to Duxford, so away we went in the old car with Sammy perched up on the back. The seating accommodation was a little limited. If Sammy was blue on the trip from Wellingore to Leicester, he was a deeper shade when we pulled up outside my father's vicarage at Duxford.

We had a wonderful couple of days and I fell completely in love with Joan on this, our second meeting. We decided to get married as soon as possible. My parents were astonished that we should want to get married after so short an acquaintance, but we convinced them we were serious. During the drive back to Leicester I asked her what she would do if her parents refused to consent. She was only eighteen and they could have argued that she was too young and that she had not known me long enough to make up her mind. However, she showed from the start that once her mind was made up she could be very determined. "Leave it to me. I can talk Mum and Dad into agreeing," she said. When we arrived at Joan's home her father was still at work and as Sammy and I had to return to Wellingore that day, we couldn't wait. I had to leave Joan to break the news to her parents.

Her parents agreed, though they thought we were mad. So Joan returned to the hospital where she had been working in Billericay, Essex, and resigned from the nursing service. Then she set off for my parents' home in Duxford to live in the parish so that the banns could be read. At Wellingore, I found everybody knew that I was going to be married. I wondered whom I should ask to be best man. Finally I asked Jackie Page, one of our officer AI operators, and he agreed. We were married by my father at Duxford Parish Church on April 15, 1941, a week after my twenty-first birthday. A number of the Squadron aircrew attended, including my C.O., Charles Widdows, and Nickie, his wife. During the service a flight of 29 Squadron Beaufighters flew low over the church in salute. They made a terrific noise and, by the look on father's face, I don't think he approved. Joan and I thought it was a fine gesture on the part of my comrades.

That night Joan and I stayed at the University Arms in Cambridge. We set off first thing next morning by train for a hotel at Minehead, Somerset, for our three weeks' honeymoon. We liked Minehead and it seemed far away from the war, although the daily news was not encouraging. The heavy German bombing attacks continued with unabated fury. One morning, as we were lazing in bed, a telegram was brought up to me. It ordered my return at once to Wellingore as the Squadron was moving to a new base. I had to leave Joan at her home in Leicester. The Squadron was off to West Malling near Maidstone to cover the approaches to London. Charles Widdows was full of apologies for having recalled me, but it was obvious that all crews had to move south. I soon forgot my disappointment for I knew we should be in the thick of it. I doubt whether Joan could have understood my thoughts. But I was still very young and the R.A.F. was my first love.

We took off on May 1 for the last time from Wellingore, a place of many happy memories and some sad ones. Pat Maxwell led B Flight and I led a section of three aircraft in his flight. Most of our groundcrew had arrived ahead of us and were waiting to guide us in to our dispersals round the airfield. A substantial mansion had been taken over as our mess just outside West Malling, and after the dreary flatness of Lincolnshire it was a delightful drive back and forth from the mess to the airfield through the hedgerows and orchards of Kent. Within a couple of days of arrival we were flying night patrols guided by our new G.C.I. stations around the Kentish coast. Now we knew we were to see action, for the enemy were flying over London every night.

II

SOON after we settled in at West Malling, Charles Widdows was replaced as Squadron Commander by Wing Commander Colbeck-Welch. But we weren't to see the last of Charles, who had won the respect of everyone in the unit. He took over West Malling as Station Commander. Colbeck-Welch, like his predecessors, was all out to get into the thick of it, but he was cursed by ill-health most of the time he was with us.

The month of May saw the Luftwaffe's last fling at mass night raids on Britain. So far they had got away with relatively light losses considering the terrible damage they had inflicted on the civilian population. It made me furiously angry to see our cities burning beneath me as I flew with other crews through the night sky, trying to stop what, at that time, seemed pointless murder of helpless people. This wanton destruction by the Germans was to bring on their heads a terrible revenge, the highest point of which was the holocaust of Hamburg in 1943. I could never see why the Germans thought these murderous bomber raids would help them. The destruction merely hardened the hearts of the British people against them. Individual combat in the air I could understand. In fact, there seemed to be something romantic and gallant about fighter versus fighter. But the bomber was a loathsome, murderous object to be destroyed without mercy. The compassion I felt some months before for the dead crew of the JU88 which Widdows shot down in East Anglia now vanished in hatred for the enemy who was destroying our beautiful country with its monuments of a glorious past.

My chance of personal vengeance came again on the night of May 8. Just after dark the sirens began to wail on the camp and in the near-by villages. One by one the Squadron's aircraft were scrambled. Ross was with me again. As always he filled me with confidence by his quiet manner in the air. The G.C.I. controller vectored us at 15,000 feet on a course towards the south-west. It was a dark night with wisps of cloud between 10,000 and 12,000 feet, but not enough for an enemy to hide in for long. As we climbed we could see the flashes and fires from the first bombs falling on London. Other night squadrons from Tangmere and Middle Wallop were already fully engaged in the fracas. When we reached height the controller told us where the enemy planes were and we closed. I told Ross, "When you get contact, bring me in so that he is just above me and dead ahead." "O.K., boss." This was our standard tactic. I could now make out heavy flak concentrations over London and fires were burning fiercely in the southern outskirts. From the G.C.I. controller I got "Creeper 42 (this was my radio call sign at the time). Bandit dead ahead, six miles, a little above. You should get contact in a moment."

I prayed that Ross's AI wouldn't fail. If it did there would be little hope of getting a visual of the enemy. "How's it going, Ross?"

"Got it, contact!" he replied. I called the G.C.I. to say we had contact and they wished us luck. Ross engaged the mute switch to cut out wireless interference from the ground stations, so that he could concentrate on giving me an uninterrupted commentary on what he saw on his radar scopes. Gradually he brought me closer to the enemy. Suddenly, as we were about 2,000 yards away, he said, "Boss, I've got two of them on the scope, both at the same range and height. One is dead ahead, the other is 10 degrees starboard."

"O.K., let's go for the one dead ahead first."

"Right. Range now 1,500 yards, 15 above, dead ahead."

So the commentary went on. By the inflexions in his voice and the slowing or speeding up of the information I could anticipate the amount of turn and whether to open or close the throttles. This was real teamwork, an absolute necessity for night-fighting. In the few months that Ross and I had worked together we had found the secret—complete co-ordination and implicit faith in each other. Now we were getting very close. I throttled back more to cut down the overtake speed to a minimum, so that I should not overshoot the target. I should see nothing until we were at about 200 yards range. Within that distance I had to see the aircraft, identify it—friendly or hostile—decide what kind of aircraft it was, and finally line it up in my sights and shoot it down.

Our speeds were synchronized at about 160 m.p.h. Gradually I opened the throttle. Ross was still passing me the vital information. "He's only about 200 yards now. The other one is 30 degrees starboard at about 250 yards. They are both slightly above you. Can you see anything yet?" I peered harder through the windscreen. My eyes were smarting with the strain of staring into space. Then suddenly I saw them both. I could make out twinkling lights from the exhausts of a two-motored aircraft, and off to the starboard out of the corner of my eye I caught a glimpse of a dark shape above me, blotting out the stars as it moved along. "I've got 'em." I didn't dare take my eyes off the one ahead of me. He took on the definite shape of a He III. I had him now fairly and squarely in view. I chanced another look to starboard at the other target which was still there. It was another He III. I quickly called G.C.I. as I manœuvred into position to fire, I pulled the nose up and shouted to Ross to watch the fireworks through his cockpit canopy. He said he could see both aircraft, and just at that moment I fired. It wasn't a very accurate burst, and although I saw some hits the enemy wasn't mortally wounded. He started a diving turn to port, smoking from one engine, and as he turned his upper rear-gunner opened fire. A thin stream of tracer passed over us. I cursed because I had hoped to finish this one off quickly and then attack the other. This was now impossible if I was to finish off my first adversary, which I was determined to do. I pulled the Beau round into a port turn and again fired a long deflection burst into him, this time with more luck. I saw the strikes and the German gunner ceased firing. Flames started to stream out behind the doomed plane. It nosed steeply towards the earth. I pulled up and turned to go after the second Heinkel after seeing a huge flash of flame as our victim hit the deck. I told G.C.I. of our success and asked for help to locate the other raider, but they couldn't help us. The situation was now confused on their scopes and other night-fighters were in the area.

After searching fruitlessly about the sky with our AI, Ross and I decided we might as well return to base. Thirty minutes later we were on the ground at West Malling. It had been an eventful night. Night-fighter forces had destroyed ten of the raiders and the flak three or four more. Next day I learned from Flying Officer Hamilton, our "spy", where my enemy had crashed. He asked if I would like to drive over and look at it. The crew were all dead. "No thanks," I said. I still remembered Widdows's crashed JU88, and could see no point in viewing the mess. But I asked Hammy if he would get me a souvenir and something for Ross. Next day he produced an Iron Cross First Class, which he recovered from the dead pilot, and a couple of German Mae Wests. I kept the medal and one of the life jackets and gave the other to Ross. The German life jackets were much less bulky than ours, although according to our experts they were not as good, because they had no kapok in them, in addition to the inflatable rubber bags to assist in keeping an airman afloat. Even so, I thought them more practical than ours and I wore my German prize until I was relieved of it when taken prisoner in June, 1944.

The large-scale raids came to a climax later on May 10, 1941. This was also the most successful night for the defences. Of about 500 German bombers sent out, 29 were brought down by night-fighters and 4 by flak. Our Squadron had its share and a number of the newer crews recorded their first successes. Ross and I were unlucky. Just after we were scrambled our AI became unserviceable. We had to return to base and there wasn't another available aircraft for us. But it was grand to see the spirits of the Squadron mounting. No longer would we have to listen to the crowing of the crews of 219 and 604 Squadrons who at this stage were the most successful night-fighters in the country. They gained that glory during the time when the Huns were numerous. We only got in at the end of this era. Our successes came in the lean years to follow, when the Germans made much rarer appearances and developed new techniques to fox the wily night-fighter.

After this last heavy raid things were much quieter and I found a home for Joan and me just outside West Malling. It was part of a delightful house in its own cherry orchard. Joan was delighted with it and we were supremely happy when for brief hours we could forget the war together.

12

DURING the spring and summer of 1941 the Squadron was built up to full strength. Some of the old hands were posted as instructors and their places were filled by new aircrew. These new men were much better trained in the art of night-fighting than we had been at first. We had to teach ourselves and experiment with techniques and tactics. These chaps had been getting the benefit of our experience. We found many of them still had a poor opinion of the Beaufighter. They thought it was a dangerous aeroplane and that, among other things, it wouldn't fly on one engine. Experience banished their fears. I was now promoted to Flight Lieutenant, remaining as Pat Maxwell's deputy in B Flight. Guy Gibson became Acting Squadron Leader at the same time and took over A Flight. Both flights were now commanded by Squadron Leaders.

During this lull in enemy night activity we had time to get to know our G.C.I. controllers better. There were several stations around the coast of Kent which controlled us from time to time. Our crews could recognize the voices of particular controllers and they recognized ours. We got to know the hot controllers and they soon found which fighter crews reacted most quickly to their instructions.

Some of the controllers were non-flying types, or World War I aircrew. Others were flying men of this war who were grounded temporarily or permanently because of injury. Two of the most successful in the sector were Squadron Leaders Hammersley and Mawhood. They were responsible for many of my early successes. Hammersley was a veteran who was badly wounded in the First World War. He was too old to start flying again so he got himself into the next best thing—controlling. Mawhood was a short service commissioned officer who had joined the R.A.F. about a year before I had. He had fought in Hurricanes in the Battle of Britain and had lost an eye in combat. These chaps got little glory for their job, but they certainly shared in all our kills, for without their wizardry we should have achieved nothing, and many more Germans would have dropped their loads of destruction on British cities.

Unfortunately, at about this time our landlady decided that she wanted us to leave. My wife was expecting a baby and she had been told when we moved into our first wartime home that no children were wanted. So we found another apartment in a large old house in the village of East Malling. It was much more fun because many of the Squadron officers and their wives were already there, and the charming landlady did everything to make life pleasant for us and her other guests.

In mid-June, Ross and I got into combat with one of the few Germans who poked his nose in the direction of England. We were patrolling at about 15,000 feet south of the Thames estuary, when we noticed plentiful flak and searchlights to the north of us. I called the controller who pointed us in the direction of the enemy, but a few minutes later my radio broke down and I couldn't speak to the ground. My intercom was still working, however, so I could talk to my AI operator. We decided to fly towards the flak and try to pick up a chance contact on our AI. We flew backwards and forwards over the area without success. Then Ross suddenly called, "Contact, hard starboard, range 3,000 yards and go down." I followed his running commentary and could picture exactly where the target was. We were still above it so I closed the range and gradually lost height, until at 9,000 feet the enemy was a little above and dead ahead at 1,000 yards.

It was very dark and there was broken cloud below us. I turned down the brilliance of my electric gunsight, so that I could only just see the reticle, and peered ahead, waiting tensely for the familiar black blob to appear. Ross's voice was getting more urgent as we closed to 600, 500, 400, 250 yards. "Can you see him yet, boss?" Suddenly there he was, a dark shape just above me at about 200 yards. "Yes, I've got him." I had to get in closer yet as I couldn't make out what he was.

I was well aware that I was poaching in Hunsdon's area, and that some of the night-fighters from that station would be about. They might be closing in on me, taking me for an enemy. Not a pleasant thought, but I didn't have time to worry about it. What was ahead of me? Friend or foe? At about 150 yards I could make out the exhaust pattern and the wing shape. It was a Heinkel. "It's a Hun, Ross. Can you see him?" Ross was now looking out through his canopy. "Yes, I've got him, Boss, give him hell." This I proceeded to do.

The smell of cordite filled the aircraft as I fired a long burst from all guns. I could see the shells striking the fuselage and wings of the enemy. He started to dive with smoke belching out astern. I followed, firing another burst. There were more sparks as my cannon shells and .303 bullets struck home. He continued to dive into clouds, then I lost him. A violent flash of light on the ground, which died down into a steady blaze, told us the end of the story. Ross and I were certain we had got him but it was going to be difficult to prove. I wasn't sure where I was, and as our wireless was dead I couldn't get my exact position from the G.C.I.

Ross estimated our position as some seventy miles east-north-east of West Malling, so I set course for home. I thought I would give the radio another try as I got closer and I managed to get a faint reply from the West Malling tower. Five miles from base reception became loud and clear. A few minutes later we were on the ground reporting our success to Hamilton, the "spy". The G.C.I. station which had controlled us after take-off had been worried because we had gone off the air. They had plotted us heading out of their area and they feared we might have got mixed up with the Hunsdon night-fighters with disastrous results for someone. Ross and I realized we had been foolish. We probably caused such confusion in the Hunsdon sector that some of the Germans got through. Our estimate of where our victim crashed was approximately correct. A wrecked Heinkel was found on the ground, but a Hunsdon fighter claimed an aircraft shot down in about the same position. It was in their sector so their aircraft got the credit. At the time Ross and I were annoyed, but we realized we had been poaching. We had learnt a lesson and we had to be content with our own conviction of victory.

At the end of June we had the great news that Ross had been awarded the D.F.M. This naturally led to more celebrations and poor old Ross was absent for a number of days. I flew with F/Sgt. Gregory—"Sticks" to his friends. Gregory had been a drummer in Debroy Somers's band for a time, hence his nickname. From the start I admired him for his cheerfulness and in the few days while Ross was away celebrating, I found that Sticks was far above average in the AI business.

Occasionally we had unfortunate run-ins with our own bombers on their way to and from targets in Germany or the occupied countries. These aircraft sometimes got mistaken for German bombers when coming in over our coastline. Dave Humphries came into the dispersal hut one night rubbing his hands gleefully and claimed a Dornier, probably destroyed. We gathered round to listen to his report to Hamilton. He had sighted the aircraft after a long AI chase just above cloud, closed the range, opened fire and saw it dive smoking into the cloud. As he hadn't seen it crash he claimed a probable. About half an hour later a Hampden bomber entered the West Malling circuit and landed. The crew reported to our Intelligence Officer and were obviously angry about something. They had been fired on by a Beau and had only escaped by diving into cloud. Nobody was hurt but their aircraft was badly damaged. Inspection showed British bullets embedded in the fuselage but Dave managed to convince the authorities that he had been miles away when the attack on the bomber had been made. The bomber crew were not impressed. In moments of excitement it wasn't difficult to mistake the identity of an aircraft, and it is to the credit of the night-fighter crews that only a few mistakes were made.

Ross and I were fired on by a Wellington bomber. It was a bright moonlight night and G.C.I. had vectored us on to a "bogey" which indicated that they were uncertain of its identity. When we got AI contact we closed cautiously. I saw the aircraft at the same time as it saw us. The night was so light and clear we had no trouble in identifying it as friendly. But I got a little too close for the liking of the bomber crew and we were greeted by a well-directed burst of fire from the tail gunner. I heard an unpleasant rattling sound as bullets bored into my aircraft. I broke away violently to the starboard, asking Ross if he was O.K. He said yes, and as nothing appeared to be seriously wrong with us we continued with our patrol. I could still faintly see the Wellington turning away towards the north and below, on the coast near Dover, there was a mass of small fires probably caused by incendiary bombs. I called control, advised them that we had intercepted a Wellington and that we had been fired on. They told us they thought the aircraft was hostile as it had dropped bombs and asked us to go and investigate again. Soon we regained contact and again as I closed, much more cautiously this time, we confirmed it as a Wellington. I called G.C.I. and said, "It is definitely friendly." But still they weren't convinced because of its apparent hostile action. So I decided to shadow it as long as possible to see where it was headed. Perhaps the Germans were using a captured Wellington to fool us, but this was doubtful. It crossed the Thames estuary heading due north and after a while started to descend. It was clearly going to land at an airfield in Norfolk. Again I broke away and headed for home after advising the G.C.I.

Our groundcrew told us there were six bullet-holes in the fuselage between Ross's position and my cockpit. One bullet had lodged in Ross's detachable chest parachute which he had put in the rack close to his seat. Our friendly bomber was certainly a most unsociable chap. We asked the "spy" to try to track down the offending friend and next day the story came out. The Wellington had taken off from Marham, Norfolk, for a bombing raid on Boulogne. The crew had lost themselves and mistaken Dover for their target. Luckily their bombs landed in fields and only set fire to haystacks. They did, however, claim to have been attacked by a JU88 and to have shot him down. I felt like sending them a congratulatory message, but realized that this would be rubbing it in too much since they must already be far from popular at their own base.

One moonlit night when he was our Station Commander, Charles Widdows flew a patrol with one of our N.C.O. AI operators. G.C.I. rang through to tell us he was being vectored on to a "bogey". This had possibilities and we hoped that it would turn out to be a German and that he would shoot it down. Some minutes later the G.C.I. informed us he had been shot up by return fire from the JU88 but was on his way back to base. We gathered outside the dispersal to greet him and find out what had happened. As he was taxiing in we saw that the AI operator's back escape hatch was open. The C.O. switched off his engines and climbed out. There was blood on his clothes. He had been slightly wounded in the leg. Then he noticed the open rear hatch and the fact that his

AI operator was missing. It must have been a severe shock to him as it was to us. We heard the story later. They had been directed on to the "bogey" over the English Channel and had identified it as a JU88. Widdows and the German crew must have spotted each other at the same time. They fired almost simultaneously. The JU88 was hit but the rear gunner got in an accurate burst of return fire. This had damaged the radio controls in the pilot's cockpit and fragments of bullet or metal from the aircraft had injured Widdows's leg. He took violent evasive action and lost sight of the enemy. Then he found he could not contact his AI observer or any of the ground stations. He did not know how seriously his aircraft was damaged or whether his operator was injured, so he decided to return to base. On arrival over base he attracted the traffic control officer's attention by flying low over the tower and waggling his wings.

We had to assume that the AI operator thought his pilot had been killed by the return fire from the JU88, since he could not contact Widdows over the intercom. The N.C.O. was proably further convinced of this by the violent manœuvring of the Beau. Was it out of control with a dead man at the controls? He must have decided to bale out. This was a hard blow for Widdows whose combat career seemed to have been haunted by bad luck. We heard some months later from the International Red Cross that the N.C.O.'s body had been washed up on the French coast. It wasn't long after this incident that our Station Commander was posted to a staff job at one of the Fighter Group Headquarters. It was a well-deserved rest for a man who had continuously shown unselfishness and courage of a very high order. We were all gratified when he was awarded a long overdue D.F.C.

In July I noticed that Ross was beginning to show signs of being tired. One day he told me he thought he had had it and would like to go back to Canada for a tour of duty. This was a blow, as I felt we had built ourselves up into a really, efficient night-fighter team. I consulted the Squadron Commander and it so happened that Group had asked for an experienced AI operator as an instructor at one of the night-fighter O.T.U.s. It was decided that Ross's experience would be invaluable in the training of night-fighter crews and that the O.T.U. was the logical place for him rather than returning him to Canada. He wasn't very pleased about it but finally agreed. The decision made, I took on Sticks Gregory as my regular AI operator.

A week or so before we teamed up, Sticks and I had our first combat. That night there was a lot of enemy activity. Just after take-off we were vectored north-east at 8,000 feet to intercept a hostile raid coming in along the Thames estuary. As we were closing with our target I heard another of the Squadron's aircraft being vectored on to a target and realized that it was Guy Gibson. Sticks called, "Contact, dead ahead and below at 2,000 yards." So down we went in a gentle dive to close the range and get below our target. I could clearly see the Thames shimmering down below us in the moonlight. Sticks continued to pass instructions until I saw an aircraft at about 500 yards. Soon I recognized it as a JU88. It saw us at the same time, started to take evasive action and fired. I told Sticks to get his head out of the "office" and watch the fireworks. Tracer was now passing close over the Beau and Sticks was urging me to open up. "No, not yet," I said. "We must get closer to make sure of the so-and-so." Later in our fights against the enemy it was Sticks who said, "Not yet, get in closer."

The return fire was getting heavy though we hadn't yet been hit. I opened up, ·trying to adjust my deflection to counter his desperate manœuvres. I fired three short bursts at close intervals and saw immediate results. His return fire ceased and the JU88 started to burn. He dived into the Thames. We were now down to 3,000 feet so we climbed, telling the jubilant G.C.I. controller the story in as few words as possible. Gibson, who had landed when we got in, had also, shot down an enemy at about 13,000 feet in the same area as our victory. He had seen the tracer ammunition of our JU88 below him as he was getting into position to attack, so he rightly assumed we were in combat. This trip and some training missions with Gregory proved to my satisfaction that he was a superb operator.

Early in August my father wrote to say Mother had pneumonia and was seriously ill. I borrowed an aircraft and flew to Duxford. Poor Mum had suffered a weak heart for as long as I could remember. My sister arrived home at the same time as myself and I believe our presence did much to cheer her up. I had to leave next day but promised I would ask Joan if she would go to Duxford to nurse Mother. Joan willingly agreed and about a week after she had left for Duxford I was in Maidstone on a night off with a bunch of our pilots and AI operators doing the round of the pubs. At 11 p.m. I returned to my lodgings in East Malling to be greeted at the door by the Squadron engineer officer who told me as gently as possible that a telegram awaited me saying Mother had died. It had been quite a party in Maidstone and it took several seconds for this news to sink in. When it did I felt all the worse for not having been around when the news came. The Squadron Commander willingly let me have an aircraft to fly home, telling me to stay as long as necessary. Sticks kindly offered to go with me. My biggest sorrow was that Mother, who had been such a good friend to me and my sister, did not live long enough to see our first son. I returned to Malling after the funeral but Joan and I had decided it would be best for her to return to her parents' home until the baby was born. This relieved my mind as I was not happy about her living near the station under combat conditions. There was too much worry for us both.

13

IN the summer of 1941 the enemy changed his tactics. No longer was he making mass attacks, his losses had been too great to keep this up. Now he was concentrating on small hit-and-run raids. The Germans had discovered that our AI-equipped fighters were less effective at low level, so many of their attacks were now delivered below 5,000 feet. We had been afraid this would happen. Our Mk 4 AI was not very effective below this height. But Britain's scientists were well aware of the problem and perfected a new AI equipment known as Mk 7, which not only made it possible to pick up low-flying targets, but also gave us longer initial pick-up ranges. This equipment was more directional than our earlier AI. It enabled the operator to pick up targets in a cone of 120 degrees around the longitudinal axis of the aircraft.

The night squadrons had the problem of low-level raiders to deal with immediately. The new AI was not available yet and, in fact, 29 Squadron was not re-equipped with it until early 1942. In the meantime we worked hard to develop tactics with our Mk 4 AI which would enable us to cope with the low-level threat. Sticks and I had an idea and in October, 1941, were able to try it out in combat. We were scrambled to intercept a target approaching the Thames estuary. As we climbed on an easterly heading into the dark sky, we broke into a cloud layer at 2,000 feet and a few seconds later were above it at 4,000 feet, continuing our climb to 8,000 feet. We were under control of one of the C.H.L. stations which had been designed to track down low-flying aircraft. The controller advised us that the target was about 4,000 feet below us.

Normal tactics to date had been to position ourselves slightly below the target as this gave us the best chance of seeing the enemy first. But during our practice against friendly aircraft, to work out new tactics at low levels, Sticks concluded that we should have a better chance of getting AI contact at a longer range if we stayed above the target until contact was obtained. We could then reduce height until we were within about 1,000 yards, when the effects of ground clutter on the radar screen would be less serious. The bomber crew would have a good chance of seeing the fighter first, but it was a chance we had to take.

The controller directed us into a position astern of our target and we reduced height a little to 7,000 feet. As the range closed, the atmosphere became more and more tense in our aircraft. Surely Sticks should have contact by now. Then from the controller, "Creeper 42, X raid now one and a half miles dead ahead and below. Any joy?" I was just about to say "No" when Sticks called, "O.K., Bob. Contact 6,000 feet slightly to port and well below. Gently port and go down 500 feet, and get your speed back." I informed the controller, who wished us the best of luck.

So far so good. I levelled off again at just over 6,000 feet; Sticks was still giving me a running commentary as if it were a horse-race. His confident voice never ceased and the fact that he repeated an instruction sometimes four or five times didn't matter to me. I should worry if he ceased talking for a second or two because this would indicate he was having trouble sorting out the picture on his scopes. "Things are working out fine. Range now just under 3,000 feet. Go down another 500 feet. The target is now dead ahead." I throttled back a little as I eased the control column forward, so as not to build up excess speed during our short descent. The enemy was flying only just on top of the cloud layer, so if he got a glimpse of us he could dive for cover and we would lose him. "Range 2,000 feet, still dead ahead. Speed just about synchronized. Down another 500 feet." Down we went again. I was now at about 5,000 feet. "Can you see anything yet, Bob?" "No, not yet." My eyes scanned ahead and below. It was very dark. What was that? I thought I saw a black shape moving across the top of the slightly lighter cloud. I couldn't be sure so I said nothing. "Down another 500 feet, and watch it! We are damn close, range 1,200 feet." Yes, there he was. "I've got him, Sticks, but keep your head in the set in case I lose him visually." "Give him the works, Chief." I called the ground controller, "Tally-ho." "Good show, Bob. What is he?" By now I was close enough to make out the twin rudders of a Dornier. "He's a Dornier 217. I am going to open fire now." With that I released the radio button and concentrated on shooting at the enemy ahead who was apparently oblivious to our presence. I fired a two- or three-second burst from my four cannons and six machine guns. Sticks had his head out of the "office" and was anxiously watching. Sparks and flame came from the Dornier and a large chunk of aircraft broke off and drifted back behind us. He dived straight down through the cloud, and a second or so later we saw through the cloud an ominous flash of light which dwindled as our foe sank into the sea. "Christ, I think his whole tail unit came off." "Bloody good, Bob. Now let's go home and have a beer. I'm dry." When we landed at base we were able to tell the rest of the chaps that the new tactic could be made to work.

September and October were busy months and the Squadron gradually built up its score of kills. Sticks and I were luckier than most. We accumulated three more destroyed and one damaged, in addition to other inconclusive combats. To give some idea of the difficulties of night-fighting it is worth mentioning two of our inconclusive combats. They were typical of what happened to numerous other crews. The first of these battles was south of London. It was a dark night with no moon and I had been persuaded to take an army officer along as an observer. This was possible in the Beau. The extra "body" had to stand behind the pilot on the escape hatch. He could see ahead over the pilot's shoulders. There was a spare intercom lead so that he could plug in his helmet and listen to conversation between the pilot and AI operator. He could also speak to the crew if he wished.

Soon after take-off the G.C.I. vectored us on to a raid and eventually Sticks got contact on AI. He directed me in and, as we drew closer to the quarry, Sticks kept telling me to throttle back, indicating that I was closing too fast. We were now at about 400 yards range and I still couldn't see the thing. A quick look showed that our speed was back to about 120 m.p.h. which, disconcertingly, was slow. Still Sticks called me to throttle back and I could tell by the rapidity by which the range was closing that I should have to do something drastic, otherwise I should overshoot and find the enemy behind us. I put the wheels and flaps down and my airspeed dropped to 110 m.p.h. At that moment I saw the target loom up just above me at about 100 yards. He was a Heinkel and must have had his throttles right back as he was only doing about 100 m.p.h.

I weaved desperately to stay behind the Heinkel, but in the process of one of these manœuvres I pulled out too far to one side and lost visual contact. Sticks quickly got his head back in the radar scope, but he was unable to pick up the target again. Probably during our manœuvring the enemy crew had spotted us and turned away. This was maddening. Our Major was the most disappointed man I had seen for some time. He thought we were sure to have a scrap because we were so close to the enemy, and then to crown things he hadn't even seen anything. That German was a wily bird. He knew that by flying just about on the stall he was making our job almost impossible. As the night was so dark he must have guessed that no night-fighter pilot would see him until he was very close. Then he wouldn't have time to check his speed to get in a killing burst of fire.

The second incident was on a bright night just off Dover. We were patrolling at 12,000 feet parallel with the coast when we were vectored to an incoming raid. Again Sticks obtained radar contact and we closed for the kill. This time I saw the enemy at nearly half a mile range. I recognized it as a single engine JU87 dive-bomber. I had never run into one of these planes before, but from all accounts they weren't much of a problem for our day-fighter boys. But he saw me at about the same moment, and as I closed to within firing range pushed his stick forward and went into a vertical dive towards the sea. For a second I lost sight of him. I quickly racked the Beau over into a half roll and hurtled down after him. I picked him up visually again but his speed was relatively slow as he had put out his dive breaks. We had no such device and, although I was throttled right back, the momentum of our aircraft took our speed quickly to 350 then 400 m.p.h. and we shot past the German before I could get off a single shot. For the next few seconds I was busy pulling the heavy fighter out of the dive, with the engines whining ominously. At last we pulled out at about 3,000 feet above the English Channel, but our JU87 had escaped, curse it. Back at Malling the ground-crew found some of our engine cooling gills had been torn off by the excess speed.

During this small revival of Luftwaffe activity I became involved in a car accident which turned a gay and happy party into a tragedy and put me in hospital for a time. To be out of action with the enemy still active seemed a disaster. With several other Squadron officers we set off for a night out in

Maidstone. My own car was unserviceable so I tagged along as passenger in Bob Willis's worn-out old Ford 8. It was a merry evening and midnight found us in a dance hall. On the return journey I had a lift in a colleague's Austin 7, which was loaded to the gunwales with four officers and two girl-friends who were returning to the mess for a final drink with us. Perhaps we were exceeding the 30 m.p.h. limit, but as I was sitting in the back I couldn't tell. The last thing I remember before the crash was seeing a vague red tail-light of some vehicle ahead—and then oblivion. When I came to I was lying on a raincoat at the side of the road with blood trickling into my mouth. This made me sick. I could also vaguely hear someone groaning. There was a crowd round the scene and a policeman helped me to my feet. Then I saw that we had run into the back of an army truck and our car was a complete wreck. The policeman helped me to his car and told me one of the girls was in a critical condition, but that the rest of us had got off with light injuries. When we arrived back I saw that I had a deep gash over my right eyebrow. It had to be sewn up in the station sick quarters. There I was told that the injured girl had died in the ambulance on the way to hospital. The officer's ward was remarkably quiet that night. It was a bitter end to a carefree evening. We were well used to the hand of death, but this shook us in a way we had never been shaken before.

14

As 1941 drew to a close, 29 Squadron saw many changes. Guy Gibson had gone to Cranfield, near Bedford. From there he returned to Bomber Command to fame and to his death. Dave Humphries followed him to Cranfield and then on to another night-fighter squadron where he was killed in a night-flying accident. We suffered a number of casualties, most of them due to the weather rather than the enemy.

Sticks and I were worried about having to leave the Squadron. We realized our turn must soon come. I had been with 29 for three years without a break. So far, every time a signal came from Group requesting a crew for the O.T.U.s, I had convinced my C.O. that I ought to stay a little longer. But I knew that soon I should be posted.

Late in November, the Squadron Commander told me I was being detached with Sticks to 141 Squadron at Ayr, Scotland, for a couple of weeks. Our job was to help them in their conversion from Defiants to Beaufighters. I doubt whether our presence was really necessary, but we were able to pass on information about AI techniques.

The Defiants had no AI. They were a single-engine, two-seat aircraft looking something like the old Hurricane, but instead of having eight forward-firing machine guns they were equipped with four machine guns in an enclosed rear turret. By manoeuvring his aircraft the pilot could bring this armament into action. At first these Defiants caught the German fighters unaware. When the enemy sneaked up behind what they thought was a flight of Hurricanes, the Defiants would turn and the rear gunner deliver a stream of bullets. One squadron of them had a big day during the Battle of Britain when they shot down twelve German fighters without loss to themselves. But the Germans soon got wise to the Defiants, and the superior manœuvrability of the Me109 soon turned the tables. Two squadrons of Defiants changed over to the night-fighter role.

Without AI gear, but by close co-operation with A.A. and searchlights, they had some successes, their best-ever performance being to shoot down eight Germans during a full-moon raid on Glasgow. During our short stay at Ayr, Sticks and I had visited the local drinking spots with the boys of 141 Squadron and enjoyed ourselves, though on occasion we nearly got into fights with some very tough gentry who frequented some of the pubs. These chaps belonged to the newly-formed Commandos who were training in the area. I am afraid we asked for trouble by criticizing in loud voices their fantastic dress and weapons, which included knives, tommy-guns and other articles of war. In turn they must have considered us a bunch of pansies. I am glad we never decided to mix it as we should have certainly been marked for life.

In December we left and, of course, I had no clue then that I should soon be commanding this Squadron. Our farewell was a riot. A very wet night included a visit to Ayr ice-rink. There, for the first time in our lives, Sticks and I put on skates and bet one another whether we could cross to the other side of the rink without falling flat. Sober it would have been difficult. In our state it was impossible. We did a most undignified crawling race on all fours across the ice.

It was fairly quiet back at West Malling. Many Luftwaffe squadrons had been moved to the Russian front. Pat Maxwell was replaced by Squadron Leader Moon who had been at Tangmere in 219 Squadron. Sticks was awarded a D.F.M. and I got a bar to my D.F.C. early in December. But I was determined to see Sticks commissioned and I found he had been recommended. At last the axe fell. A signal arrived saying that Braham and Gregory were transferred to 51 Nightfighter O.T.U. at Cranfield. I had had a good run, having been with a combat unit continuously since the outbreak of the war. The Squadron Commander knew how I felt about going and promised he would do all he could to get me back to the Squadron.

Though Sticks and I were disappointed, Joan was happy to see me out of the line for a while. She rarely let me know she was worried but I knew she was very unhappy at times, especially as we were living apart and she was shortly expecting our first child. I am afraid that at the time I was very selfish. The R.A.F. came first and my wife and family second. She knew this and I shall always be grateful to her for her unselfish understanding.

Our job for the next six months was to train new fighter crews. Sticks and I got to know many of the staff and students well and some of them were to serve with me later. Outstanding among them was Flight Lieutenant Henry Jacobs—Jacko to his friends—who was Jewish. He was the chief AI instructor in 3 AI Squadron, and he or Sticks flew with me on most of our instructional missions. I had met Jacko briefly at Tangmere. He was already making a name for himself as an expert in the AI business, and although he was older than Sticks and me he impressed us with his tremendous keenness to get at the enemy. The three of us were to become firm and lasting friends.

Cranfield was about twelve miles from Bedford. This was the nearest town on which we could let loose our pent-up emotions. At the Key Club we were able to drink, dance and get an excellent meal up to one or two in the morning. Jacko soon enrolled Sticks and me as members and there we spent many a pleasant evening off. We also met there the first

American aircrew we encountered. The newly-arrived U.S.A.A.C. 8th Air Force had taken over a number of airfields in the area and their officers had already been enrolled in the club.

A meeting between the Allies in this club once nearly led to a riot. Luckily both sides sobered up before serious physical or material damage was done. A group of Cranfield instructors were chatting and drinking round the bar, when four or five American officers arrived. Everybody was minding his own business when one American made some crack about annexing Australia as the forty-ninth State. One of the AI instructors in our party was an Australian named Hawkins. He was exceedingly short, but what he lacked in physique he made up for in aggressiveness. He leapt out of his chair and before we could stop him he was about to take on all the American visitors single-handed. Harsh words were exchanged and the Americans decided to leave, but Hawk wasn't satisfied. He took off down the stairs after them. We dragged him back still fuming.

February, 1942, was a lucky month for Sticks and me. He had his well-deserved commission, and Joan and I had a son. I got a few days off and drove to Leicester to see my new family. My wife was in the nursing home and had had a bad time, but the little boy, whom we named Michael, was thriving. Poor Joan had indeed suffered, but she made a rapid recovery. She would have liked me to find a home for her and the baby near Cranfield, but I pointed out that my stay at the O.T.U. was likely to be short. Besides, it was better for her to be with her mother just then. We were luckier than many service families who were separated for years.

Next, Sticks and I were ordered to 219 Squadron at Tangmere, near Chichester, to get experience with a new type of AI equipment known as Mk 5. Some of the Squadron's aircraft had been fitted with it and Fighter Command wanted opinions as to its value from other experienced crews. It was a good feeling to be back in a squadron again and flying the old Beaus. But this new AI gear was little, if any, better than the Mk 4. Its main difference was that it incorporated a pilot's radar scope. When the AI operator picked up a target he could transfer the information to the pilot who could then, in theory at least, continue the interception with the operator monitoring his progress. But there was one major drawback. The pilot still had to look up and fix the enemy visually. His eyes could not change focus rapidly enough from the 18-inch range of his instrument panel to a distance of 100 to 700 yards. After a few trials Sticks and I decided the best way was to ignore the pilot's scope and let the AI operator talk the pilot into visual firing range. Generally our views were shared by the 219 crews. The equipment never went into large-scale production.

Shortly after this I had a narrow escape in the air. Jacko's rapid appreciation of what was going on saved us both. I flew one of our station doctors in a Dominie to Ibsley on the south coast. Jacko and Sticks came along for the ride. I hadn't been feeling well, but I didn't think much of it. The trip to Ibsley was uneventful. On the way back Jacko sat just behind the pilot's seat with Sticks dozing in one of the other seats. I started to sweat and felt faint. Next thing I knew was Jacko leaning over my shoulder, gently pulling back on the control column with one hand, and slapping my face with the other. This brought me to. I was feeling ghastly. So Jacko and Sticks kept a close watch on me for the rest of the flight. When we were safely back on the ground at Cranfield the doctor took my temperature, which was 101 or so. He said, "Well, my lad, you've got German measles. Off to bed with you." This kept me off flying for two weeks. I always thought it a little ironic. It might at least have been ordinary measles!

15

IN early June Sticks and I took a few days off to visit 29 Squadron. Ted Colbeck-Welch allowed us to fly as much as we liked. Since I had left, new Beaus with the Mk 7 AI had been issued to the Squadron, so Sticks and I decided to master this new equipment for low-level interception. One night there was a lot going on in the Canterbury–Dover area and we were anxious to have a go. But there weren't enough Beaus with the Mk 7 equipment. So, as visitors, we had to be content with the older Mk 4. Something big was brewing as all the aircraft were scrambled one after the other. Our turn came and off we went. We could see heavy flak round Canterbury but the G.C.I. put us on a patrol line. The controllers had their hands full controlling the rest of the Squadron, and naturally they favoured crews who were flying with latest AI as they would be most likely to get the enemy. It was maddening having to hang about knowing the enemy was near. We saw many fires burning in and around Canterbury and the flak was the most intense I had seen up to that time. Sticks and I decided to fly a zigzag course over Canterbury, gradually easing over towards the coast and out to sea. For some time we picked up nothing except some near misses from our own flak. Suddenly Sticks came over the intercom with a slightly excited inflexion: "Contact." "Christ, don't lose him, Sticks." "Hard port, and down." The commentary continued. "More speed. We are only just holding him." By now we were down to about 12,000 feet and the throttles were wide open. "O.K., Bob, we are gradually closing. He is about 2,000 yards dead ahead and a little below. Down a bit more."

We were clear of the Canterbury flak heading out towards the coast. I remember thinking, "This swine is on his way home. He has dropped his load." During a moment's pause in Sticks's commentary I passed a message to G.C.I. saying we were closing on a target. "Good show, but make sure that it is hostile," was the reply. This was a sobering thought. It hadn't occurred to me. Well, we should soon see. Instructions from Sticks became more and more rapid. "Keep your eyes open, Bob. You should see him in a minute. He is 10 degrees above and dead ahead at about 200 yards." I adjusted my gunsight and searched for tell-tale exhaust flickers or a black object blotting out the stars. One second there was nothing, then, as if from nowhere, it was there. Twin rudders, and very faintly I made out the red glow from the exhausts of twin engines. "It's a Do 217, Sticks. Get your head out of the office and have a look." Just as I opened fire he said, "I can see him, Bob. Give him the works." One burst was enough. He caught fire and dived steeply into the sea off Sandwich.

G.C.I. told us that 29 Squadron fighters had been in a number of successful combats. Bad weather was now closing in rapidly at West Malling and we were advised to go to Manston. I pushed the nose down through a stratus cloudbank to 1,000 feet and soon saw the Manston flare-path. Fog was rolling in from the sea. It was obvious we should have to get down very quickly. The control tower cleared me to come straight in to land, but in the hurry and excitement I made too close a circuit and was over the edge of the runway too high and too fast. "Tighten your straps, Sticks," I called. "We can't go round again or we'll never get in with this weather." "O.K., cock, but watch it." I side-slipped to get rid of height and kicked the rudders from side to side to get rid of as much speed as possible. At last the main wheels hit but we were much too far down the runway. We passed the last flare lights doing about 60 m.p.h., then blackness as we bumped over rough ground. There was a rending crash as my starboard wing hit the top of a small building. We came to a stop in what appeared to be a ploughed field.

We scrambled out shakily and in the distance vaguely made out the lights of a crash-truck heading to us. We were amazed that the Beau was still on its undercarriage. The only visible damage was to the starboard wing and flap. Everything else seemed O.K., except that the props were festooned with barbed wire.

The crash-truck crew were amazed to see us in one piece. As we drove back we saw how close we had been to disaster. Our landing run had taken us through a gap formed by a revetment, which housed a Hurrie fighter-bomber waiting to be flown on an early-morning mission, and a number of buildings. There had just been room to get through. If I had veered slightly to the left, we should have crashed into the Hurrie bomber. If we had turned a little the other way we should have crashed into solid buildings and might have killed many of the inmates as well as ourselves.

Because of this incident we were going to be late getting back to Cranfield. Most of our stay at Malling had been over a week-end, so I hadn't bothered to advise my Station Commander where I was going. Trouble ahead! After our pleasant and exciting visit to the old Squadron they flew Sticks and me back to Cranfield but on landing I was told to report to the C.O. immediately. The Adjutant ushered us into the Old Man's presence. He seemed bad tempered so we braced ourselves for what we thought must be coming. "Where have you two been?" I told him we had taken the week-end off and spent it with our old Squadron, but because of the mishap at Manston we were late getting back. I also told him of our success and this seemed to mellow him. His main interest for the next few minutes seemed to be whether 29 Squadron or the O.T.U. should be credited with the kill. I don't recollect this problem ever being solved. Then he said, "All right, you two, before you go off again on one of these jaunts, just let me know. Now off with you." We were flabbergasted. We had expected at least to be put under open arrest.

That night a party was arranged in our honour and what a party! Somebody got hold of an exceedingly large silver goblet and filled it to the brim with champagne. We were dragged forward and had to consume this vast quantity of liquor between us. I recollect that eventually I retired to the men's room and locked myself in, feeling terribly ill. There I must have fallen asleep for I remember Jacko climbing through the window to see what had happened to me. As he guided me to my room he told me Sticks had also been led off to bed feeling no pain.

In June, 1942, Squadron Leader Watkins, my immediate boss at the O.T.U., was posted and I was granted the acting rank of Squadron Leader to take his place. Watty had run a damn good training squadron and there was little for me to do but carry on. But the instructors were a problem. They had no outlet for their desire to get at the Germans so I decided to start a standing patrol of one AI Blenheim each night we were on duty for the use of instructor crews only. Our chances of catching the odd German who broke through the perimeter defences in one of our old Blenheims was a little remote, but the hunt added zest to our rather trying but essential job.

As the months passed I became more restless to get back to an operational unit. Sticks and I had been with the O.T.U. for just over five months. I had a few more weeks to go before my six months were up so decided to be patient, which was as well, because my frequent inquiries about a posting were beginning to irk the acting C.O. The C.O. was away at the time and his deputy didn't take too kindly to Sticks or me.

We suspected he had a bit of a complex about operational types. At last, to my joy the Station Adjutant told me there was a posting for Sticks and me back to 29 Squadron at Malling. I was to go as a Flight Commander. This was great news. Ted had kept his word. It was six months almost to the day since I had left the Squadron for Cranfield. The C.O. was still away, so I went in with Sticks to say farewell to his deputy, whose first words were, "I suppose you realize that you will lose your acting rank?" This seemed an unnecessary comment and in the tone that it was made confirmed my suspicion that this officer, who had not seen any action, had no love for those who had. I pointed out that I couldn't care less about the rank but, for his information, all night-fighter flight commanders were Squadron Leaders, so it was most likely that I should retain my rank. With that Sticks and I left his office to set out for Malling as quickly as possible.

Even though I didn't enjoy instructing, I had made many friends at Cranfield. Jacko in particular was one for whom I had a great regard. It never ceased to amaze me that some experienced pilot hadn't grabbed up Jacko. He was without doubt one of the country's most efficient AI operators. I put him on a par with Sticks who, in my opinion, was the best.

16

STICKS and I returned to 29 Squadron at a time when the Axis Powers were at the peak of their success. On all fronts the Allies were fighting desperately to hold positions against a confident enemy. In Russia the southern group of German armies were advancing into the Caucasus. In North Africa General Auchinleck's Eighth Army was back in Egypt, harried by Rommel's Afrika Corps. In the Far East the Allies were faced by the victorious Jap, who had already overrun our Far Eastern Colonial Empire and was at the gates of Australia. Only in the air were there signs of hope. The R.A.F. was a match for the Luftwaffe in every theatre of operations. The bomber offensive was building up nightly and with the support of the newly arrived U.S. 8th Air Force Germany was being punished for her indiscriminate bombing of British and European cities in a way she had never dreamed of. Goering's boast that no bombs would ever fall on Germany was now causing him great embarrassment. Spitfire and Hurricane pilots, after the great victory of the Battle of Britain, were again seeking out enemy fighter opposition by luring him into combat over his own ground in occupied France, Belgium and Holland. The costly losses inflicted on the Luftwaffe by our night-fighters and A.A. artillery had stopped any serious large-scale attacks on Britain. However gloomy the overall picture looked, in the R.A.F. there was confidence of ultimate victory. We were mastering the enemy in the air.

There had been great changes in 29 Squadron while Sticks and I were away. Most of the aircrew were new arrivals, but many were familiar to us as they had passed through Cranfield during my tour. Colbeck-Welch was replaced by Wing Commander Cleland and once more 29 was lucky to get a very popular and likeable boss. Wing Commander "Pop" Wheeler, D.F.C., M.C., of First World War fame, was the new Station Commander. He had just completed a most successful tour in a night-fighter squadron and was champing to get back on operations. He had done more than his share in two wars. Later he managed to get back to operations in Bomber Command where he was killed. He was a great airman.

In spite of my views about Joan living with me near the airfield while I was on combat duty she persuaded me to bring her down to Malling again. We found excellent accommodation in a house in East Malling where she settled down to the chores of a wartime wife with our young son. I was rarely at home though there was no major enemy activity. The Germans still sent over aircraft to drop mines in the Thames estuary. I was now Flight Commander of A Flight. All our aircraft were fitted with Mk 7 AI which had been giving the Squadron good results. Sticks and I adopted Beaufighter 8284 as our special charge and with the co-operation of our ground-crew soon had it in excellent shape.

Just after I returned to 29, Squadron Leader "Dickie" Richards was posted supernumerary to the Squadron. The idea was that after some operational experience, he would take over a flight in another night-fighter squadron. Dickie was a most amusing individual. He looked like a typical English gentleman farmer. He was stocky with a ruddy complexion and an enormous handlebar moustache. I think he felt a bit out of things because he hadn't seen as much action as his younger confrères. His ambition was to get one Hun, then he would be satisfied. It wasn't long before his wish was granted and the story he told about the combat was price-less. He intercepted his German on a bright moonlight night over the Thames estuary and after a lengthy chase under radar control saw the aircraft and began to position himself for attack. The enemy saw him, too, and opened fire with his rear armament. When Dickie was asked what he did he solemnly replied, "I saw this odd line of lights coming towards me, so I flies up them and presses the tit (firing button) and in no time at all she's a flamer." Dickie's complete disregard for such things as enemy tracer bullets was typical.

Outstanding night-fighter crew of the Squadron at this time were Flying Officer Pepper and AI Operator Sgt. Toone, affectionately known as Pepper and Salt. Both of them were in my Flight. Pepper was a Canadian who raced motor-cycles in peacetime. He proved he could fly a Beaufighter better than anyone in the Squadron, sometimes perhaps a little dangerously.

Soon Sticks and I were in action again. On the night of August 8, 1942, we chased a solitary German aircraft over the North Sea, but we were too far behind to catch him. Pepper and Salt were patrolling south of us and they shot him down. Next night we were scrambled again and G.C.I. told us there were several "bandits" approaching the Thames estuary. We got AI contact and closed in on a Dornier 217 at 7,000 feet. This aircraft didn't see us and we opened fire at very short range from below, sending it crashing into the sea. Immediately afterwards G.C.I. put us on to a second aircraft. Again we closed and saw another Dornier 217. We were both at about 8,000 feet and coastal searchlight batteries began to illuminate us. The Dornier took violent evasive action and momentarily I was blinded by the searchlights and I lost him. This was our second chance of getting two in one night and again we were thwarted.

During mid and late August it looked as though things were really going to blow up. The temporary increase in "trade" was brought about by the Dieppe raid on August 19. It would be impertinent of me to attempt to write about this famous attack. More qualified writers have written reams on the subject. But there is no doubt that valuable lessons about amphibious attack were learnt in this operation and they were put to good use in planning the Sicily and Normandy invasions. During the Dieppe attack, Fighter Command, in support of the soldiers, forced the Luftwaffe into a heavy daylight battle. The results were even. Both lost about 100 aircraft. For a few nights after Dieppe, night-fighter activity increased as the Germans sent numbers of aircraft, chiefly JU88s, to reconnoitre for shipping movements in the English Channel and on our south-coast ports. For me this was an exciting time. In the space of four nights I was engaged in three combats which resulted in one enemy JU88 being destroyed, two others being damaged and my navigator and me nearly getting killed. The day after Dieppe I flew Sticks to his home at Newcastle on leave and picked up Jacko from Cranfield to fly with me in Sticks's absence.

At West Malling most of our effort was switched towards countering these dawn and dusk reconnaissance aircraft. Our chief problem was that the enemy, by using a radio altimeter, could fly extremely low, most of the time below 1,000 feet and often as low as 50 feet above the water. At the time we had no such accurate low-level altimeter in our Beaufighters. Mk 7 AI also had limited range at these very low altitudes so that extremely accurate ground radar control was necessary. The normal G.C.I. units could not see targets at these low altitudes. We had to rely on C.H.E.L. stations (Chain Home Extra Low), the function of which was to track such raids. It was soon found that the C.H.E.L. was extremely good and our successes were largely due to the excellence of the individual controllers at these stations.

Jacko and I had our first encounter with a low-flying JU88 at dusk on the evening of August 24. We switched our radio over to receive control instructions from a C.H.E.L. station near Beachy Head. We stayed at 5,000 feet until we crossed over the south coast between Dungeness and Beachy Head. The controller told us there was a "bandit" about thirty miles south of us flying along the Channel on a south-westerly course. "Dollar 42, vector 210 degrees and descend to 1,000 feet." (Dollar was then my call sign. It was changed from time to time for security reasons.) Opening-up the throttles, I dived towards the sea, where I could dimly see "white caps" as dusk gave way to night.

After several more changes of heading Jacko called, "Contact one and a half miles. He's below you, Bob." Gently I eased the stick forward again, till my altimeter read 500 feet. At this height, even in the darkness, we could make out the waves which seemed awfully close. A slight lack of concentration and we would both be in the drink. Gradually the range closed. "He's still below you, Bob. 300 yards, dead ahead." "Christ, he must be clipping the waves." Then I saw him. He was just a little below. To get in a good shot I ought to fire from slightly below and gently pull up. If I tried this I should be in the drink as there just wasn't room to get below him. So I tried a shallow diving deflection shot from above. The four cannons and six machine guns roared and Jacko and I saw a few flashes from the JU88 as our shells went home. Then I hit the slipstream from his propellers and for a few seconds I fought to gain control of our aircraft which was threatening to roll over on its back into the sea. During these few seconds I lost sight of the enemy and couldn't pick him up again. I called the ground radar and they told us they could not help us any more, so we returned to Malling disappointed. The most we could claim was a "damaged", probably not badly at that. However, from this attack we gained valuable experience in countering very low-flying aircraft at night.

At this time, a Lieutenant Kelly of the U.S. Army Signal

Corps was attached to the Squadron to get experience with our radar technicians. Later Kelly became ground radar officer in one of the newly-formed American night-fighter squadrons. His duties did not require him to fly, but he was keen to see how the AI worked in the air, so Jacko and I took him with us on a dusk patrol on August 28. We had been airborne for a little over an hour and nothing seemed to be happening. Our boredom was suddenly relieved by the ground controller's voice over the radio. "Dollar 42, I have a bandit for you 15 miles south of your present position. He is at 1,500 feet. Descend to 1,000 feet and steer 210 degrees." This was Flight Lieutenant Hill, the C.H.E.L. controller at a station near Beachy Head.

Throttles wide open we headed on the course. Over the intercom I told Kelly what was happening and that with any luck he would see his first Hun. This was the last thing he expected and he was more excited than Jacko and me. Gradually the range closed, with Hill giving us a running commentary. At two and a half miles Jacko called "Contact. Dead ahead and below." As usual he passed me a continual flow of instructions in his calm way, until at last I saw the faint glow from the exhausts of two engines. I recognized the silhouette of a JU88. By now we were down to 150 feet above the water and again it was impossible to get in a shot from the night-fighter's favourite position below the target. So I opened fire in a shallow dive from above and at close range. I don't think the crew of the JU88 saw us as they took no evasive action nor did they return our fire. Kelly was looking over my shoulder and shouting encouragement over the intercom as flashes appeared all over the fuselage of the enemy aircraft followed by a large explosion. A second or so later it fell burning into the sea where the wreckage glowed on the surface. By this time Kelly was beside himself with excitement. Joyously we returned to base to a meal of bacon and eggs.

As all the crews on duty had flown once during the night or were still in the air, it was our turn again to take the dawn patrol. "Kelly, how about coming along? You never know, we might have some more fun. Besides, you bring us luck." "No thanks," he said, "that was enough for me." He was obviously tired and had other work to do on the ground. We missed him as he was good company. Jacko and I were asleep in arm-chairs in the flight rest-room when we were awakened at 02.45 to take off for the dawn patrol. We scrambled into our Mae Wests and, only half awake, ran out to our Beau. It was still pitch black as our groundcrew strapped us in. We climbed through the smooth night sky and set course for Beachy Head at 5,000 feet and were soon in radio contact with the C.H.E.L. station.

We were directed to a patrol line east and west of Beachy Head about twenty miles out to sea. It looked as though we were going to have an uneventful trip. To pass the time Jacko and I discussed what we were going to do with our day off. Meanwhile the sky to the east was getting lighter with the approach of dawn. Soon we should be relieved by the Spitfires. The next call from the ground controller shook us out of our reverie: "Hullo, Dollar 42, I have a customer for you. Vector 180 degrees. Descend to 1,000 feet. He is 15 miles from you." I pulled the Beau round in a tight diving turn and opened the throttles. A few more instructions came from C.H.E.L., then Jacko called, "Contact. Two and a half miles ahead and below." Following Jacko's commentary I descended to about 150 feet. By now it was getting quite light and at 2,000 yards I suddenly made out the shape of a JU88, probably from the same squadron as the one we had shot down a few hours earlier. Closing the range to nearly 200 yards I opened fire. I saw a few flashes on the fuselage of the 88, then he started to take evasive action and to return my fire accurately from his top rear-gun position. The fight continued for a few seconds but the cleverness of the German pilot caused most of my shots to miss him. Suddenly he pulled hard around in front of my nose with his starboard wing nearly in the sea. His rear gunner fired a long burst and tracers were flashing all about us. At the same time there was a most unpleasant clatter like someone kicking over a dustbin. I could see that my port engine was on fire. I called Jacko over the intercom to make sure he was all right. At the same time I switched off the burning engine and operated the built-in fire extinguisher.

Now we were the hunted. A few miles away I could see the French coast. "Jacko, where is the 88?" "I can't see him, Bob. Maybe he dived into the drink." "Well, for Christ sake keep your eyes open. We shall be lucky if we get this kite back home." The fire in the port engine had died down but the aircraft was full of the smell of burning. I was having difficulty in keeping it in the air, even with the other engine going full bore. Luckily for us the JU88 had either had enough and high-tailed it for home or had dived into the sea when he turned so sharply in front of us. Our main worry now was to get as far away from the French coast as possible. We were in no shape to fight off avenging German fighters.

The C.H.E.L. controller gave me directions to steer for a little crash strip at Friston, on the top of Beachy Head, the nearest airfield. "Jake, tighten your straps. We may not be able to make it and have to ditch." He yelled back, "To hell with that, let's get a little closer to home." We were just skimming the tops of the waves. With Jacko's encouragement and the last bit of power from the one remaining overworked, smoking engine, I gained a little height. "Dollar 42, you're coming along fine. Friston is only ten miles ahead." Our controller was also willing us home. At last there was the coastline with the cliffs of Beachy Head to my left. I thought I might stall and crash if I tried to pull up over them, so I flew in over the flat coast just to the east, then gently turned port, coaxing the old Beau in one final effort in a slight climb to the top of the Head and Friston.

It was nearly broad daylight and there right in front of me was the perimeter hedge of the little airfield. It was too late to lower the undercarriage and my speed was too slow, so I gently bellied the heavy aircraft on to the grass at about 120 m.p.h. At this stage the overworked good engine was showing signs of fire and, as we hit the ground and slid along with a bumping and rending sound, it caught alight. We ground to a halt quite close to the edge of the cliff-top with the airfield fire engine and the doctor on his motor-bike roaring along behind us. They had been warned of our arrival in plenty of time. Jacko was out of the aircraft almost before it stopped rolling and was directing a small fire extinguisher on the fire in the starboard engine, as I climbed wearily out through the top escape hatch. Our Beau was a sad sight. Propellers were bent under from the belly-landing, and here and there I saw the bullet-holes our worthy enemy had pumped into us. One bullet had passed through my seat. I don't know how it missed my back.

The doctor led us over to a small hut where we contacted our Squadron by phone and also called through our report of the action to the intelligence officer. We couldn't be sure whether the JU had crashed or not so we claimed a "damaged". At about 8 o'clock after a wonderful breakfast of numerous eggs and bacon, our Squadron Oxford, a communication aeroplane, arrived piloted by Wing Commander Cleland to pick us up and take us back to Malling. Jacko and I were very tired, and the reaction was beginning to set in. But the personal interest of the Squadron Commander in our well-being did much to relieve our worries. An hour later we were back at Malling. I had arranged for Jacko to pick Joan and me up in his car in East Malling that evening for our planned visit to Maidstone so I hurried off home. Joan had no idea what we had been up to, but as details were bound to leak out through her friends, I told her something of our adventure. However, I was ill at ease because I knew she worried. She was remarkably brave and she managed somehow to keep her feelings to herself most of the time. But again I wished she had been able to stay with her parents where at least she would not be harrowed by details of my flying operations.

17

Two weeks after Jacko's return to the O.T.U. at Cranfield, Pop Wheeler, the Station Commander, called me to his office and told me that I had been awarded an immediate D.S.O. and Jacko a D.F.C. for our work against low-flying enemy reconnaissance aircraft. I sent a telegram of congratulations to Jacko and set off by car with the C.O., Wing Commander Cleland, Sticks and several other Squadron friends for a lunch-time session at the Star Hotel in Maidstone to celebrate. I am afraid we left an indelible mark on that establishment. The barmaid wished to close up at two o'clock in the afternoon as usual, but we had other ideas. Gently but firmly we removed her from behind her bar and took over. Eventually a worried management convinced us we should leave. After some argument we agreed and piled happily into our waiting cars, all somewhat the worse for wear. I insisted on driving my own car and forthwith collided with a small island in the middle of the main street, to the consternation of a watchful policeman. The damage appeared to be slight so I backed off and proceeded on my merry way to Malling, after a wave to the policeman. Some weeks later I received a summons to appear in court for dangerous driving and for damage to property in the city of Maidstone, namely one island. It cost me five pounds, which didn't seem much for such a splendid party.

During the last quarter of 1942 the enemy, in addition to his sporadic night raids, sent over his bombers and fighter-bombers singly or in small numbers in daylight when the weather over Britain was considered too bad for our Spitfires to be out. There were many days when the weather over our south and east coasts was poor, yet conditions were good at the Luftwaffe airfields in occupied Europe. As they approached England the enemy used cloud cover, then dropped his bombs blind or dived through the cloud to make a visual bombing and machine-gun attack at low level. Without airborne radar it was nearly impossible for day-fighters to tackle these aircraft. Our G.C.I. and C.H.E.L. stations were only able to direct them to within about a mile of the enemy, so to counter the threat the R.A.F. began to use night-fighters by day. With their airborne radar they could follow these targets closely in and out of cloud, and at least have a chance of attacking them. Further, the Beaufighter, with its vastly superior radius of action over the Spitfire, could take off in the worst of weather and, if unable to get back to its own base, could be diverted to almost any airfield in Britain where the weather was reasonable. The new development meant long hours on duty for us but the night-fighter crews welcomed any chances of getting at the Germans. The only German aircraft I had been close to in daylight up to this time was a JU88 scurrying away from an east-coast convoy in 1940. Then our Blenheim couldn't get close enough to open fire. I eagerly awaited another chance.

Sticks and I were not kept waiting long. We were chatting in the crew room on October 19. The weather was foul. The ceiling was about 200 feet and visibility barely a mile. At 10.15 orders came through to scramble one Beaufighter. In a few minutes we were airborne. I had to go on to instruments almost at once, as we entered cloud as soon as we were off the ground. Sticks checked his radar and I contacted Biggin Hill Sector control. We had levelled off at 3,000 feet just on top of the cloud. The Sector Controller directed us to patrol a line just off the coast. Above the cloud there were blue sky, bright sunlight and unlimited visibility. After fifteen minutes or so of this the Sector Controller told us to call C.H.E.L. at Foreness. This looked like business. I called and recognized the voice of Dave Mawhood, now one of the R.A.F.'s ace controllers.

"Bob, I have a bandit for you at 3,000 feet. Steer 010 degrees. Range 5 miles."

I whipped the Beau around and opened up. Even before Sticks had AI contact I saw an aircraft skimming the top of the clouds four or five miles ahead. I called "Tally-ho" to Dave and, as the range closed, recognized it as a Dornier 217. By now Sticks had radar contact. When we were about two miles away the Germans must have seen us. They dipped into the cloud. "Damn it, Sticks, it's up to you now." "O.K. Bob, I have him at one and a half miles. Turn port and descend 500 feet."

Sticks brought me to a position about 800 feet astern and 100 feet below, but cloud was so thick I could see nothing. I hoped the Dornier would think he had shaken me off and climb back up into the clear again. But he was a wily bird. The only thing to do was to attempt a blind shot at him in cloud. Chance of success was slight but it was better than nothing. After a few minor corrections Sticks said, "Now." I gently eased back on the control column and pressed the firing button for about three seconds. The guns roared and the Beau rocked as we flew through the enemy's slipstream, but I could see nothing. No flashes, no explosions. "Is he still there, Sticks?" "Yes, 700 feet ahead." "O.K., let's try again. This time we will close to 600 feet. Tell me when he is dead ahead and 100 feet above."

We were still heading north—two aircraft playing hide-and-seek in thick cloud and only a few hundred feet apart. Now after about fifteen minutes, concentration on accurate instrument flying, my eyes were beginning to blur. I shook my head and blinked to clear them.

"O.K., Bob, we are coming up into position. He is about 100 feet above and at 600 feet."

Again I eased back very slowly with my speed set at about 180 m.p.h., the speed of our Dornier. I pressed the firing button. The Beaufighter shuddered as the four 20-mm. guns and six machine-guns blasted out pounds of armour-piercing and incendiary shells. Again we hit the German's slipstream and I saw flashes in the cloud ahead. "Sticks, I think we've hit him. Watch your radar and see what he is doing." "He's going down to starboard. Hard starboard and lose height. Range 900 feet." Down we went, still in cloud. "Have you still got him?" After a second Sticks called, "He's gone, Bob. I haven't anything on the scope." I told Sticks I was going down to get under the cloud to see if there were any sign of wreckage. "O.K., but for Christ sake watch it. The cloud's nearly on the deck." I knew we were over the sea somewhere just north of the Thames estuary so wasn't worried about flying into high ground. Still, it was a tricky moment when at last we broke out of ominous grey cloud at about 200 feet with the slightly darker grey ocean beneath us.

We seemed to be right on the waves. Forward visibility was less than a mile so it was difficult to watch for wreckage and still fly the Beau safely around in circles at a reduced speed of 150 m.p.h. After a few minutes it was clear we were not going to find anything. "Bad luck, Sticks. I don't think we can claim more than a 'damaged' for that one. Still, he didn't get to his target." Back we climbed into the soup and soon we were out in the sunshine on top. I called Mawhood and told him what had happened but all he could tell us was that after the combat the enemy aircraft had disappeared from his scopes. We could only assume that it had turned for home at very low level, probably damaged, or had dived into the drink. We would never be certain. Now our problem was to get

Wing Commander J. R. D. Braham, D.S.O., D.F.C., A.F.C., C.D.
Belgian Order of the Crown and Croix de Guerre

Battle of Br
fighter-pilot
scramble fo
their machi

Germany launched her first big air raid of
the war on London during the night
of September 6–7, 1940. Here, R.A.F.
and Luftwaffe planes make vapour
trails during the ensuing battle

A low-level attack by Beaufighters
on a German naval escort in the
Bay of Biscay

...thor, right, plans
...d with navigator
..."Sticks" Gregory

...Squadron, com-
...by Wing Com-
...Ted Colbeck-
...centered, who is
...by Flt. Lt. Guy
...V.C. (*on his*
...and the author

...thor, left, and
..." after a public
...s lecture in 1943

Luftwaffe-eye-view
British fighter whi
dived through a fo
of HE 111Ks

The rear-gunner of a
Heinkel prepares
for combat

The Mosquito, ideal for
intruder raids, carried
four cannons, four ma-
chine guns and four
500-lb. bombs

(*Above*) : The author with his wife outside Buckingham Palace in 1942 after receiving the D.S.O. The photographer is Flt. Lt. "Jacko" Jacobs, who had just been awarded the D.F.C. for distinguished navigational work with Braham

(*At left*): The men behind the scenes: radar technicians of 141 Squadron to whom, says Braham, much of the Squadron's success over enemy territory was due

(*Below*): The majority of the author's night-fighting was done in Beaufighters; here he is flying one over Kent in 1942. The Beaufighter carried six machine-guns and four cannons

Tribute to the "Few" . . . the author at a Battle of Britain commemoration service. Mrs. Braham is standing behind him

Interviewing German pilots immediately after the war

The author's P.O.W. card, issued after he was shot down over
Denmark in 1944

The man who did it: Robert Spreckels in the cockpit of his FW 190

Robert Spreckels flying
plane in which he sho
Wing Commander Bra

My friend the enemy. A reunion with Spreckels early in 1961. Wing
Commander Braham is on the left, next to Mrs. Spreckels. Mrs. Braham
is next to Herr Spreckels, now a successful businessman in Hamburg

Officer commanding 432
All-Weather Fighter Squadron at Bagotville, Canada

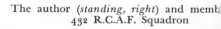

The author (*standing, right*) and memb
432 R.C.A.F. Squadron

home. Mawhood checked the weather at Malling and advised us that conditions had worsened since we took off. So he diverted us to Bradwell Bay on the northern shore of the Thames estuary where the weather was a little better. There we landed without any trouble in time for a late lunch. We were both disappointed, but at least the enemy hadn't reached his target and, if he made it back home, the story he would tell his comrades wouldn't encourage them in the future. No longer were they immune from attack in bad weather.

One morning a week later I was at the flight office checking over the aircraft and as nothing seemed to be doing I gave Sticks the day off. It was raining hard, but the cloud base was quite high, so it was anticipated that day-fighters would be up if necessary. I was wrong. Just after eleven we were requested to send off a Beau on a routine patrol because our Intelligence Services had information of enemy air activity over Northern France. Only myself and a new N.C.O. AI operator were immediately available. He was Sgt. Heywood who had arrived in the Squadron only a week before and wasn't very familiar with our Mk 7 airborne radar. But we paired up and were soon under radio control by Squadron Leader Guest, Chief Controller at Wartling, a G.C.I. on the south coast. He told us he had a bandit for us at 10,000 feet fourteen miles away, approaching the coast near Eastbourne.

I was familiar with the AI set as I had flown as AI operator with other pilots of my flight on training missions, so I could give Heywood advice when he queried me. He was obviously nervous so I did my best to encourage him. At 10,000 feet we were in and out of cloud and there was broken cloud all the way down to 2,000 feet with heavy rain which reduced forward visibility out of the Beau to about a mile. When we were three miles from the target Heywood called "Contact" and took over the intercept from the G.C.I. Controller. He soon settled down and his commentary on the enemy's position was calm and efficient. I couldn't see our target until we were only 300 yards away. Then it suddenly appeared, a JU88 at 6,000 feet in a gentle starboard turn slightly above us. "O.K., Heywood, I've got it." At least I hoped I had. The rear gunners in the Junkers fired at us wildly and the pilot desperately sought solid cloud. I opened fire too soon and not very accurately with no results. However, my Luftwaffe friend wasn't too difficult to follow. By now I had calmed down and fired two accurate bursts. The JU88 caught fire and dived steeply into the sea making a tremendous splash and leaving a gradually spreading oil patch. I flew around the scene, which was five miles or so off the coast between Eastbourne and Hastings, but there was no sign of life, so I set off for home. Heywood was blooded sooner than he thought and greatly elated with our success. He had done a fine job. After putting in our intelligence report to Flight Lieutenant Ham, our "spy", Heywood and I took the rest of the day off, he to enjoy his success with his pals and I to await an irate Sticks Gregory. By the time Sticks got into work next morning he had heard about our success and the expletives started before I could get into the security of my office. "So my clever bloody pilot thinks he can perform with all and sundry AI operators, does he? Deliberately sending me off for the day to show everyone I'm not indispensable. I have news for you, Squadron Leader Bob Braham, sir. Never again will you get rid of me so easily." By this time the Flight was in an uproar and I had to endure Sticks's friendly banter for several days.

October, 1942, was "Pepper-and-Salt" month for 29 Squadron. This relatively new crew had proved themselves outstanding night-fighters. They had destroyed three German bombers since their arrival in the Squadron in the summer. On the last night of the month they doubled this score by shooting down three more in two sorties. At the time this was a record for an Allied night-fighter crew. It was only surpassed once throughout the war, when our new Squadron Commander shot down four aircraft in one sortie a few months later, thereby keeping the record for 29 Squadron.

Activity began early on this memorable night of October 31. By nine at night most of my Flight were airborne. Sticks and I quickly ran into trouble with a faulty radar, so we asked the C.H.E.L. station at Foreness to scramble another of our aircraft from Malling in our place. Meanwhile we were told there was a bandit for us so we agreed to carry on until our relief arrived. Our target was approaching the Thames estuary at 6,000 feet and the C.H.E.L. Controller quickly brought us into a position astern. But the troubles with our radar prevented Sticks from taking over the intercept until we were within about a mile range. At last we got contact, just when I had given up hope of getting anywhere. Sticks's experience now told. The night was clear. I got a visual on an aircraft at 1,000 yards range and a little above. As the range closed I recognized it as a Dornier 217, one of Germany's standard two-motored bombers with twin fins and rudders, not unlike our own Hampdens. The crew of the Dornier didn't appear to see us. At 150 yards range I fired two long bursts and the German immediately caught fire and crashed into the sea five miles off Broadstairs.

We were filling out our combat report when "Pepper and Salt" landed. They had also shot down a Dornier 217 and the Squadron's air and groundcrews were elated. Most of our Beaus had landed and it appeared that the excitement was over when the operations phone rang again. The boss rushed to pick it up and shouted to us that there was another raid on the way and we were to scramble as many aircraft as possible.

"Pepper and Salt", the Squadron Commander and two

other crews took off immediately. We had to wait for about half an hour while the radar technical staff repaired our AI. At last we were airborne, but too late. The raid on Canterbury had been and gone. We returned home in time to slap "Pepper and Salt" on the back as they had shot down two more Dorniers on their second trip of the night. In a few weeks Pepper was awarded a D.F.C. and Toone ("Salt") the D.F.M. for this superlative performance.

A few weeks later the Squadron were stunned to hear that "Pepper and Salt" had been killed in a crash not far from the airfield. While making a daylight air test before night-flying they had got into a spin from which the pilot could not recover. It looked as though poor old Pepper had attempted some manœuvre which was beyond the capabilities of the old Beau. A Beaufighter would normally take a lot of abuse, but if a pilot overdid it she could be a most unforgiving aircraft. This tragedy was particularly painful because Pepper and his young wife were close friends of Joan and myself. It fell to me to tell her. She proved she was as brave as her gallant husband.

The rest of the year was uneventful for me in the air. But in late November I was surprised to get a letter from the Air Ministry telling me that I was to attend an afternoon party at Buckingham Palace. I was to be a representative from Fighter Command to help entertain a group of American officers on their Thanksgiving Day. I imagined it would be very formal and, frankly, I didn't look forward to it. When I presented myself at the Palace I was ushered in with many other officers to be presented to the Royal Family. We shook hands with the King and Queen, the two Princesses, Mr. Churchill and other Government and military figures. Finally, we were conducted to a large banquet hall where afternoon tea was laid out on a vast array of tables. I noted with interest that there were also bottles of liquor on each table.

The Royal Family came to join us for a most enjoyable and

informal stand-up tea. Everything was done to make us at home. During this pleasant gathering I became friendly with a Colonel of the United States Army and later, after we had taken our leave, a very happy group went to his flat where the jollifications continued. I was introduced for the first time to Bourbon. Later that night I caught a train back to Malling, a little befuddled perhaps but wondering why I ever worried about attending that delightfully friendly party. The Royal Family, like thousands of other families in Britain, opened their doors and their hearts to our Allies and helped to bring to them some memory of their homes. A week or so later I was again a visitor at the Palace. This time I was with Joan and Jacko. Jacko and I received our recent decorations for our effort against German low-level reconnaissance aircraft from the hands of the King.

A few weeks before Christmas I was summoned to 11 Group Headquarters at Uxbridge for an interview with the Air Officer Commanding. What had I done? On the train I tried to think what this call could mean. I was ushered in before Air Vice-Marshal Saunders who, after a few friendly remarks, told me I had been promoted to Acting Wing Commander and was to take over 141 Squadron at Ford on the south coast near Chichester. The A.O.C., a big friendly man who had risen from the ranks, then outlined to me the problem. 141 was in the doldrums. It had been necessary to post the Squadron Commander, one of the Flight Commanders and the Adjutant. The Air Vice-Marshal told me to report there as soon as possible and said a new Flight Commander and Adjutant were already on their way. "Get it back in shape and if there is anything you want you will be given all the help you require," he said.

This was quite a challenge, and much more so than being given command of one of the famous night-fighter squadrons. When I left Headquarters to return to Malling I was already determined that 141 should be the best night-fighter unit in the R.A.F.

This promotion to Squadron Commander had come at a time when at last the Allies were gaining ground. The famous Eighth Army had won a lasting victory in the desert and was now well on its way to joining up with Anglo-American armies in Tunis. The Russians had annihilated the German Sixth Army at Stalingrad, and even in the Far East the clouds of defeat were lifting slowly. Indeed, to quote Churchill's words, this was "the turn of the tide". Yet how different the situation had been only six months before. Then the only signs of hope were in the air. On land and sea the Axis seemed dominant.

My mind turned to more personal problems. Ever since our marriage I had been worried about having my wife and family living with me near the station. I felt it was bad for both of us. If anything happened to me I would be happier if Joan were with her parents. As Squadron Commander I should have to spend much more of my spare time with the Squadron than I had as a Flight Commander. Only in this way was it possible to get the feel of a unit and encourage and lead by personal example. I knew my wife would be unhappy at the prospect of parting again. I wasn't looking forward to telling her of my decision. Joan was delighted about my promotion and I think she guessed what my plans were for her even before I told her. At least she made it clear she understood, which lifted a great weight from my mind.

I still had a number of things to clear up in 29 Squadron and it would be necessary for me to fly back and forth between Malling and Ford for at least two weeks. Joan and I decided she might as well stay in our lodgings at East Malling until the new year and then return to her parents' home near Leicester. This meant that I would be able to see something of my family at Christmas. My parting from 29 was a sad one. I had served with it since December, 1938, nearly four years, with only a break of six months when I was instructing at Cranfield. I was the last of the original 1938 Squadron to move. As it was one of the ace night-fighter squadrons of Fighter Command, I was proud to have shared its success. Now my loyalty must change.

I was given the usual round of farewell parties, during which I was presented with a model Beaufighter by our groundcrew. This I still have. It was made from one of the propellers of my Beau, No. 8284, the aircraft which Jacko and I crash-landed at Friston. The model was beautifully made. It was mounted on a Hercules engine-bearer by half a piston-ring from the same engine. This was a touching gift into which the makers had put many hours of detailed and careful work. The token indicated to me, though I was well aware of it anyway, how close was the link between air and groundcrews of 29. Every success and misfortune was shared. This spirit I was determined to take with me to 141.

18

BY taking command of 141 Squadron at the age of twenty-two, I shared with Paddy Finucane the honour of being the youngest officer of Wing Commander rank in command of an R.A.F. combat unit. At the time this meant little to me. At Ford, after introducing myself to the Station Commander, Paddy Maxwell, an ace of First World War fame, I went down to the Squadron offices where I was greeted by the new Adjutant, Flight Lieutenant Dickie Sparrow. I had a long talk with him and was soon put in the picture. The Squadron was in a rut. Most of the senior crews were married and lived off the station with their families, so supervision and leadership were lacking. But a number of them had received posting notices and it remained for me to instil some spirit into the rest. Dickie, who was in the wool trade in civil life, impressed me immediately as the right man for his job. He was older and more mature than the aircrew and more tolerant. His advice on administrative and personnel matters was invaluable. Without his unselfish guidance I dread to think what would have become of the paperwork, as I was no good at it.

Dickie introduced me to the rest. Squadron Leaders Beal and Cooper were the Flight Commanders. Beal was a new arrival like myself. Buster Reynolds was the "spy", a man of Sparrow's calibre and just as helpful. Dougal, the "mad Irishman", was the doctor. In spite of his crazy games he was invaluable in the months to come. The aircrew were a mixed bunch including New Zealanders, Australians, Belgians, an

Indian and other nationalities with a smattering of British. One thing was obvious. They were keen to get out of the rut and make a name for the Squadron. So in a short speech I outlined to them what I expected. It was simply this: that 141 should become the best night-fighter squadron in the R.A.F. This speech, with modifications, I also gave to the groundcrew and it was with pride that I sensed they got the point, although I believe anybody could have put it across better than myself.

A few days later the A.O.C. decided to inspect the station. This caught me napping. I hadn't yet got to know all the aircrew by name, nor was I sure where certain sections on the station were. This visit led to some amusing incidents. Dickie quickly gathered our crews together and I told them if I couldn't remember particular names they would be Flying Officer Smith, Brown or Jones. If they objected to these temporary names they would have to grin and bear it. They did. I got most of the names right but a few were made up on the spur of the moment. Whether the Air Vice-Marshal saw through this dodge I never found out. The visitors were then shown round our operational area. To avoid major bloomers I had Dickie at my elbow throughout. Even so I was caught out. The A.O.C. wished to be shown our armament section. I knew it was in one of two huts. But which? Dickie was also new and wasn't sure either. So hopefully I asked the A.V.M. to follow me and opened the door. "The armament section, sir." A heavy silence followed. I had shown the A.O.C. our wash-rooms and a latrine. "Very interesting, Braham. Now where's the armament section?" he said. It had to be the other hut so I tried again and this time I was right. Before I had time to say anything the A.O.C. spoke to an airman who had his back to us, loading 20-mm. cannon shells into belts. "What are you doing, my man?" he asked. To which the airman replied, "What the hell does it look like?" We were all in a state by now and when the airman turned and saw whom he had spoken to he looked as if he were going to faint. However, the A.V.M. was a most understanding individual. He made a joke of it, but how grateful we were when he left.

Buster Reynolds and Sparrow tackled me shortly after my arrival at Ford about a V.C. citation for one of the Squadron's Warrant Officer pilots who had been killed by enemy action. The navigator survived. They intercepted a Heinkel III over the Channel and in the combat the pilot was badly wounded. He continued to fire at the enemy until it was destroyed and then turned for home. He was in a bad way but knew his navigator couldn't swim, so he headed back towards the coast which he eventually crossed. Then calmly he ordered his navigator to bale out. The navigator argued that he wanted to stay and help, but at last realized there was no point in arguing. So he jumped and landed safely by parachute. The gallant pilot, who remained calm throughout the ordeal in spite of his serious injuries, crashed the Beaufighter and was killed.

A citation had already been forwarded but it had apparently been turned down by the Sector Commander. Buster and Dickie felt that this officer was out of sympathy with 141 Squadron because of its poor performance. I agreed with them that we should take the matter up again. We rewrote the citation and forwarded it with a covering letter, requesting that the subject be reconsidered. We were unlucky again. Up to this time in World War II there had been only one V.C. awarded to a fighter pilot. This went to Flight Lieutenant Nicolson during the Battle of Britain. We all felt that, apart from the obvious merit of the case, an award would have done much to boost morale for Fighter Command as a whole and the night-fighter force in particular.

After the New Year Joan wrote to say her parents were ready for her to go to their home in Leicester. I took off in a Beaufighter with Sticks for West Malling to help her with the move. We had two wonderful days together at our adopted home in East Malling. Joan told me she was expecting another child, probably in June. This was great news and did much to soften the blow of our separation. We both hoped for a daughter and tried to agree on a name for her. We settled for "Wendy".

On the second evening of my visit the air-raid sirens sounded in Malling. I phoned 29 Squadron to ask if Sticks and I could help as we had a Beaufighter available. Joan was angry. I had only come home for two days and here I was trying to go off flying again. I must admit it was most selfish. The Squadron Commander of 29 turned us down anyway. He had enough crews and aircraft to cope. At the time I thought it was my duty to have a go. My thoughts strayed back to the Squadron as I lay awake listening to the Beaufighters taking off from the near-by airfield. Next morning we learnt that the Germans had made a small raid in two waves on parts of Kent and the south coast and that 29's boss had shot down four aircraft. This was great news, but I wondered how my own Squadron at Ford had fared. I am afraid these thoughts dominated my mind as I hurried Joan and Michael off by train to Leicester. Thank God for an understanding wife. Our happy days together were over and from now until the end of the war I was a very infrequent visitor to Leicester.

I hurried back to the airfield at West Malling where Sticks was waiting for me. He had contacted 141 at Ford and been told that Cook, one of my New Zealanders, and his AI operator had been shot down by a Beaufighter during the night's activity, but that they had baled out and were safe. As soon as we arrived Buster Reynolds met me with Cook who seemed none the worse. From an intelligence appraisal it looked as though my crew had been accidentally shot down by 29 Squadron's Wing Commander and that ours was one of the four aircraft he claimed destroyed. This was unfortunate, but in the heat of the combat it wasn't difficult to understand. A Beaufighter could look like a Junkers 88. There were several such mishaps during the war.

My Squadron shared the airfield at Ford with the Fighter Interception Unit and a small Naval Air Fighting Development squadron. With the Navy organization we had little to do, but we saw a lot of the F.I.U. people. They were organized to try out new and modified AI equipments and to develop night-fighter tactics. Ford was an ideal location for them. They often tested out their theories and equipments in combat.

Friendly rivalry existed between F.I.U. and 141, and sometimes Sticks and I and some of my more experienced crews helped in their trials. We were able to provide them with useful information. Sticks and I had only been with the Squadron three weeks when we were engaged in another night combat which was to be our last defensive air battle. My successes in the future were all over enemy-occupied Europe or Germany itself. There had been little night activity for several weeks and most of my Squadron were stood down. Many of the aircrew were having a party in Worthing that night. We were thoroughly enjoying ourselves when the siren sounded. I rang Ford and found that the enemy was active and that F.I.U. had already shot down one aircraft. Promptly the party ended and we filed into our cars and sped back to the airfield. Sector ordered one of my aircraft off, so Sticks and I ran to our waiting Beau. It was a beautiful moonlight night and I remember thinking how stupid the Germans must be to send bombers over on such a night which was ideal for night-fighters. The interception followed the usual pattern and eventually the joint efforts of the G.C.I. and Sticks brought me to within visual range of a Dornier 217 flying at 15,000 feet. The night was so clear that the enemy saw our Beau at the same moment. He took evasive action, turning one way then another while his rear gunners sprayed tracer in our direction, luckily not very accurately. I was a bit excited and probably suffering a little from the party which we had so hurriedly left, with the result that I opened fire at too long a range with no results. Sticks soon stopped my foolishness by caustic comments over the intercom. It took four long bursts which used up nearly all our ammunition before the Dornier began to burn and dive. He ended up with a tremendous splash in the sea a few miles off the shore. I wasn't pleased with myself as we clambered out of the aircraft. The Dornier nearly got away because of my poor shooting. Still, 141 had held its own with our friendly rivals F.I.U. and between us we had shot down two of the three or four attacking aircraft. One other was destroyed but nobody claimed it. It was probably hit by our A.A. but did not crash for some time so we could not determine who got it.

Night raids were small and infrequent at this time but the Germans took every advantage of bad weather to attack coastal targets by day, using FW190 fighter-bombers, JU88 and Dornier bombers. These attacks, in addition to our night readiness and training commitments, put a heavy load on the Squadron, particularly as we now had a great many inexperienced crews. There were only five or six experienced hands left, and the brunt of both day- and night-fighting fell on them.

Cook and his AI observer, ranked as old hands, had an extraordinary experience during one of the German day attacks. After a short chase they saw their quarry, a Dornier 217, flying at tree-top level near Chichester. Cook's Beaufighter was rapidly overhauling the German, who, in his eagerness to get away, failed to see a gas-holder and flew into it with an enormous crash. Cook hadn't fired a shot but after some haggling with the authorities he was rightly credited with its destruction. There was little time to train the increasing number of new boys. The O.T.U.s were still turning out crews with basic night training on the Blenheim. Training courses had been cut to a minimum because an ever-increasing number of night-fighter squadrons were being formed not only in Britain but also in the Middle and Far East. So I regretfully decided that 141 must be withdrawn to a quieter area to bring all our crews up to combat standard. I discussed this with the Flight Commanders, the Adjutant and Buster Reynolds, and they all agreed that if we stayed at Ford much longer the experienced crews would burn themselves out. The enemy would then have a clear field.

Having made up my mind I requested an interview with the A.O.C. He was sympathetic and agreed that 141 should be withdrawn to a quiet area. After a pleasant and friendly discussion it was settled that 141 would change places with 604 Squadron at Predannock, Cornwall, in mid-February. A few days before the move Sticks and I flew to Predannock to discuss the change with Wing Commander Woods, the boss of 604. The airfield was close to Land's End. One of the runways ended not far short of the rocks overlooking the sea. The airmen were billeted a few miles from the field and the officers lived in the beautiful Mullion Cove Hotel, which had been requisitioned. From its windows on the north side you could look out over the ocean. I met the Station Commander as well as the Squadron Commander of the coastal Beaufighter Squadron who would share Predannock with us. Their task was to attack enemy shipping and aircraft in the Bay of Biscay. Woods told me my Squadron would be able to work with two G.C.I. stations, both of which had excellent controllers. This information put me in a good frame of mind for the trip back to Ford. I was confident that two months at Predannock would get the Squadron into top shape. Then I would badger the Higher Command to get back into action.

19

Our Squadron had to hand over our newer Mk 7 AI Beaus to 604 Squadron at Ford, while we took over their older aircraft, many of which were still fitted with the earlier Mk 4 AI. This was a bitter experience as we were fond of and accustomed to our aeroplanes. But my depression vanished when I learned from the engineer officer that there were enough Beaus with Mk 7 AI for the Squadron to run a satisfactory night-fighter training programme.

We landed at Predannock on February 17, 1943. Conditions there were ideal for training, thanks to the co-operation of the two G.C.I. stations at Treleaver and Newford. In a matter of weeks, by flying practice interceptions day and night, 141 began to shape into an efficient Squadron. Up to this time the newer crews had not been able to benefit from the experience of the older hands who were always overworked. Now things were different. The two G.C.I. units not only helped us to improve our efficiency unhindered by action against the enemy, but also offered social relaxation. Many of the charming and talented W.A.A.F. plotters became firm friends of our personnel.

I found myself constantly hankering after action. Up to this time only two squadrons of night-fighters not equipped with AI were permitted to roam over enemy-held territory in search of aircraft landing or taking off. They were known as intruders. Because of their lack of AI and the ingenuity of the Germans in using dummy and decoy airfields, the success these two squadrons had achieved was very limited.

At conferences at Fighter Command and Group Head-quarters I had urged that it was time we sent AI-equipped fighters over occupied Europe to back up Bomber Command. German night-fighters were beginning to inflict very heavy losses on our bomber forces and I felt that if the R.A.F. would allow our night-fighters to work with the bomber streams perhaps we could shoot down enough German fighters to reduce casualties. But my arguments were of no avail. Even the suggestion that we only use older types of AI was turned down, at least for the present. When I was satisfied that our night-training programme was sufficiently advanced, I decided to try again for some limited offensive role for the Squadron. So I visited our Group HQ near Bath and sought an interview with the A.O.C. He was away sick at the time so I was ushered in to see his deputy, Air Commodore Basil Embry, later Air Chief Marshal.

I had met this remarkable man with the piercing blue-grey eyes once or twice before, and was aware of his reputation as an aggressive leader. I felt he would be sympathetic to my suggestions. Some of us felt in 141 that if we couldn't operate AI-equipped fighters over enemy territory, then perhaps we could swell the ranks of the two intruder squadrons by using our older Beaus and removing the radar. I proposed to the Air Commodore that to maintain Squadron spirit and contri-bute something to the war effort, the experienced crews should be allowed to raid rail and road traffic over the Brest Peninsula on moonlight nights. These operations were to be known as Rangers. I further suggested that we should be per-mitted to patrol in daylight in the Bay of Biscay to help Coastal Command in tracking down the large FW200 (Condor) reconnaissance bombers which were flying out of the Bordeaux area and homing U-boats on to our merchant shipping. To my joy Embry agreed in general to my request, on condition that we maintained our night-fighter efficiency. This I promised we would do. When I returned and told the Squadron the effect was miraculous. Never had the morale of 141 Squadron been so high.

We waited patiently for the next moon, and on the night of March 20 the first offensive Ranger missions were flown. Only three aircraft were sent out and I took part in this first sortie. We were told by a staff officer at Group the area of France we should patrol to look for "trade". For this first effort we were given the railway system in the Brest Peninsula. These east-west rails were the lifeline for the garrisons at St. Nazaire, Brest, Lorient and La Rochelle, all centres of German U-boat activity. Our AI operators now became navigators and together we planned our routes and patrols with Buster, our Intelligence Officer.

Our plan was to fly low over the English Channel, then climb to 1,500 to 2,000 feet over some isolated part of the rocky Britanny coast and then proceed to the selected railway line and look for trouble. The distance to our target area was about 130 miles, so we should have enough petrol for an hour or so. Sticks was away from the Squadron for nearly two months and I was unable to get hold of Jacko, who couldn't be spared from Cranfield, so I took Flight Sergeant Blackburn, a New Zealander who was relatively new to the Squadron, as my navigator. Buster had been badgering me for a trip so he came along as passenger. As soon as it was dark we started up our Beau and took off. This was our first effort at carrying the war to the enemy. It was a grand feeling. We flew at about 300 feet above the sea to reduce the possibilities of being picked up by German ground stations. Blackburn was experienced as a navigator and after about thirty-five minutes I spotted the rocky coast of Britanny.

So far no opposition. Continuing south we spotted occasional farms, woods and villages, then I saw the glint of the moon on the main railway line from Rennes to Brest. This was our target. I pulled the Beau around in a steep turn so that we were flying eastwards along the line. I searched ahead for the tell-tale stream of smoke from a locomotive.

Cruising at 180 miles an hour, I weaved the heavy fighter from side to side to reduce the possibility of a surprise attack from a German night-fighter, although at this level it was unlikely. We had been on patrol only a few minutes when I saw a thin streak of smoke shining in the moonlight. It was obviously a train travelling at speed. I wanted to catch it on a straight stretch of line, so I manœuvred the Beau around in a gentle turn until the train was just east of the town of Guingamp. Now I would have an unimpeded shot. Buster reminded me to watch for flak as most trains in occupied Europe had a flak car attached. This was a small risk we had to take.

Everything was now set. I eased the Beau into a shallow dive from 2,000 feet setting my sights on the engine. At 1,000 feet, diving at 240 m.p.h., I pressed the button on the stick for a long burst. The four cannons and six machine guns roared and the Beau slowed slightly from the recoil. We could see the shells and bullets kicking up sparks and flame on the locomotive, which suddenly burst into gouts of steam and smoke. Easing back gently on the control column and still firing I let the stream of lethal fire power drift back along the partially smoke-hidden train.

Broken lines of red tracer ammunition started to drift up towards us, and as it got closer it flashed past like a whiplash. We circled at 3,000 feet just out of range of the flak and saw the train stop. The engine was expelling steam in great clouds from its torn entrails. Satisfied, we turned for home, and in forty-five minutes were back at Predannock. The other crews returned shortly after us. One had beaten up another train and the other saw nothing of importance to attack. Our first forays over enemy territory had been successful. Two trains had been damaged with no loss to ourselves. The effect on both air and groundcrews was tremendous.

March and April gave us generally good weather. Sometimes on days off a few of us flew to the Scilly Isles in the Squadron Oxford, a communication aeroplane, and landed at the small airfield on St. Mary's Island. I eagerly looked forward to this pleasant relaxation. I loved the daffodil-covered Scillies and the almost tropical climate. It was difficult on these occasions, as we drank a pint of bear and lunched on cream and jam sandwiches in the warm sunshine, to imagine that war was so close. Not so far away thousands of men of many nationalities were locked in bloody conflict. At other times we visited Lt. Davies and his merry band of Motor Torpedo Boat crews in the small harbour at Penzance, where temporarily they were resting from operations off the French coast. Now they were being used in an air-sea rescue role. They took us for rides in their speedy craft out into the waters of the Atlantic. In the evenings we gathered in one of the small cabins to drink and swap yarns into the early hours. If any of us were a little under the weather after roistering in Penzance, these tiny boats became our hotel. Their long-suffering boss and crews always welcomed us aboard, and provided us with a bunk for the night. In turn, these kind friends of the Senior Service visited us at our airfield and were sometimes taken for a ride in a Beaufighter. I think they enjoyed their visits as much as we looked forward to seeing them in Penzance.

The time required to bring the Squadron to a respectable standard of night-fighting turned out to be less than I had originally imagined, in spite of the influx of new crews. By the end of March, a month and a half after we arrived at Predannock, I felt that we were in pretty good shape, so I stepped up our offensive activities. The majority of crews were given a chance to visit the German over his own ground.

We also flew a number of patrols into the Bay of Biscay. These we flew in daylight, usually sending two aircraft out in loose formation for mutual protection. We weren't lucky with them and suffered our first combat casualties. A relatively new Flight Commander and an experienced Sergeant Pilot took off with their navigators for a patrol off the Gironde estuary. They apparently ran into a large number of JU88 long-range fighters and both our Beaus were shot down. The information came to us from our Intelligence Service, who had picked up the radio chatter of the German squadron involved. It left no doubt as to the result of the battle.

This was a serious blow to the Squadron. The crews we lost were popular so we thought in terms of revenge. Later information from Intelligence revealed a possibility that the Germans had been alerted to the presence of our aircraft by so-called neutral Spanish fishing boats. Those of us who had flown in the Bay had noticed these boats. The thought that my crews had been shot down because of the treachery of these people made my blood boil. Next morning I decided that regardless of the strict regulations concerning attacks on neutral shipping, these people would have to be taught a lesson. I again selected Blackburn as navigator and briefed another of my experienced crews for a mission of revenge. Group were told we were merely off on another routine patrol.

Just before lunch we set off, flying at wave-top height in line abreast about fifty yards apart. Our course took us to the Scillies then south-west, fifty miles off the coast of western Brittany, then due south, finally cutting in towards the French coast near the mouth of the Gironde. From here we would patrol some fifty miles out to sea. The southern extremity of our mission would take us to within sight of the north coast of Spain. We flew as low as possible to elude German-manned ground radar units along the coast of France. To ensure surprise I had briefed that unless we were in combat or some emergency arose, radio silence would be maintained between aircraft.

It was hot work in the Beau in these southern waters, with the sun turning our glass and perspex-covered cockpits into greenhouses. Soon we were sweating freely. "What was that?" I asked Blackburn over the intercom to look towards the eastern horizon. Yes, masts of ships. I waggled my wings in our pre-arranged signal and banked sharply towards them, climbing to 1,500 feet. My number two followed. In a few seconds we were over several fishing boats. I confirmed they were Spanish from their flags. Right, you bastards, we'll teach you to help the enemy. Climbing again, I banked round with the other Beau following. I selected one vessel as my target and dived again. My gunsights were set and I flipped the switches to arm my guns. The range rapidly closed and then I noticed someone lying in the stern of the boat, arms behind his head, obviously sunning himself. I moved my thumb from the firing button. Whoever the figure was he or she was awfully small. In the fraction of a second while I was taking all this in, it dawned on me that it was a child—probably the son or daughter of the owner of the boat and quite oblivious of our evil intent. When I saw the child I knew I couldn't do it. I broke radio silence and called Davis. "Hold your fire." As we roared by at masthead height the child waved, quite unafraid. With that my anger against the treachery of these supposed neutrals left me. Even though some of them might have been responsible for the death of my two crews, I couldn't commit murder. Two hours later we landed back at Predannock. I started to explain to the pilot of the other Beau what had stayed my hand but it was unnecessary. I could see he understood.

Throughout March and April we stepped up our Ranger sorties over France and also increased the number of trips into the Bay. Flight Lieutenant Le Boutte, one of our Belgian pilots, was becoming adept as a train strafer. Soon he led the Squadron in this field. Before the war Le Boutte had been a major in the Belgian Air Force. He escaped through France into Spain before the advancing German armies in 1940. He had had a rough time in various prisons before he got to England where he was received into the R.A.F. with a temporary commission as a Flight Lieutenant. He was a man in his forties who wore glasses, but had more spirit and courage than many a younger chap. I never ceased to admire him and was glad to hear after the war that he became Chief of the Belgian Air Staff. His one desire was to get at the enemy as often as possible. It must be admitted that he put the fear of God into many of our groundcrew at night. His poor eyesight made his judgement of speed on the ground at night very unreliable. He tended to taxi his aircraft towards dispersal at high speed, to the consternation of the airman who was walking backwards trying to direct him into position with a torch. The airmen became very proficient at running backwards!

One moonlit night we were returning from a late patrol looking for the elusive Condors in the Bordeaux area. Flying over the sea at 500 feet I saw ahead a long cigar-like object in the water. I recognized it as a submarine. As we were only sixty miles from La Rochelle we thought it must be a U-boat charging its batteries on the surface. I pulled the Beau round into a climbing turn. As the sub hadn't dived, the crew must have assumed we were a German aircraft. How I wished we had bombs or depth charges. But at least our 20-mm. shells would pierce the oil tanks and ballast compartments and possibly kill some of the crew. At 500 feet I fired a long burst. The Beau shuddered and I saw flashes and sparks as our shells struck the vessel. The Germans returned our fire with an inaccurate burst from the conning tower. I climbed away and turned for another attack, but my quarry had started to dive. We were too late. We had the satisfaction of seeing a growing patch of oil on the water, which meant the U-boat was at least damaged and would probably be docked for a time for repairs.

There wasn't much social activity at Predannock. Once the Squadron was invited to the Church Hall for a dance, and many of us attended. Dickie, the Doc, and I thought we should make an appearance, so after a few jugs of ale in the Mullion Mess, off we set for the dance. It was a pleasant night and we decided to walk. On the way we espied a horse in a field having its evening nap. It struck us that if we were to borrow the animal and arrive at the dance on it we might liven up the proceedings. With a little coaxing the Doc and I mounted the surprised animal. Dickie led it by a rope to the dance hall. There we knocked, the door was opened and we entered mounted on our steed. Pandemonium broke out. The horse became frightened and riders, horse and our attendant adjutant left in rather a hurry. We returned the fractious animal to its field where it was pleased to see the last of us.

For a long time a solitary JU88 reconnaissance aircraft had been flying unmolested out of Brittany, just skirting the western fringe of our ground radar cover and from there continuing up the west coast of Ireland. Among other things this aircraft was collecting weather data for the Luftwaffe and German Navy.

Our friends in 248 Coastal Beau Squadron, who shared our airfield, had several times tried to intercept this aircraft. On one occasion they succeeded but at a heavy cost. They lost one Beau and the other returned heavily damaged. But they destroyed the JU88. However, the place of this worthy adversary was soon taken by another aircraft. Something had to be done. Unfortunately he stayed for such a short time within our G.C.I. coverage that unless Beaufighters were in the right position at the right time, it was virtually impossible to intercept him.

Our Group Headquarters, in conjunction with the Royal Navy, worked out a plan for a naval picket-ship to be located out at sea on the line of flight of our wily friend. This ship was fitted with a primitive radar set and carried a R.A.F. controller to work the equipment. Provided the sea was relatively calm and the radar serviceable, this plan seemed to have promise. As soon as information came that the JU88 had taken off we were to scramble a Beau, fly out and contact the controller on the picket vessel and then patrol and wait for the enemy to appear on the radar screen. This particular enemy became known as "The Milk Train", because of the regular schedule he kept. But hard as we tried we never got really close to him. The German squadron responsible for these missions were extremely experienced and up to all our tricks.

We were a happy and contented Squadron. Only once did I have to lay down the law, and this was to one of our Australian pilots. I was having lunch with the Station Commander in our hotel mess when we saw a single Beaufighter coming straight towards the building from the sea at window height. For a second I thought he would hit us, but he pulled up, roaring low over the roof. The Old Man was livid. "Get that man's name and I will see he is court-martialled." I cooled him down and he finally agreed that I should deal with him. When I saw the culprit I laid it on in strong terms. The Aussie seemed genuinely repentant and, remembering a similar misdemeanour of my own in earlier days, I left it at that.

Up to this time cowardice was something I hadn't come face to face with. I had heard of it in other units, but never expected it to occur in my own Squadron. After I had briefed two crews for a patrol into the Bay, I returned to my office and the Adjutant announced that Sawyer, one of our newer pilots, wished to see me. He was one of the crew members I had just briefed. He was obviously ill at ease, but after a little friendly coaxing he said that my briefing had been changed after I left the Squadron dispersal and he knew that it would be impossible for them to reach the patrol area. I thanked him for his loyalty and said that I would look into it. I sent for the senior crew who had been detailed to lead this sortie and asked them what they meant by changing my briefing. The navigator, who was the stronger personality, spoke up and said that he thought my routing was too close to the enemy coast and consequently too dangerous. I pointed out that they would be at zero feet over the water and no closer than fifty miles to the French coast at any time. There was one chance in a thousand that they might be seen by a patrol of German fighters and this was considered an acceptable risk. We had flown this same route before and it was the only way that would permit us to reach our patrol area in the southern parts of the Bay and stay there for any length of time. To my astonishment the navigator then said he had been trained as an AI operator on the assumption that he would always fly over Britain. He didn't wish to risk his neck or experience farther afield. I could hardly believe my ears. Were we, or were we not, at war? Regretfully, I lost my temper. I told him to get out and wait in the Adjutant's office.

The pilot, a Squadron Leader, had obviously been influenced by his navigator. He now appeared to be a little worried, saying that if I insisted he would carry on with the mission as briefed. However, it seemed that he was not happy flying the Beau. He felt he wasn't master of the aircraft, but would like a transfer to a Stirling Bomber Squadron. I could understand his possible phobia regarding the Beau. It had happened before that someone was afraid of one type of aircraft but would operate others happily. I pointed out that flying a Beau in the Bay was a far safer operation than driving a bomber, particularly a Stirling, over Germany. But he insisted he would like to fly Stirlings. I told him I would see what could be done, but I was most unimpressed by the general lack of tact and spirit shown by changing a briefing in front of a new crew.

Obviously I couldn't send this crew on the trip, so I selected another crew to lead the mission and both of them returned safely to Predannock after an uneventful patrol. Meanwhile, after a discussion with my father confessor, the Adjutant, a letter was prepared to Group Headquarters about both officers, indicating a "lack of moral fibre", to quote Service terminology. Because of the seriousness of the affair and the possible repercussions on the less experienced men in the Squadron, I preceded the written word with a telephone call to Embry. The Acting Group Commander wouldn't accept the pilot's plea for a transfer, saying that if he wouldn't fly Beaus it was more than likely he didn't wish to fly anything in combat. I didn't entirely agree with the Air Commodore, but I lost the battle. Within twenty-four hours both officers were off the station and posted to other units on probation. I never heard of them again. A replacement crew arrived and to my joy the pilot was my old friend Winn of Debden days, now a Squadron Leader. He brought with him his AI operator, Flight Lieutenant Scott. Scotty provided the Squadron with some amusement at first because of a facial twitch, but he could give as good as he received in ragging. His attitude to the twitch was, "What do you expect, if you have to fly with a clot like Winn?"

20

Sticks arrived back with the Squadron from a course in time to go with Buster and me to visit the Bristol Aircraft Company's factory at Filton. We were to represent crews flying the company's aeroplanes and were expected to speak to a large gathering of aircraft workers in one of the canteens. I dreaded public speaking but managed to mumble a few appropriate words, thanking them on behalf of the aircrews for furnishing us with such a fine aircraft as the Beaufighter. I spoke with sincerity, but as I felt inadequate as a speaker I then dropped a bomb for Sticks, by calling on him to say something. From the look he gave me I should have dropped dead. But in his completely uninhibited manner he soon had the crowded canteen laughing at his jokes, most of which were at my expense. I deserved it for springing the surprise speech on him. These visits no doubt did a lot of good and encouraged the workers, who received little credit for their hard work.

On the afternoon of April 10, information came from a near-by coastal Group HQ that one of our long-range reconnaissance aircraft in the Bay had sighted a large German armed raider with naval escort approaching the Gironde River from the south-west. Immediately a strike force was organized by the Group consisting of a R.C.A.F. squadron of Hampden torpedo bombers and six Beaus from the coastal squadron at Predannock. The Beaus were to act in an anti-flak role. I was asked by a staff officer if I would like to help with three of my Beaus. The answer was, "Yes." Our job would be the same as the Coastal Beaus—to shoot up the naval escort. This time Sticks was on leave, so again I took Blackburn as my navigator. He had proved himself very able at this sort of work. Doc Dougal had also been badgering me for a trip, so he was told he could come as a passenger. Two other crews were selected and, after co-ordinating plans with the Coastal Beau Squadron, I briefed my crews.

We were off the ground on time followed by our Coastal friends at a short interval. We spread out into two wide formations a few miles apart, with 141 in the van. When we arrived at the point over the Scillies where we were to meet with the torpedo bombers, there was no sign of them. I decided to fly the planned route in the hope of eventually locating them. For forty-two minutes we sighted nothing but empty sea as we skimmed fifty feet above the Atlantic swell. I began to think the trip was to be a waste of time.

The Doc, standing looking over my shoulder, was the first to see something. "What's that over on the horizon?" I noticed little puffs of smoke in the far distance. "My God, it's flak. The Hampdens must be there already." I wheeled my formation round and opened the throttles wide. A few seconds later we made out the masts of ships—a big one surrounded by several smaller ones which were pouring out a terrific barrage of light and heavy flak at the torpedo bombers. The whole convoy of ships was manœuvring wildly to escape. Things didn't look too good. An enormous splash followed by oily smoke marked the grave of one of the torpedo bombers and as far as we could see none of the ships seemed to be damaged.

We were still some miles away and as yet the Germans hadn't spotted us because we were approaching fast and low, our props throwing up a light salt spray. I quickly called the leader of the Coastal Beaus to join us in attacking the escorts. Between us we should be able to split up the heavy flak barrage if we attacked different ships simultaneously. To my chagrin he answered that he thought it wasn't worth it as the torpedo attack was practically over. He was going to lead his aircraft home. There was no point in arguing over the radio, so I called my two crews and directed them in for an attack on the escort vessels.

A small destroyer was about a mile ahead of me, so I selected this as my target. Up to now none of the flak seemed to be directed at us. The ships were concentrating on the Hampdens. When I got to within half a mile I started firing and as I did so my ship turned to starboard, showing us his stern to give us a smaller target. At the same time a stream of red balls of fire flashed towards us, not only from his flak guns, but from other ships in the convoy. The air was full of flying metal and I couldn't see how we could escape being hit. I kept my thumb on the firing button and the four cannons spewed out streams of armour-piercing and high-explosive shells at the rate of 700 rounds a minute per gun. The inside of our aircraft filled with cordite fumes which I hardly noticed as I concentrated on keeping my sights on the ship. At first there was a fountain of spray just astern of the vessel.

My fire was falling a little short. With my thumb still on the button I eased back ever so slightly on the control column to adjust my aim. Then the ship was smothered in flashes and smoke as the shells from our guns struck home. We bore in at 230 m.p.h. and the Nazi ship grew larger and larger. But no longer was there any return fire from his guns. The crew must have been killed or were seeking shelter from our murderous fire. The air was full of bursting shells as the rest of the convoy tried to shoot my comrades out of the air. For a second or so I was spared the fire from the other ships as I was too close to their own vessel. I kept as low as I dared, firing all the time until, at the last minute when it looked as if we might crash into the stern of the ship, I hauled back on the stick and just cleared the mast. Then turning hard to starboard we dived back down to water level, heading west away from the convoy at full throttle.

When we broke away all hell broke loose. The Nazis threw everything at us to avenge their damaged comrade. "Make it difficult for them, Sir. Weave." Blackburn's voice broke in over the intercom, reminding me to take evasive action. Great gouts of water shot up all around us as the heavier naval guns joined in with the light flak. One or two shells burst in large black puffs alongside of us, rocking the aircraft dangerously. There was a sharp metallic rattle as fragments of hot steel buried themselves in the vitals of our good old Beau. At last we were out of range. "Everyone O.K.?" The Doc and Blackburn said yes. "Blackburn, did you see our other two aircraft?" "I think one of them bought it, sir. I saw him for a second surrounded by flak bursts as we were closing in on our target. Then there was a large splash in his area. I didn't see the other one at all." My heart sank. This wasn't so good.

It was getting dark. The ship we had attacked seemed to be out of control, going round in a slow circle, smoking but still afloat. All the other vessels seemed to be unharmed. My immediate concern was to try to contact my other two crews. I called them both over the radio. MacAndrew, the pilot of one of the Beaus, answered at once and said that he was O.K. and was also heading home. The other crew failed to answer. I hoped and prayed they had survived even though it would mean being taken prisoner. Later I heard they had been shot into the sea by heavy flak and went down with their aircraft.

Two hours later Mac and I landed our Beaus back at Predannock. Both had been hit by flak fragments, but no serious damage had been done. I had fired 520 rounds of 20-mm. ammunition in one long burst, nearly six seconds of continuous fire, the longest burst I fired throughout the war. The average single burst in combat was two to three seconds. It had paid off for we had seriously damaged the German naval vessel.

In general, however, the mission was unsuccessful, chiefly because of the failure of the rendezvous and the consequent lack of co-ordination during the attack. The armed raider got away scot free. On the debit side the mission cost us one Beau and one Hampden destroyed and several Hampdens severely damaged with wounded crews. I was angry about losing our crew and felt that if the Coastal Beaus had participated it might not have happened. I expressed my views rather harshly to the Squadron Commander of the Coastal Beau Squadron who, I felt, should have been leading his aircraft personally in view of the importance of the mission. In fact, his aircraft were led by one of his experienced N.C.O. crews. This incident caused some ill-feeling between the two squadrons at Predannock for some days. Things were soon back to a happy state, however, when soon afterwards the Squadron Commander was removed from his command. His place was taken by one of his excellent Flight Commanders who was an outstanding Beau strike-force leader.

I now received a call to visit Fighter Command Headquarters at Stanmore for a briefing. The Staff Officer said he couldn't divulge the purpose of the conference over the phone, so naturally I was left wondering. I set off next morning with Buster Reynolds in one of the Squadron Beaus. We were met at Northolt by a staff car and whisked off to Bentley Priory, the rambling old mansion which served as headquarters and brain centre of Fighter Command. Buster and I were ushered into one of the conference-rooms and confronted by a number of senior staff officers and two civilians, one of whom I recognized as a member of the Telecommunication Research Establishment at Defford, near Malvern. I was told at once that my Squadron had been selected for a new operation to be known as "Serrate".

A special R.A.F. flying unit which had aircraft fitted with secret electronic gear spent its time trying to monitor and locate enemy radio and radar frequencies. At times it undertook hazardous trips over or near enemy territory to gain this valuable information. It appeared that they had found out the frequency of the AI equipment used by the German night-fighters. With this information the scientists at T.R.E. had evolved a device which, if used in conjunction with our AI, would enable us to locate German night-fighters whenever they switched on their AI. Fighter Command had decided to equip 141 Squadron's Beaus with this "black box" and send us out with the bomber streams. Our job was to shoot down or drive off as many as possible of the large number of German night-fighters which were beginning to take a heavy toll of our bombers. I suggested that other squadrons should be equipped with "Serrate" at the same time so that we could send out a large number of aircraft to combat the German night-fighters. However, the meeting decided that as we knew so little about the "black box" only my Squadron would be used. As Predannock was not an ideal location for this sort of operation, the Squadron would have to be nearer the centre of things. It was agreed, therefore, that we should move to Wittering at the end of April, where the aircraft would be fitted with the "black box".

We then got into a discussion about our own AI. It was felt that we still couldn't afford to risk losing our later AI equipments over enemy territory, so my Beaus would have to use the Mk 4. The few aircraft I had fitted with Mk 7 would be replaced by the older variety. I accepted this only as a minor setback after the great news of this operation. Now the Squadron would get into the thick of things, and if we could save even a few of our bombers from the enemy it would be most satisfying.

By the time the conference was over I was fairly jumping

with excitement and could hardly wait for the day to move to Wittering. But I could tell only my two Flight Commanders —Davis and Winn—since the operation was so highly secret. On return to Predannock late that evening I sent for them both and gave them the gist of what had been discussed, with a warning to keep quiet until we arrived at our new base in two weeks' time. Then the rest of the Squadron could be brought into the picture.

During the last two weeks at Predannock I flew on one more Ranger sortie. I took Blackburn as navigator and Buster as a passenger. It was a bright moonlit night and again we were seeking out road or rail movement on the Brest Peninsula. The only transport we saw on this patrol was a lorry on the road to Cahaix, south-east of Brest. One short squirt from our guns and it crashed into the ditch at the side of the road, a smoking ruin. On the way home we saw a line of three E-boats, which from the appearance of their wakes were travelling at speed. I manœuvred the Beau into a position for an attack on the last boat in the line and started a dive from 3,000 feet, opening fire at around 1,000 feet. There was a loud bang and a bright flash which momentarily lit up the inside of the Beau. This was followed by a blast of wind. At first I thought we had been hit by flak from the boats or fired on from an unseen German fighter. Pulling out of the dive I turned towards the English coast and called Blackburn and Buster over the intercom to find out if they were both O.K. Buster answered, "There is a large hole in the floor of the fuselage." "All right, we had better return to base." "Keep your eyes open, Blackburn, there may be fighters about." The hole in the fuselage would account for the wind blasting into the aircraft, but I wasn't sure what had caused it, so for some time I staggered our aircraft from side to side just in case a German night-fighter was around. Forty-five minutes later we landed our damaged Beau at Predannock.

Investigation showed that a 20-mm. shell had exploded in the barrel of one of our guns when I pressed the firing button to fire at the E-boat. The damage was not very serious, but certainly spectacular. The gun concerned had snapped in half and a large hole was blown in the fuselage directly beneath it.

Once a month the Sector Commander at Portreath asked the Station Commander and myself over for a meeting to discuss administrative or operational problems. During the Squadron's last few days at Predannock we received such an invitation and flew over. It was a routine meeting and after lunch we set off back for our own airfield. Circling Predannock for a landing, we noticed to our horror the smoking scattered remains of an aircraft near one of 141 dispersal areas. I called the control tower and asked if it was one of my aircraft. "Sorry, sir, I'm afraid so." I landed as quickly as possible and drove over to the scene. The fire-fighters were still playing their hoses on the smouldering wreckage which covered a large area. The pilot was the Aussie I had bawled out only a few weeks before for beating up the officers' mess at Mullion. With him was poor Blackburn who had been in so many combats with me.

I was told that the pilot, who was a Deputy Flight Commander, was leading two other Beaus in formation practice. They were flying in a V and during the practice the Aussie led them in a number of low beat-ups of the airfield, in spite of warnings from the control tower not to do it. On one of these passes he came too low and the wing-tip of his aircraft caught the roof of a Nissen hut. The Beau smashed into the ground at high speed. The crews of the other two aircraft realized he was too low and broke off from the formation. This stupid accident which cost the lives of the aircrew could easily have been more disastrous as there were airmen in the hut.

I suppose I should have sorrowed over the death of the pilot but all I felt was anger. He had been given one chance for a serious low-flying offence, but as soon as my back was turned he had let the Squadron down again. He was also responsible for the death of a fine navigator who had just won the D.F.M. and he nearly killed many other people. Next day Blackburn's wife arrived at Predannock and I told her as gently as possible that it was an accident and that her husband had been killed instantly. At least the last part of my words was the truth. Unfortunately I don't think she believed me as she had already been in contact with some of her husband's N.C.O. friends. They had dropped some sort of hint that he was killed by the foolishness of the pilot. Later she agreed to the funeral arrangements. Then I had to tell her that Blackburn had just been awarded the D.F.M. for gallantry. There were no tears in her eyes as she bitterly said, "What good will that do now?" Blackburn had meant a lot to me as a man and the way he died affected me to the extent that I was unable to say anything helpful in reply to her question. Dickie and Doc came to the rescue and did what they could to ease the poor woman's suffering.

21

O̲ UR few remaining days at Predannock were spent in polishing up our night-fighter training and preparing the aircraft for the move. In the interim the few Mk 7 AI Beaus were replaced by the Mk 4 versions. I also received a letter from Air Commodore Embry congratulating me on the award of a second bar to my D.F.C. for successes in our recent offensive operations. Personally I felt the gong belonged to the Squadron as a whole as every man-jack of them had put up a fine show. Before leaving for Wittering, I made the promised visit to T.R.E. at Defford to discuss the technical details of Serrate with Mr. Williams, the brilliant little Welsh scientist who was to give us much help in the months to come. Finally, on the last day of April, 141 Squadron took off for the last time from Predannock to fly to Wittering. As our sixteen aircraft set course in formation for our new abode, I had a feeling of regret. At Predannock the Squadron had been rejuvenated and had lost forever its sense of inferiority. But it was no good looking back. Besides, the future looked even rosier.

Wittering was a large grass airfield with one of the longest landing runs in the country. Because of its length it was a popular diversion for bomber aircraft returning damaged from raids over Europe, as it permitted the tired and sometimes wounded crews the maximum room for errors. There was little fear of over-running the field.

Group Captain Legge, a tall, friendly man, was our new boss and he and his staff immediately set about making us feel at home. Wittering was a pre-war station with substantial permanent hangars and barracks which had suffered only slight bomb damage. However, as a necessary precaution our aircraft were dispersed some distance from the permanent buildings and only housed in the hangars when it was necessary to do major repairs. We were liberally provided with vehicles to move about the station.

The first couple of weeks were taken up in local practice flying and fitting the aircraft with the Serrate device. Much of my own time was spent in planning our future operations. I soon found that 141 was to be given a remarkably free hand. Operationally the Squadron reported directly to Fighter Command Headquarters, by-passing the usual channels of Sector and Group. Bomber Command contacted Fighter Command Intruder Control at Stanmore during the morning or afternoon before a raid. The staff at Intruder would then phone 141 Squadron giving the bomber target, pertinent routes, types and numbers of bomber aircraft and time over the target. Sticks, who was now a Flight Lieutenant and the AI leader of the Squadron, Buster Reynolds, the Intelligence Officer and I, would then plot this information on a master-map in the briefing-room and plan the Squadron's tactics for the night.

When most of our aircraft had been fitted with Serrate, Mr. Williams advised that we should move to an airfield more distant from the enemy coast to practise with the device against some Defiants which had been equipped with a gimmick to simulate the German AI. It was thought that if we trained at Wittering there was a possibility that the enemy would detect what we were up to through his radio and radar intelligence service. If he got wind that we were on to his AI frequency he would have time to make adjustments and nullify our chances of success. The importance of the advice was appreciated by Fighter Command, who arranged for the

Squadron to be moved to Drem, near North Berwick in Scotland. This move was to take place in mid-May.

In the meantime, with my two Flight Commanders, Winn and Davis, and Sticks, I visited Bomber Command and Nos. 5 and 8 Group Headquarters to advise their staffs how we intended to operate, and to pick up any useful information about the tactics of both our bombers and the German night-fighters. In general everyone was most helpful, although we got the feeling that they thought that one squadron of aircraft was not enough to be of much use. We didn't agree. Even a few of our night-fighters flying in and around the bomber stream would cause confusion to the German defence organization. It was also likely that our presence would worry some of the German night-fighter crews so that their attacks on our bombers would be ineffective. However, we all agreed that it would have been better if we could have entered into this phase of operations in a big way rather than with one squadron. The argument in favour of this had been lost some time ago. One other problem that seemed to bother the bomber boys was that we were certain to be fired upon by our own bomber crews. In the heat of battle, they could not help mistaking us for enemy fighters. It was pointed out that this was an acceptable risk. We couldn't expect the crews of the bombers to wait for positive identification. It would probably then be too late if the fighter turned out to be a German.

Until we moved to Drem we continued our night-fighter training, putting the emphasis on "stalking" fighter-type aircraft. We expected that the German fighter-crews in their Me110s and JU88s would be able to detect our presence on their AI as we closed in on them, so the chances of a surprise attack were unlikely. After a week or so the Squadron became quite proficient at night dog-fighting. Pairs of Beaus chased one another around the dark heavens, with the AI operators reeling off running commentaries of the position of the other fighter to their pilots, as both crews tried to close the range until a visual was obtained. Usually the pilot who first obtained a visual won our practice combats. Gunnery was now more important because we should generally be firing on a manœuvring target. All our aircraft were fitted with cine-cameras, harmonized with the gunsight, so that when we practised attacks in daylight our shooting accuracy or inaccuracy could be recorded. In this way we could see if we were allowing too much, or too little, deflection in our shooting and the experience gained enabled us to do better on subsequent practice trips, and later in combat.

In the third week of May, when the last of my aircraft was fitted with Serrate, we flew up to Drem. Landing at this airfield recalled memories of 1940, when with 29 Squadron I flew convoy escort in and out of the Firth of Forth. At that time things were very black for England. We were about to be kicked unceremoniously out of Norway. Now, in the spring of 1943, the Gods of War were smiling on the Allies and everywhere there were signs of victory. I met the Commander of the special Defiant unit with which we were to work for the next few weeks. I was pleased to see he was a friend of 29 Squadron days, Ian Esplin, an Australian Flight Lieutenant. He had served with me as a Deputy Flight Commander. Ian was an experienced night-fighter pilot and well aware of the urgency of getting us up to scratch on the new device. Together we worked out a flying programme which would enable all the Squadron crews to get the hang of how best to use Serrate with their AI.

Despite a tight training programme at Drem, 141 found plenty of time to play. We played as hard as we worked and at times our high spirits got us all into a little trouble. The manageress of the Station Hotel in North Berwick took the Squadron under her wing, and the pleasant bar of the hotel became a favourite meeting place. In this bar we encountered a Naval officer who insisted on making disparaging remarks about the R.A.F. and 141 Squadron in particular. He was silenced rather roughly. Later in the evening we met him again at a local officers' club and once again he had to be dealt with forcibly. He was stubborn and wouldn't shut up. Our methods of silencing the Navy were not altogether approved of by the local Scottish officers and their ladies, so we had to leave. Still, honour was satisfied and we were content. I learned later that word of our adventures must have reached the ears of the Station Commander at Drem.

On another occasion about a dozen of the Squadron officers set out on bikes for a near-by pub. After a pleasant evening of darts with the locals, we returned to Drem. It was dark and we had no lights but we felt that a race back to the mess was in order. Eventually we straggled puffing up to the mess in time for a meal of good old bacon and eggs. Last to arrive was Charles Winn with bloody and swollen face. "What happened to you?" "Oh, I thought I could do better with no hands. Apparently I was wrong." Winn's bike went out of control and he hit the road with his chin, knocking out one of his front teeth. His now unhandsome face cracked into a toothless grin as he tossed this gory trophy on to the dining-table in front of me. "A souvenir," he said. My interest in the bacon and eggs suddenly waned.

Information reached us that a JU88 night-fighter had landed intact with its crew at an airfield in Britain. They had had enough of the war and decided to sit it out as P.O.Ws. The interest of this for us was that we now had a working German AI set from which our boffins were soon able to confirm that the frequency of the equipment was as they had previously surmised from the findings of our radio and radar reconnaissance aircraft. The lucky windfall gave us all the feeling that our future operations against the enemy night-fighters would be blessed with immediate success.

I had to fly down for another briefing at Fighter Command Headquarters. The Group Captain of Night Operations, Tubby Pearson, wanted to know first-hand how we were progressing with our training. I told him I thought we had picked up all the available information and developed tactics as far as possible under trial conditions. When asked if I thought the Squadron was fit to have a crack at the enemy I said "Yes." I was then told that I could take them back to Wittering within the next few days and be ready for operations within two weeks. This was great news. I was about to leave Pearson's office when he detained me, saying that he had heard we had been overdoing the drinking at Drem, and what did I think about it. I asked where he got his information and he said the Station Commander had phoned him personally about it. This had never been brought to my attention by the C.O. at Drem, although I was aware that on occasions some of us had been a little too high-spirited. I managed to convince Pearson that all was well under control. He took my word for it and I never heard any more about it. But on returning to Drem, I took the precaution of warning all our personnel. We didn't want to prejudice our chances of being the first squadron to take on the Serrate job.

A day or so before leaving Drem I became a father again. The baby was not "Wendy" as planned, but another boy. We had never thought of a suitable name for a boy. Perhaps the answer was to have a real Bob in the family, so I wrote to Joan to suggest we called him Robert. I couldn't get home at the time because of urgent work but "Robert" was agreed upon when I wangled a few days off on return to Wittering. We soon accepted Wittering as our new home. In spite of wartime rationing we lived well, thanks to the abundance of partridge and pheasant in the area, which we poached with complete abandon.

To landowners of the district I offer abject apologies, but at least they can be sure that this illegal supplementing of our rations did much for our morale, besides keeping our eyes in for shooting of a more serious kind. Our Group Captain was also most generous. He was an ardent fisherman and would get up at most unearthly hours of the morning to fish near-by trout streams. He often offered us some of his catch for dinner or breakfast. His hobby, unlike our poaching, was above-board. He had permission to fish the local streams.

22

WE were soon committed to our first Serrate operation. On the afternoon of June 14, word came that a large force of bombers would be attacking industrial targets at Oberhausen in the Ruhr. We were given complete freedom of action as to how the Squadron would operate, so after I had jotted down all the information on bomber routes and timings a meeting of the Squadron's senior officers was called. There was disappointment when the engineer officer said only six aircraft could be counted on, but as was to be expected with new equipment such as Serrate we had our teething troubles. Sticks and I were to fly on this trip and my Flight Commanders selected five other crews. It was agreed that we should be able to stay in the air longer with our bomber friends if we started out from an airfield as near the east coast as possible. So we decided to fly to Coltishall, near Norwich, and refuel there.

Despite all we had learned at Drem and from the boffins, there were many unknowns which could only be solved in combat. It was felt that the best way to achieve surprise would be to climb into the bomber stream and then set our speed to that of the bombers. In this way the enemy ground radars and night-fighter crews would be unable to detect high-performance fighters until we were engaged in combat. The crews selected were then called in for a briefing. I noticed there was a lack of the usual forced gaiety before a sortie. We all had a sense of serious concentration. We weren't fooling ourselves. On paper at least, the odds against us were tremendous. There would be at least 100 German night-fighters to our six. However, it wasn't as bad as it sounded because our trump card was surprise and the confusion that the few of us could cause. The main German defences consisted of a number of radar belts encircling the Third Reich. The outer one was the most effective. It ran around the north coast of Holland down over the Zuider Zee, through Belgium and France to Paris, then cut back eastwards near the Franco–German border to Switzerland. The Luftwaffe defence organization was capable of controlling very large numbers of night-fighters scattered liberally on airfields throughout Germany and occupied Europe. They also deployed heavy flak and searchlight concentrations at strategic points, chiefly around industrial areas and cities. Our briefing map showed a large blob of red extending over the whole of the Ruhr, an indication of one of the heaviest of these flak concentrations in the world. Air combat would most likely take place on the route to and from Oberhausen, as the German night-fighters tended to keep clear of the main target-areas to give their flak a free hand. We believed that the anti-aircraft fire was only a minor worry compared with the enemy fighters.

At Coltishall we ran into old friends. This airfield was the home of 68 Squadron, one of the many defensive night-fighter units. They had a rough idea of our new job, but no details, and they were obviously envious of our luck. However, this squadron had seen more fun than most of the other night-fighter squadrons because they were near coastal shipping lanes and only a short distance north of Harwich. They had occasionally mixed it with German mine-laying aircraft. We weren't due to take off until 11.30 so had ample time for a leisurely meal, but in our excitement we didn't tarry long over it. I am sure our feelings were appreciated by our hosts at Coltishall. We wanted to make sure everything was O.K.

with our Beaus which we inspected with fond attention. Then we waited impatiently for the off.

The moon was high and the night beautifully clear, when at about 11.15 we heard the rumbling of many aero engines passing over. We could faintly make out ten Lancasters or Halifaxes a few thousand feet up and still climbing on their easterly course towards Germany's arsenal, the Ruhr. Hundreds more of these huge machines loaded with destruction would meet them over the North Sea and the stream of aircraft would stretch in a seemingly endless line for about 100 miles. Those who straggled off to one side because of faulty navigation would be easy targets for enemy fighters.

I checked my watch. "O.K., let's go." Sticks and I climbed aboard our Beau. Once cleared by the control tower we were to maintain radio silence until our return to England. As we climbed, Sticks watched his AI for signs of the masses of bombers that must be in our vicinity. Soon he told me over the intercom that he had many contacts all around us. The bombers were scattered between 10,000 and 18,000 feet. We decided to level off at 12,000 feet because the information we had from Bomber Command Headquarters was that the enemy tended to hit the lower-flying bombers hardest. We droned slowly over the North Sea and below us I could see the moon shimmering on the unfriendly waters. Thirty minutes later the faint outline of the Dutch islands at the mouth of the Scheldt hove into view. We were bang on course. As usual, Sticks's navigation was perfect.

The countryside below us was completely blacked out, although on a night like this it was easy for us to find our way. Rivers, canals and even rail lines stood out clearly. Up ahead I could see the beams of a few wavering searchlights, but nothing else that looked hostile. Yet we knew that on the ground Luftwaffe defence centres were issuing orders to night-fighter airfields to scramble squadrons of night-fighters. At this moment Me110s and JU88s would be roaring off the landing fields throughout Holland, Belgium and western Germany to meet their hated adversaries, the bombers. Only this time, unknown to them, six Beaufighters were lurking in the stream.

Sticks was now continuously scanning the Serrate and AI scopes. "I've got a number of indications of night-fighters, Bob. I'm taking the strongest-looking signal. Turn starboard 10 degrees and let's see if we can get this one." We were now flying towards the signals emitted by a German night-fighter's AI. The technical limitations of Serrate gave us no idea how close or far the aircraft was until we picked up contact on our own AI, but we could tell his relative position to us in space. Flak appeared in the distance and bombers ahead of us were now under attack. "Sorry, Bob, that signal has disappeared. But I have another. Port 20 degrees." I banked the Beau round to our new course and the aircraft rocked suddenly as we hit the prop-wash of another aircraft in front of us. I couldn't see anything but it was probably one of our own bombers. Again after a short chase, no luck. The Serrate signal disappeared, but always there were others indicating the presence of large numbers of enemy fighters. It seemed that the enemy left his AI on only for short periods.

By now we were approaching the Ruhr and the flak ahead was becoming more intense as the bombers started to unload. Fires and explosions could be seen from many miles away as Oberhausen received mortal blows. But this wasn't a one-sided battle. Off to the right there was a vivid flash in the sky, then a flaming comet streaked earthwards. I noted the position and cursed. It was probably one of our bombers. "Keep a good check on the equipments, Sticks. There are plenty of Huns about." Up ahead was another fire in the sky, gradually sinking lower and lower to crash in a sheet of flame, marking the grave of another aircraft. Things were getting hot.

We were close to the flaming ruins of Oberhausen and the sky above us was filled with bursting anti-aircraft shells and the flares released by the Pathfinders to show the main force where the bombs should be dropped. There were so many bombers over the city that the German gunners couldn't hope to aim at individual aircraft. They threw up a curtain of steel in the hope of driving off their tormentors. It was in vain. The attack continued.

By now the leading bombers were turning away from the target and setting course for home. So skirting the flaming city, we headed back among their track. So far, I had only seen fleeting glimpses of dark shadows as we passed close to one or two of our bombers, although we flew through the prop-wash of many as we criss-crossed the stream in what seemed a fruitless search for the many German fighters.

Then there was excitement in Stick's voice, as he called, "Bob, I've got another signal, turn gently port." As I manœuvred the Beau I counted three other aircraft on fire in the air within my range of vision. I knew our bombers rarely shot down a German night-fighter so I could only assume the enemy was exacting vengeance for the raid.

"Bob, I think this one is behind us. The signal is strong."

"Have you anything on the AI yet?"

"No, but keep turning."

It was an eerie feeling, knowing that we were playing a deadly game of hide-and-seek with an unseen foe.

"Bob, I've AI contact 2,000 yards behind. Hard as possible port."

"Are you sure it isn't one of our bombers?"

"Yes. It isn't. The Serrate and AI signals match up. Keep turning, he's only about 1,000 yards and 20 degrees on your port and a little above. Now ease the turn a little, and watch it. You're closing fast, you should see him in a second. He's only 600 yards and still well over to port."

"I've got him, I've got him," I yelled excitedly.

In the moonlight I caught a glimpse of an aircraft on my port beam. At that moment he straightened out, heading south at 10,000 feet. An Me110. Perhaps he had lost me on his AI. At 400 yards range I opened fire, gradually easing off the deflection so that as I rolled in astern of him the dot of my electric gunsight was centred on his fuselage. Explosions appeared all over the Me. Burning brightly he dived steeply towards the earth. By now Stick had his head out of the "office" and was shouting encouragement as he watched our enemy crash in a mighty flash of flame. This was no time to relax. "Keep a look-out on your set, Sticks. There are lots of the blighters about." Checking the position of our fight, I noted that the Me110 had crashed on the north-east shore of the Zuider Zee.

We had been flying for nearly three hours and our petrol was getting low. I decided to call it a day. With throttles wide open and in a gentle dive, we headed towards home, crossing out over the island of Texel. Sticks was still picking up indications on his Serrate and I hoped the rest of the boys were having luck, too. In case any enemy night-fighters tried to pick us up I dived to within a couple of thousand feet of the North Sea, with Sticks still keeping watch on his equipment.

If nothing else, we had proved that Serrate worked. And we had probably saved the lives of one or more of our bomber crews by writing off the Me110. We were both tired out, particularly Sticks. He had spent most of the trip gazing into his cathode-ray scopes. I knew what a strain this could be, having tried it myself. At nearly 3.30 a.m. we contacted Wittering control tower and were soon on the ground surrounded by excited Squadron comrades. All but two of our aircraft were back and the control tower was in contact with both of these. I sighed with relief. We had lost none.

I waited for the other two crews to land, then we all drove over to the mess for a meal of bacon and eggs, during which we discussed the operation. Sticks and I were the only successful crew, but several of the others had been close to combat, only to have either the Serrate or the AI fail at the crucial moment. However, our experiences promised well for the future. What we couldn't assess was how much confusion our presence had caused to the Luftwaffe defence set-up. We felt that although we had only shot down one aircraft, our presence in the stream may have drawn off some enemy aircraft which would otherwise have attacked our bombers. It was six weary crews who finally wandered off to bed as dawn broke. Later in the day we learned that thirty of our bombers had failed to return from the attack, but we drew comfort from the fact that more might have been lost but for 141's effort.

Throughout June and July, 1943, Bomber Command increased the tempo of its attacks against the Ruhr and Hamburg. In these two vital German centres of industry and production little was left but death and destruction. The vengeance being exacted on Germany for her attacks on cities of occupied Europe and Great Britain was indeed terrible. When the bombers flew, we flew, regardless of weather, and our successes slowly mounted. Gradually, as our technical personnel became more proficient at ironing the bugs out of the Serrate equipment, we were able to increase the number of aircraft we sent aloft. By the end of July, several squadron crews had shot down two or more of the enemy. Sticks and I increased our personal score by damaging a JU88 on a trip with our bombers to Côlogne. On another occasion we destroyed a Me110 near Elberfeld. So far we had not had serious casualties ourselves, although several of our aircraft had been hit by flak or machine-gun fire from our bombers as we flew close to them. On one of the raids on Cologne, my

Beaufighter was attacked by two JU88s during the night and we were damaged. One engine was set on fire. By diving steeply we not only succeeded in eluding the enemy fighters but also put out the fire and eventually landed successfully back at Wittering on one engine.

During short lulls I commandeered one of the station's communication aircraft, usually a little Tiger Moth, to fly to Leicester. It was good to get away on these short visits to see Joan and the kids, leaving behind me the strain of operations for a few hours. But in some perverse way, after a day with the family I felt I had to get back with my comrades. Relaxing in Leicester filled me with a sense of guilt when I knew other members of my outfit were fighting it out against the enemy. My feelings must at times have been obvious to Joan as I certainly showed signs of irritation and sometimes outright anger towards my two young sons. They, like all very young children, were prone to cry and grumble about minor things, and I was incapable at times of appreciating their little problems. This sometimes led to harsh words between my wife and me and when I returned to the Squadron I would try to forget my selfish conduct either by flying on another op, or by drowning my remorse with friends in one of the local pubs.

Not long after our arrival at Wittering, Paddy Englebach joined us. Paddy was a brilliant linguist, but not the most proficient of pilots, although he had the heart of a lion. He was one of the few people I have met who managed to bend over the tips of the metal propellers of the Beau on take-off. After three such incidents in rapid succession during his first few training flights in 141, I decided that enough was enough. We couldn't spare the aircraft, nor did we wish to see him kill himself. But when I saw him to tell him that he was being taken off flying, I was so impressed by his obvious desire to have a go at the enemy and his utter dejection that I relented and agreed to give him one more chance. His piloting still

178

left much to be desired, but he flew many trips over enemy territory. He did not get any "kill" but managed not to bend any more props.

The many long operational sorties were beginning to tell on some of the crews. With the advice of Doc Dougal I noticed many of them before it was too late and sent them off for short leaves to rest. Unfortunately I didn't appreciate how tired Sticks was getting until one night we had to return early from a trip over Holland because he was feeling unwell. I deeply regretted my lack of foresight, as Gregory was one of the ablest AI operators in Britain. In my insatiable desire to get at the enemy I was unwittingly burning him out. He badly needed a rest. Towards the end of July I told him that I was going to ground him for a while to give him a chance to get back in shape. I asked him meanwhile if he would take over as Squadron Operations Officer, responsible for the planning and briefing of our missions. Poor old faithful Sticks was in tears as he argued against my suggestion but eventually saw that there was no point in going on without a rest. He then mentioned in his unselfish way that this would be a good opportunity to get Jacko back again from Cranfield and give to him the break on operations which he had wanted for a long time. I rang the personnel people at 12 Group and asked if they could help us to get Jacko transferred to 141. A few days later a very happy Jacko joined our Squadron.

23

OPERATION Serrate gave us no respite. We were duty-bound to fly whenever the bombers went out and as this was nearly every night we were all beginning to show signs of fatigue. The Squadron had enough crews to ensure that individuals stood down about every other raid, but the nervous strain of these operations was great. Our losses were still light but every night we flew we had to face searchlights, flak, enemy night-fighters and sometimes fire from our own bombers. The time spent over enemy territory was long—at least two hours—and of course there was the knowledge that if we were shot down and able to bale out we were unlikely to get back until after the war. On defensive operations we knew that if we had to take to the parachute, we could be back with our comrades within a few hours.

Yet only one crew member cracked. One of my gallant Belgian pilots came to me obviously upset, complaining that on the last few trips he had to return to base before crossing the enemy coast because of Serrate or AI failure. He suspected his AI operator was deliberately saying the equipment was unsatisfactory. This was a serious accusation, but I was convinced of the pilot's keenness. I decided to send them out again that evening and if they returned for the reasons the pilot mentioned, the aircraft would be quarantined until the next trip when it would be flown by another crew. If the new crew found nothing wrong with the equipment, we should have fairly conclusive proof that the AI operator was "windy".

Sure enough the Belgian and his operator returned early from their trip. The following night the same aircraft was sent out with Winn and Scotty. No work had been done on the equipment and they completed a sortie over enemy territory without finding any fault in the Serrate or AI.

I sent for the Belgian's AI operator who soon broke down and admitted he didn't like the job. He convinced me that he couldn't be salvaged and that, to put it bluntly, he was yellow. I had little sympathy for him because I knew that we all felt fear at some stage of the game and many of us had much more to lose than he had, but by self-discipline we managed to conquer or submerge our fear. This officer was removed from the Squadron and my Belgian pilot was re-crewed with another operator. It was a tragic irony that soon afterwards they were shot down in flames near Bremen.

Letting Sticks fly too long without a break taught me a sharp lesson and I tried to ensure that all crews were given short spells off. It began to be apparent, too, that I needed some drastic change. My temper was getting short and I was overdoing the flying to a foolish degree. One day the Squadron received word that the Royal Navy would welcome two officers aboard one of their destroyers at Harwich for a few days. The destroyer was part of the escort for an east coast convoy. This was the sort of change I required and I decided that hard-working Buster, my "spy", should come with me. We joined H.M.S. *Whitshed*, a rather ancient ship. As we clambered up the gangplank I suddenly remembered some old custom about saluting the quarter-deck. Turning to Buster I asked him where this deck was. He shrugged. An officer and two or three ratings were waiting to receive us on deck, so I must try to do the correct thing. I didn't want to start our holiday off with a major "goof". Trying to look nonchalant I gazed at the mainmast and threw up a hasty salute, hoping this would be acceptable. Looks of disdain on the faces of the members of the Senior Service showed that my ignorance had not gone unnoticed.

The Captain was a young Lieutenant. I remember being surprised by his lowly rank. It seemed to me that his responsibilities merited at least the rank of Lieutenant Commander but this was none of my affair.

The trip up the east coast with a convoy to the Firth of Forth, which lasted two days, was invigorating and I found that in the company of the Navy I was able to forget completely the problems that had been crowding in on me during the past few weeks. We were given the complete run of the ship. Occasionally we were asked to identify aircraft and it was then that we appreciated how touchy the Navy were about aircraft in their vicinity. We soon saw that if they waited positively to identify friend or foe, it was often too late. The aircraft would be in a position to attack. So there was a justifiable tendency to shoot first and ask questions later.

At the mouth of the Firth of Forth the *Whitshed* said farewell to her charges and in company with another destroyer and a cruiser headed back for Harwich at speed. Throughout the trip the sea, thank God, was relatively calm and I wasn't sick. But when the old *Whitshed*'s engines were running at full bore the vibration they set up brought me very close to nausea. I managed to save the R.A.F.'s honour. When we got back to Harwich I felt like a new man and was grateful to our Naval friends for wonderful hospitality.

While Jacko was settling in at Wittering and getting acquainted with Serrate, Sticks and I flew one more trip together. This was to be our last operation as a team for seven months. A very large force of our bombers was to attack the industrial centre of Mannheim in South-Western Germany. We decided that Bradwell Bay on the Thames Estuary would be our most suitable refuelling and starting-point. Dave Blomeley, my brother-in-law, was stationed there with 605 Mosquito Intruder Squadron. I hadn't seen him since the early days of the war and was looking forward to our meeting again. We spent a few happy hours reminiscing while I waited for take-off time. Dave was enjoying his job with the intruders, but was envious of my Squadron with its AI and Serrate. The intruders flew long and hazardous trips far into enemy territory at low level at night, trying to seek out enemy aircraft. But as they had no airborne radar their successes were few.

Just before midnight my nine aircraft took off at intervals of a few minutes, climbing south-eastwards to make contact with the masses of our bombers which were forming up into a stream ahead of us. Soon we had the usual indications that we were in their midst. North of Dunkirk we could see flak and searchlights. On the Belgian–German border the darkness was broken only by anti-aircraft shell-bursts. The puff-balls of smoke from the shells bursting nearer could be clearly seen and once or twice our aircraft was rocked by explosions.

Aircraft could be seen burning in the sky around us, some heading slowly towards the earth while the crews fought vainly to retain control. Others fell like flaming meteors. Sticks sent us chasing after a night-fighter which switched off his AI, so we had to chase another. Near Liège, Sticks picked up a firm indication and after flying round at 10,000 feet we at last got AI contact. It was obvious that the enemy wasn't unaware of our presence but in a masterly way Sticks, by quick interpretation of his radar scopes and his running commentary, got me into a position astern.

At 150 yards range I vaguely made out a dark object. I couldn't identify him at this range so, turning to keep inside him, I closed until we were barely 100 yards apart. Then the object blossomed suddenly into the familiar shape of an Me110. At this range I couldn't miss. I fired two short bursts from our aircraft's ten guns. Strikes appeared all over the rear of the 110. It flicked on its back and spiralled to earth in flames.

At that moment a white flare soared into the darkness, fired from another aircraft close to us. Perhaps it came from a German night-fighter pilot who was marking the position of the crash, thinking it was the funeral pyre of one of our bombers. We searched for as long as petrol would permit for this or another German fighter, but in vain.

With Mannheim burning furiously in the distance, we turned for Bradwell Bay and landed three hours after take-off, tired but successful. One of my other crews saw the white flare and the explosion from the crash of our victim. They were able to confirm our air victory, which brought my total to fifteen, fourteen at night. Gradually we were catching up John Cunningham's score of eighteen at night. For Sticks's sake I was particularly happy about this success. He could now take his rest knowing he had done well. For his untiring courage and determination as an AI operator and navigator, I recommended him for a bar to supplement his already well-earned D.F.C., and D.F.M. We were a very happy crew when we celebrated the official announcement of this "gong" a few days later.

Our very popular C.O., Group Captain Legge, was now posted. He had endeared himself to the Squadron by his interest in our operations and general welfare. He made a habit of waiting up at our dispersal for the last of our aircraft to return, usually in the early hours of the morning. He then joined us for the usual meal of bacon and eggs, listening to our stories of the night's work. We decided to throw a special farewell party for him, with a dinner and presentation. We defeated rationing by devious means. Thanks to Winn we got a large number of pheasants and for the main course a very special bird! I was not told about this surprise until the last minute. It was roast swan, by courtesy of Winn. We had a glorious party but were saddened by the fact that the Group Captain was leaving us. Wittering was lucky to get another likeable boss in his place.

During a spell of really bad weather, when neither Bomber Command nor ourselves could fly, we ran a ground-defence exercise to keep everyone on his toes. The aircrew, headed by myself, were to act the part of paratroopers. We were dropped by vehicles some miles from the aerodrome in the late afternoon to make our way back and "destroy" aircraft and vital installations. The Station administrative staff and the Squadron ground personnel, lead by Dickie Sparrow, were responsible for defence. It was a wet evening. Each mud-covered group made its way, by devious routes, back to the airfield. We had blackened our faces and hands. When my unit reached the dispersal area it was pitch black, but every so often light beams swept the airfield and thunder-flashes cracked to show that the defenders were alert. Both sides had been issued with thunder-flashes to simulate grenades.

From the cursing and shouting it was obvious that the defence was making it hot for my commandos! Eventually we worked our way forward and chalked a cross on two Beaus indicating their destruction. Then we were surprised and captured, but not before Sticks had tried to lob off a thunder-flash. Unfortunately he hung on to it too long and it exploded in his hand, splitting the palm open. The defenders were true gentlemen. Instead of bumping us off they sent old Sticks to the Doc and unceremoniously dumped the rest of us into a room in one of the dispersal huts which was being used as a P.O.W. cage. It was already full with the majority of my aircrew who had been captured. Except for Sticks there were no other casualties. The exercise was considered a draw. Some aircraft were "destroyed" and the ground installations were "blown up". Against this, all of my "commandos" were either captured or "killed". It was not only a lot of fun and good physical exercise but we all learned useful lessons. The chief one was that it would be almost impossible to stop a determined enemy from attaining his purpose, even though it might cost him the entire attacking force to achieve it. It made one wonder what would have happened if the Germans had been prepared to sacrifice a few experienced airborne soldiers for attacks on some of our key Early-Warning Ground Radars during the Battle of Britain. Perhaps the outcome of that famous battle would have been different.

One of my worries since the Serrate operations began was the limited radius of action of the Beaufighter. Attacks by Bomber Command on Berlin and the North-Italian industrial areas showed us clearly that we could only accompany our friends along part of the route.

Our practice was to send half our available fighters out with the stream to fly as far as they could. The rest took off later during the night to meet the returning bombers, again as far out along the return route as possible. This wasn't very satisfactory. It split our small effort in half, but it was the best we could do. In discussing the problem with staff officers at Fighter Command, I requested that our Beaus should be replaced by the longer range Mosquitos. This they promised to look into, but they could do nothing immediately. They still weren't prepared to send Mosquitos with the latest AI over enemy territory.

When we first arrived at Wittering there was only one other flying unit on the Station, an instrument training flight equipped with Oxfords. Their task was to run small courses for selected Fighter Command pilots, to improve their instrument flying and bring them up to date with latest developments. Later in the summer, our ranks were swelled by the arrival of an American P38 (Lockheed Lightning) long-range fighter squadron, part of a U.S.A.A.C. Fighter Group dispersed between Wittering and the satellite at near-by Kingscliffe. This squadron, although direct from the States with no combat experience, soon impressed us with their eagerness and spirit. Their role was to escort the ever-growing numbers of daylight bomber formations of the U.S.A.A.C. 8th Air Force. We didn't envy them their job. It was soon apparent from their losses that the Lightning was no match for the Me109s and FW190s.

Major McGovern, the Squadron Commander, and I soon became firm friends, and possibly because of this our two squadrons got along well. Only one problem arose and that was gambling. Our allies were inveterate card-players and the stakes were usually high, certainly well beyond the means of the average R.A.F. type. Some of my men thought they could compete, and found themselves in the red. It was easy to see that my chaps didn't want the Americans to think them penny-pinchers but I had to stop them gambling to ensure good relations between the two squadrons. I was worried, too, that a heavy loss was bound to lower the fighting efficiency of an airman. Experience had shown that a worried pilot could make fatal mistakes. McGovern saw my point and was helpful. Both squadrons accepted the decision with good grace.

It didn't take Jacko long to become acquainted with Serrate. We were soon flying together again. The first few trips were easy ones. Bomber Command was hitting targets in Northern Italy and this gave Jacko time to orientate himself. We took off for these sorties from Ford. They were very boring and uneventful. In three of these missions our only excitement was when, in a moment of boredom on the way back, we attacked the German airfield at Melun outside Paris. It was a clear, moonlit night as we dived our Beau to a low level and strafed the hangars. We couldn't see what damage we did but we certainly awakened the defenders. They filled the sky with streams of flak, but their aim was poor. It was quite a firework display with orange lines of tracer criss-crossing the sky as we withdrew.

Bomber Command then switched its effort back to Germany. Here the opposition was very different and there was always a chance of a scrap with one of the multitude of German fighters.

24

For some time the British Government and Air Staff had been worried by information that the enemy was developing two powerful new weapons; one a pilotless aircraft, the V1, and the other a medium-range rocket, the V2. Both had large, high-explosive warheads. From intelligence sources and the interpretation of photographs taken by our reconnaissance aircraft, it was apparent that the major development and testing of these new missiles was taking place at Peenemunde, on the Baltic coast. Further, unless countermeasures were taken urgently the enemy would have one or both of his V weapons in full-scale production within a short time and would be able to bombard Britain on a scale undreamt of before.

During the early afternoon of August 17 an urgent call was received from Fighter Command by Sticks, my new Operations Officer. The order was that 141 was to put up a maximum effort that night in support of one of Bomber Command's most important raids of the war. It was to be a very heavy attack on the weapons experimental establishment at Peenemunde. At the time the true significance of this raid was not entirely known to us, but we had enough information to be impressed with the importance of putting up as many fighters as possible.

We began planning our tactics while Sewell, the engineer officer, rallied the groundcrews to give their best. Because of the complexity of the AI and Serrate equipments, we were lucky if we got twelve of our nineteen aircraft off on any one

189

night. Invariably one or two of these had to return early because of some trouble. Sewell returned to the briefing-room and surprised us all by saying that he thought we could count on sixteen for the night. This was really something, as the Squadron had been on operations five nights running and both ground- and aircrews were very tired. The hard work and loyalty of our airmen never ceased to amaze me. Even during the dull periods of the past when there was little action their spirit had been wonderful. In recent months, with our increased chances of action, morale was the tops. They worked excessively long hours without moaning as long as there was a hope for their aircrew to have a crack at the enemy. Pouring over the planning map with Sticks and Buster we saw that the bomber stream was routed over the North Sea, some eighty miles north of the Frisian Islands, over Denmark and then south to the target. Return route was much the same. With the limited range of the Beau we could only hope to fly to about a line running north and south through Heligo-land. Eventually we decided to send half the force out with the bombers and the rest to meet them on the way back.

On previous missions we had always flown either within the bomber stream or straggled along its fringes. Now it was decided we could do more good if we patrolled between the enemy and our bombers. Eight fighters were to take off at about the same time as our large friends. Four of these would patrol a line east and west some twenty miles north of the Frisians to Heligoland at between 12,000 and 18,000 feet. The other four to patrol a line south of Emden to the causeway over the northern part of the Zuider Zee. This presented the Germans with two "thin red lines" between their night-fighters and our bombers. Our remaining fighters would be similarly deployed later during the night to meet the returning Lancasters and Halifaxes. On paper it sounded a logical plan. Time would tell.

A general briefing was called for 4 p.m. I drove to the officers' mess to awaken Jacko, who was trying to catch up with lost sleep. Like the rest of us he was worn out, having flown on the three previous nights. It took some not too gentle persuasion to get him out of bed. We took off for the short flight to Coltishall, which was again the starting-point for the night. There we had plenty of time for last-minute checks on the aircraft and the weather. The Met man promised us a fine night with a full moon and only small amounts of high cloud. This was good for us, but I didn't envy our big brothers, because such conditions also favoured the Luftwaffe night-fighters. Jacko and I snoozed for a while in chairs. Then at 9.30 p.m. I gathered all the crews for a few final words and wished them luck before climbing into my Beau with Jacko to lead off the first wave.

We crossed the English coast near Cromer, heading over the North Sea for Heligoland. I temporarily forgot my tiredness, although it was to hit me later that night. For once, we couldn't pick up the bombers on our AI as they were many miles to the north, but Jacko was checking our radar to make sure everything was in order. He also had to make sure we hit the patrol line north of the Frisians at the right point. Throttling back to about 160 m.p.h., approximately the speed of the bombers, I hoped to persuade the German defences into thinking we were a straggler from the main stream, and so to draw off a night-fighter or two.

After fifty minutes' flying we reached the western end of our patrol. Even the small amounts of cloud had now dissipated and visibility seemed endless. On our starboard we could see the dark outline of the islands and farther south the coastline of Holland itself, with the mouth of the Ems river ahead in the distance. Not a light was to be seen, yet by now hundreds of our bombers were droning relentlessly towards their target, Peenemunde. Surely the German defences must

191

have detected something. I faintly made out the heavily-defended fortress of Heligoland. There was no point in drawing fire from its guns, so I eased to south a little. Every few seconds I asked Jacko if he had picked anything up. So far there was nothing.

At the end of the patrol line I turned and headed back. I had just straightened out of the turn when Jacko called:

"Bob, I have a Serrate contact. Turn port and climb 200 feet."

I could tell by his voice that he had picked up something definite.

"Bob, I think we have one of the so-and-so's. Keep turning port. O.K., now straighten out. It shows dead ahead and a little above."

"Have you AI contact yet?"

"No, not yet, but keep going on this course, we are getting closer; keep your eyes open. There are a lot of the blighters about."

We were closing in on a night-fighter, but we shouldn't know exactly how far away he was until we got an AI contact. From the number of indications on the Serrate scope it was obvious that the enemy was now alerted to the presence of our bombers and heading in large numbers, with throttles wide open, to intercept them.

Minutes passed as we closed in, flying north-east towards Heligoland. I scanned the sky for some enemy who might be sneaking up on us. "Bob, I've got AI contact at 5,000 yards a little to port and above. Buster (fly as fast as possible) and turn gently port."

Jacko's commentary now poured out in a continuous flow as if he were willing us to the target. I adjusted the brightness of my electric gunsight and strained to see ahead and above. Now we were at 400 yards, and previously on moonlit nights I had picked out visually my quarries much sooner than this.

"Bob, he's only 400 yards dead ahead and a little above. You must see him now." Jacko was getting impatient. Why wasn't I seeing him? Perhaps my tired state was affecting my vision. My eyes were smarting. Suddenly there he was as clear as could be—twin engines, twin tail, our opposite number, a Me110 night-fighter. He was turning gently to port.

"Take a peak, Jacko."

"O.K., I see him. Give him the works."

At 250 yards I eased gently back and the Beau shuddered as I pressed the button. The enemy started a gentle dive towards the sea beneath. We followed and gave him another squirt. He burst into flames and dived vertically.

I climbed back to 16,000 feet, heading again towards Ameland. Before we had straightened out Jacko called urgently: "Hard starboard, there's another only a few hundred yards away." I hauled the Beau round in a tight turn when Jacko called, "Look out, he's only 200 yards ahead and slightly above. You're closing too fast."

"Christ, I've got him," I yelled. Above me in a tight turn was another Me110, and at the speed we were travelling we looked as if we were going to ram him. I eased back the stick, put the sights on him and fired at the point-blank range of about fifty yards. There was a blinding flash as the Me exploded in my face. Our Beau rocked violently, threatening to flick over on its back. My windscreen was flecked with oil from the exploding wreckage which hurtled seawards. "God, that was close," was all I could say. Then as we circled I saw in the light of the moon a parachute floating gently downwards. Something made my blood boil. Perhaps it was the narrow escape from the collision that angered me, or maybe it was because I was exhausted. I called Jacko on the intercom. "One of the bastards must have been blown clear, I'm going to finish him off." I had turned towards the parachute when Jacko said, "Bob, let the poor blighter alone." This brought me to my senses and I felt ashamed at what I had intended to do. As we flew past the forlorn figure dangling on the end of the 'chute and falling towards the sea I wished I could call out to him to tell him that his life had been spared because of the compassion of my AI operator—a Jew like many of those the Nazis had slaughtered in the ghettoes and concentration camps of Europe.

Again we climbed back up to 16,000 feet and headed back towards Ameland. Jacko was still getting indications on his Serrate but by now reaction was setting in and I was so tired I could hardly see. "Jacko, I've had enough; let's go home. The rest of the boys should chalk up quite a score." Jacko was tired, too, but he wanted to stay on patrol. "Bob, we've lots of ammo. Maybe we can shoot down a couple more." I'm afraid he lost the argument. Two worn out, but satisfied airmen dived towards the North Sea and headed westwards for home. Nearly four hours after take-off, we landed safely back at Wittering.

Some of the crews had landed, but more than half, including the second wave, were still airborne. We had had a fairly good night. In addition to our two destroyed another crew claimed one destroyed and one damaged. Exhausted as we were from several nights without proper sleep, Jacko and I were determined to wait up for the rest to return. By 3.30 they were all back and I was thankful we had suffered no losses. The enemy had lost four destroyed and one damaged to my Squadron. I was a bit disappointed. I thought we might have had more but there was no doubt our very presence caused much confusion. We probably saved the lives of many of our bomber crews. Later we learnt that the raid on Peenemunde had been most successful. About 700 personnel had been killed on the site including many of the expert technicians. But of greater importance was the fact that the development and production of the V weapons had been set back about nine months. The cost to Bomber Command was high. More than fifty aircraft were lost out of about 600. Most of these were lost near or over the target, which again pointed to the need for an aircraft of longer range than the Beaufighter.

Soon a few early marks of night-fighter Mosquitoes were allotted to the Squadron for tests. But they were a sorry bunch of worn-out aircraft. They had been used in squadron, then in O.T.U. service before reaching 141. The engines gave us endless trouble at high altitude. Yet these few planes got the crews accustomed to the Mosquito, which in general performance was superior to the Beaufighter.

Nothing could compare with our beloved Beaus for ruggedness. On many occasions they brought us back when other aircraft would have failed. We never used these first few Mossies on operations because of their unreliability, but we did appreciate their value if we were to be given newer versions. During some of our daylight trials we engaged in friendly dog-fights with McGovern's American Lightnings and even allowing for our lack of experience in the Mosquito the Lightnings would have had a slim chance with us in combat.

Because of our mounting score of successes, Sticks, Jacko and I were frequently named in the daily press. These articles amused us at times but they could also be most embarrassing. I would have liked to know where the information came from. On the evening after the Peenemunde raid I was asleep in my room when the door burst open and in came Winn with a newspaper in his hand and a leer on his face. "Have you seen this, sir?" He knew well I hadn't. I seized the paper and noted that Jacko and I had hit the headlines for our recent exploit. Included in a not very accurate account of our combat experience were details of my life. Apparently I was an angel, described as an avid reader of the Greek classics and a rigid teetotaller. No wonder Charles Winn was leering. At the time I was exceedingly angry, but later I saw the funny side of it. Some well-meaning reporter had interviewed my proud father and I am afraid he had misinterpreted what was said. The fact was that I gave up reading Greek the moment I left school and in all honesty I could hardly say I was a teetotaller. It took me many a day to live down the myth of my puritan existence.

25

SOON after the Squadron's success on the night of the Peenemunde raid, I was awarded a bar to my D.S.O. To quote a sentence from the official citation, "for his brilliant leadership of 141 Squadron and exceptional skill and gallantry on operations". High-sounding words, to which I hoped I could live up. My successes were due to teamwork between pilot, my AI operators and groundcrew, therefore I considered the decoration belonged to the Squadron. There was a hectic celebration in which the whole of 141 took part. We were high-spirited and young and probably overdid the drinking at this party as on previous occasions. For this I make no excuse. Some may think we seriously overdid it. I agree, but I believe there were good reasons for this sort of behaviour. There has been a tendency by many authors, particularly the British, to play down this side of war service. It would appear that Air Force officers were paragons of virtue, past whose lips nothing flowed but heroic words and milk! Except in a few cases, the facts were very different. Let's face it, there were many reasons why we drank too much. For some, drinking was a means of escapism, or a way of hiding fear. For others, perhaps with less imagination, the attitude was, "Let's enjoy life to the full, tomorrow we may be dead." In my own case I have never tried to analyse the reasons in detail, but I think fear was at the root of it. Not only the fear of "buying it", but also the fear of showing fear to others. Though I make no excuses I remind the reader of the terrible responsibility that was thrust on a generation of young men, some not much more than boys.

The stepping-up of the war against the enemy meant that my visits to my family in Leicester were becoming few and far between. I knew I had reached a stage where my responsibilities towards them were taking second place to my job of running the Squadron. For Joan, this was a hard and difficult time. I tended to be a touchy and not too understanding a mate. The effect of long periods on operations was leaving its mark, though at the time I didn't appreciate it.

Some of our bomber raids hardly required escorts, such as those on Italy or the Channel ports. German fighters rarely appeared, as the target areas were not within the main Luftwaffe defence belts. Retaliation was left to the German flak. Yet we always sent out our Beaus just in case.

It was during one of these easy missions, flying with the bombers to attack Channel ports, that we suffered one of our few casualties to enemy action. No enemy fighters were detected, but flak was intense. During the return flight one of our Beaus was severely hit by flak. Flight Lieutenant Ferguson, the pilot, dived his badly-damaged aircraft out towards the Channel, hoping to get back to England. Whether he was wounded or not his AI operator, Flying Officer Osborne, never knew. Only a few miles from the coast and at a height of two or three hundred feet, the pilot told his operator they would have to ditch.

From then on the story is hazy. The Beau went out of control and dived steeply into the sea. Osborne remembered nothing of the crash but he found himself floating, supported by his Mae West life jacket with his one-man dinghy attached by a cord. He blew up the dinghy with its CO_2 bottle, climbed in and found to his amazement that he was only slightly bruised and shocked and seemed to be in one piece. There was no sign of the pilot, only bits of wreckage and oil. In his shocked condition, Osborne spent a cold and uncomfortable night bobbing up and down in the Channel, almost in sight of the French coast and wondering if he would be rescued by us or by the enemy.

At Wittering, all we knew was that one of our aircraft was long overdue and had not landed elsewhere. We had to assume the worst. The dreaded telegrams were dispatched to the parents of the crew informing them that their sons were missing in action. Osborne's father decided to visit the Squadron next morning to get more details. He was bearing-up well under the worry and I told him the little we knew. I didn't want to build up false hopes.

Meanwhile, Dickie, my Adjutant, was in contact with the Air-Sea Rescue Squadron that covered the area of the previous night's target. Mr. Osborne and I were talking about the war in general and trying to keep away from further discussion about the fate of his son, when Dickie burst into the office. An Air-Sea Rescue Walrus, an amphibious biplane on patrol off the French Coast, had spotted a dinghy and picked up Osborne close to an enemy minefield—a very gallant rescue. A few hours later Osborne arrived back at Wittering, a little sunscorched, but apparently none the worse. Rarely have I felt happier than at the moment when I saw this father and son reunited. I am sure the father had assumed his boy was lost. It was a great moment, but marred for me by the knowledge that the gallant pilot had gone down with his plane.

As the summer of 1943 progressed, the Squadron built up a respectable number of kills against the enemy night-fighter force. As in other squadrons, most of the successes went to one or two crews only. The others only got a kill here and there. I believe the main reason for this was that only a few crews attained the extremely high standards of co-operation and co-ordination needed for night-fighting. The "aces" were also complete masters of the AI and Serrate equipments. They got out of these intricate radars enough information to seek out the enemy even when the sets were only partially serviceable. In 141 Squadron the names of Flight Lieutenant Howard Kelsey and his operator, Sgt. Smith, and Flight Lieutenants White and Allan, another outstanding crew, were beginning to appear regularly in the combat reports. Both crews had destroyed more than five aircraft apiece at the time of Peenemunde over enemy territory and been decorated for their exploits. Before the end of the war their successes mounted and they stood high in the list of night-fighters.

In early September, 1943, rumours began to filter through to the Squadron that I was to be sent off for a rest to some non-operational job. To me this sounded like the knell of doom. My Squadron was everything to me, more even than my wife and family. I was obviously overtired but couldn't see it. I hoped against hope that this was just a rumour. As if to show my defiance of fatigue, I increased my sorties and once nearly killed Jacko and myself through lack of judgement, probably caused by exhaustion.

We were flying with the bombers on a raid on the Mont Luçon tunnel in South-Eastern France. There had been no enemy night-fighters so I decided that on the way back we would fly low and strafe trains. Roaring along at 220 m.p.h. at 2,000 feet in the bright moonlight, we spotted one not far from Paris on the main Dieppe–Paris line. It was travelling at speed. Down we went firing a long burst from all guns at the engine, which exploded in a cloud of steam and sparks. There was no answering flak from the train, and as it had stopped we circled once and set off for further targets. Very soon we saw another travelling towards Paris from Amiens. I dived again firing long bursts from our powerful armament. In my desire to wreck this train, I completely forgot my height. There was a rending crash. Reflex action took over as I desperately hauled back on the control column. We had hit the tops of trees lining the railway embankment.

We got back to two or three thousand feet, very shaken. But the aeroplane still seemed flyable, despite a hole in the bottom of the fuselage between myself and Jacko. We landed an hour later and gazed in wonder at the mess, then hastily retreated to the bar for some Dutch courage. Something told me that if I didn't take it easy we shouldn't live long.

It seemed like an answer to my thoughts when I was sent on a short rest a few days later. My orders were to go to Kenley airfield, of Battle of Britain fame, to practise drill for Battle of Britain ceremonies in London. R.A.F. and W.A.A.F. contingents were gathered to brush up their marching on the tarmac and runways of this now rarely-used base. I learned I had been selected to lead the contingent of Battle of Britain veterans through the streets of London. This was a shock. I felt there were many more qualified for the job. My contribution to the famed battle was one enemy aircraft destroyed at night in August, 1940. I suggested that one of the better-known aces of the time should lead, and I would willingly follow. My pleas were ignored, so for a couple of days under the eyes of drill instructors and senior Air Force officers I led my detachment of pilots and navigators in marching and counter-marching.

On the appointed Sunday we were driven by bus to London. We formed up with many other contingents representing A.A. gunners, Police, Firefighters, Civil Defence Workers, Women's Volunteer Service, Nurses and W.A.A.F.s. There were more than 3,000 of us. Bands interspersed the parade and the whole column stretched for about a mile. The bands ensured that we were out of step most of the time. The music echoed off the buildings along our route to our confusion. Then the short steppings of the W.A.A.F.s immediately ahead of us turned my detachment into the original double-shuffle boys. Much as I admired the girls in the Service, never again do I want to have to march behind them. The problem of constantly changing step and the cheering of the thousands of onlookers completed my embarrassment. We marched down Pall Mall in front of Buckingham Palace where the King received our salute. More by luck than judgement, this was about the only time during our march when we happened to be in step with the contingents ahead of us. A few minutes later I thankfully dismissed my portion of the parade at Wellington Barracks and swore I would sooner meet any number of Huns than run the gauntlet of cheering crowds again.

Rumour of my transfer now became fact. Braham was ordered to attend No. 12 course at the Army Staff College, Camberley, beginning October 21, 1943, barely a month away. I argued in vain against this posting and even went so far as to request a personal interview with the C. in C., Air Marshal Sir Roderick Hill. Over a cup of tea in his office this kindly man told me he fully understood my wish to stay with the Squadron, but it was also obvious that I urgently needed a rest from operations and four months at the Staff College would do me a power of good. I had to admit to myself that he was right.

My replacement, Wing Commander Roberts from Training Command, wasn't due at Wittering until early October, so Jacko and I had a few more weeks of flying together. We took an active part in several more trips against the enemy, chalking up two more kills and one damaged and bringing my total score to twenty. Nineteen of these were at night and one by day, in addition to a "probable" and six damaged. With the able help of Sticks and Jacko, in particular, I had now equalled John Cunningham's record for night kills. Our night scores were to remain unchanged for the rest of the war, and only to be surpassed by Brance Burbridge and his AI operator, Skelton, who shot down twenty-one at night.

My last combat sortie with the Squadron was on the night of September 29. Flying with our bombers on a raid to

Bochum in the Ruhr, we destroyed an Me110 and damaged a JU88 in separate battles within ten minutes over the Zuider Zee. This trip, besides being a grand finale to my tour with 141, also provided my American comrade, Major McGovern, with his first experience of night-fighting. Mac had been badgering me for some time to take him along. He brought us luck. But for the failure of my guns, which jammed after a very short burst, our second enemy of the night, the JU88, would also have been destroyed instead of merely being damaged. However, our worst foe on this particular sortie was our own light flak. The gunners of a Bofors light battery on the Norfolk coast, between Hemsby and Winterton, did their best to shoot us down on our way back to base at 1,500 feet. After much cursing at the "pongoes" we flew out of range. As we had been in contact with our base for some time we couldn't understand why we should be treated as hostile.

Although I commanded 141 for only ten months, it was during a time of varied and hectic activity. The morale of the Squadron had been low, but I was fortunate to see it rise until it was second to none, thanks to the determination of every man on the unit. It may be unfair to pick out individuals for comment when all did so much, but I was particularly lucky in Flight Lieutenant Bernard "Dickie" Sparrow, my Adjutant, and Buster Reynolds, the "spy". Unlike the aircrew, neither of these ground officers received any tangible credit for their hard work. Yet they did a tremendous amount for the Squadron, and always gave me good advice. From defensive operations the Squadron had switched to the offensive with outstanding success. Our losses had been relatively low. In truth 141 had lived up to its motto *Caedemus Noctu,* we kill by night.

Before leaving Wittering, I solemnly promised Sticks and Jacko, both of them unsurpassed in their trade, that I would do all I could to have them posted to whatever unit I was to go to after the Staff College. This was a little disloyal to Wing Commander Roberts, my successor, but he appreciated my feelings towards these two officers who had shared most of my triumphs and escapes from danger.

26

As I was leaving the Squadron more Mosquitoes arrived, still old marks but a little better than the first few we had been allotted. They were fully-equipped with Serrate and gradually replaced the faithful old Beaufighters. In spite of the higher performance of the Mosquito, the Squadron's successes tended to dwindle at first. The enemy was becoming wise to our Serrate and AI capabilities and adopting tactics and techniques to reduce our effectiveness. For the rest of the war it was to be a battle of wits between our technical personnel and his, in radar development. Sometimes the Germans had the edge. Then it was our turn and 141's kill rate went up.

I spent a few days in Leicester with my family before leaving for Camberley. I suppose I was a pain in the neck to my successor during those days. I constantly badgered him for an aircraft to "fly just one more OPP." Roberts was willing but Headquarters were adamant. The order came: "Braham is not to fly any more combat missions until after his course." So I returned to Leicester for the rest of my short leave.

My association with my "first love", 141 Squadron, was now broken for good, and with it comradeship such as I have never known since. Naturally Joan saw things in a different light. At least for a while she would not have to worry whether I would return from a flight over enemy territory. Though we were still apart, the knowledge that I was safe was a comfort to her.

The whole of the Camberley area lived and breathed in the

tradition of the Army and many of the beautiful homes near the staff College housed retired Generals and their families. I was a little awed but on arrival learned that there were five other R.A.F. officers on the course, most of whom I knew well. This was a relief, as the "pongoes", or Army types, seemed by comparison to be a staid and superior lot. This opinion of mine was to be changed in the near future. I settled in quarters which I shared with Ras Berry, who had just returned from North Africa, where he had become one of the R.A.F.'s most able fighter Wing Leaders. We then repaired to the Cambridge Arms, a pleasant hotel almost opposite the main gate of the College. This was to be a favourite haunt.

Commandant of the College was a Major General Wimberley, who had recently returned from the Middle East, where he had distinguished himself as the Commander of the 51st Highland Division in Montgomery's victorious Eighth Army. Our instructors were mainly officers of Lieutenant-Colonel rank but there was one R.A.F. Wing Commander. Many of them had been in combat in various theatres of war. Men on the course were mainly Army officers, but in addition to the small R.A.F. contingent there were representatives from the Royal Marines and from Canadian, Australian, United States and Czech forces. Our studies were done in syndicate groups. The six R.A.F. officers were allotted to six of these groups and, in effect, became air advisers.

Days at the Staff College passed quickly, and unexpectedly I enjoyed them. My first impression of the "pongoes" was wrong. They were not as wild as our R.A.F. boys but they were a gay and friendly crowd. At Camberley we studied the three main phases of warfare—the withdrawal, the advance and the attack. During the first years of World War II the British had become expert at the first of these phases. The withdrawal is regarded as the most difficult and intricate aspect of warfare. A commander must maintain high morale among his troops when everything is going wrong. If he fails, the withdrawal becomes a rout. The British Army could be proud that this never occurred, because leadership was good and the plain British soldier had plenty of guts. The Allies had recovered from the first heavy blows of the aggressor and we could now plan for advance and attack. Rumours of a second front were rife. With the terrific build-up of British, Dominion and U.S. Army divisions in Britain it seemed that it could not be long before these rumours became fact.

I was still able to get my hands on aircraft to fly in my spare time, thanks to the proximity of Farnborough. At week-ends there was a choice of a Percival Proctor,★ Tiger Moth, Avro Tutor† and even an old Gladiator. Several of the Army students and staff flew with me in one or other of these aircraft on visits to Joan and the children in Leicester. On one of these occasions, Joan had her first unofficial ride in a Service aircraft, an Avro Tutor. She enjoyed it immensely. Her only worry was that she had to draw up the parachute strap between her legs. As she wore a skirt this exposed rather a lot of nice leg to my Army captain friend who was trying not to notice.

We were lucky to be given talks by many high-ranking military commanders during the Camberley course. They included General Montgomery, of Eighth Army fame, and General Anderson, commander of the First Army in North Africa. I remember these two particularly well because of the marked difference in their personalities and the tremendous interest and competitive spirit they engendered among all of us at the Staff College. Many of the students and staff had served either with the Eighth or the First Armies and the rivalry between the two groups was hot. During his talk "Monty", later Field Marshal Viscount Montgomery of Alamein, exuded cockiness and confidence, and justifiably so because of his

★ Percival Proctor: a single-engined, two- to three-seat monoplane trainer.
† Avro Tutor: a biplane two-seat trainer similar to the Tiger Moth.

many fine victories, at least one of which—Alamein—changed the course of the war in our favour. Anderson, in contrast, seemed dour and even a little bitter. The reasons were easy to understand. His First Army was largely new to combat. It consisted of a hodge-podge of British, French and American divisions, all loosely knit together and using different types of weapons and equipment which made logistics a nightmare. Also, because of political pressures, he was forced at times to commit his Army piecemeal, with poor results. As an interested onlooker, I felt that General Anderson had won a tougher battle with all too little strength nearly all the time. Yet in the end, the First and Eighth Armies joined hands in Tunisia and kicked the Afrika Corps and the Italians out of Africa. Many were the arguments among us, sometimes heated, on the pros and cons of the campaigns of these two Armies after we had heard their respective commanders talk to us.

On field exercises with my syndicate, each officer was allotted a position on an imaginary divisional staff. Once I found myself a Brigade Commander of tanks. These cumbersome weapons were supposed to be lagered before breaking out for an attack. I thought I had selected an excellent lager. I had noted a sunken road, lined with trees on each side. It seemed ideal natural cover against air reconnaissance. It was too easy! Perhaps they would offer me a permanent job as an Army Brigadier! My enthusiasm was soon shattered by one of the umpires, who told me as kindly as possible, so that not many of my comrades could hear, "Sorry, old boy, your tanks are written off. They can't possibly climb those banks, they're too steep. They would turn arse over tip." Well, that was that. My dreams of leading tanks into battle were smashed. Somehow the rest of the course heard of Braham's bloomer and much was the ribbing one "air adviser" received for the next few days.

Perhaps some of us didn't take the course as seriously as we should. While many students were working over problems in their rooms until late hours, a few of us regularly went to the Cambridge Arms. Here we passed the time talking among ourselves and with the local inhabitants and quaffing the ever-popular but weak beer. On return it became our habit to hold a cigarette lighter under the chin of the white marble bust of Julius Caesar, who was perched at the bottom of the main staircase in the entrance hall at Camberley. This had the effect of blackening the chin, and gave this soldier of the past the appearance of having a beard. Without fail one of the hard-working cleaners gave the old gentleman a "shave" early next morning, and he was all prepared again for another beard. Such pranks relieved the monotony of study.

At this stage of the war I had been lucky enough never to have had to use my parachute. One of our visits was to the paratrooper training school on Salisbury Plain. We were shown the equipment and training methods of these elite troops. In a field was a practice jumping tower 80 to 100 feet high, from which paratroopers leapt into space suspended in a harness. Speed of descent was controlled by a pulley which simulated the speed of fall from an aircraft. We watched demonstrations by fearless men in red berets. Then an instructor called for a volunteer from among our course. We looked at each other and smiled sheepishly, but nobody answered the call. After an embarrassed silence, my Army friends fixed on me and indicated that I was the volunteer. After all, they said, I was a "blue job" (airman). I cursed them and shrugged.

Apprehensively I climbed the ladder to the platform at the top where the grinning instructor helped me into the harness. "There's nothing to it, sir. Just bend the knees and keep your feet together, then you won't break an ankle." Encouraged by his kind words, I braced myself on the platform and peered down, pale of face, at the leering visages of my comrades far below. Next moment I felt a shove in the back and I was falling at an alarming rate. I hit the ground with a thud which knocked the wind out of me. As soon as I was sure I was still in one piece, I got up from the sandy soil grinning triumphantly and cocked a snoot at my Army friends.

In December, 1943, I learnt that 141 Squadron, which was now completely equipped with Mosquitoes, had moved from Wittering to West Raynham, Norfolk. Its long ties with Fighter Command and more lately with Air Defence of Great Britain had now been severed. With two other Mosquito squadrons, 239 and 169, 141 Squadron became part of the recently-formed 100 Group, under the control of Bomber Command.

The story of 100 Group merits a book of its own. I will only briefly outline its role. The Group was responsible for direct and indirect support of Bomber Command's offensive. Some squadrons, such as the three just mentioned, were charged with shooting down enemy night-fighters. Others, equipped with a variety of aircraft, flew with the bomber streams or acted as diversionary attackers, jamming the enemy ground radars and communications and generally making life as difficult as possible for the enemy defence. At last we had what a few of us in the night-fighter business had been clamouring for—a strong force of offensive night-fighters able to range anywhere over the Third Reich.

At the end of January of the New Year, 141 threw a reunion party at its new base at West Raynham. My invitation enabled me to take three of my new-found Army friends, including two Canadians. West Raynham thoughtfully sent an Oxford to Farnborough to pick up the Army types, while I flew along in an old Gladiator single-seat fighter as "escort".

It was a grand feeling to be back with old comrades again. Squadron Leader Davis, who had been one of my Flight

Commanders, now commanded the Squadron, replacing Roberts who was in a staff job. Charles Winn and the old originals, Buster Reynolds and Dickie Sparrow, were all there. The reunion was a roaring success. As the evening progressed the party games became rougher and rougher but no serious injuries were suffered. Winn fled during the latter stages of the party and locked himself in the toilet. He was being chased by irate Squadron members whom he had squirted with a fire extinguisher. The problem of winkling him out of his sanctuary was soon solved. Someone produced a Very pistol and cartridge. This was fired into his refuge through a window. It created a fantastic amount of smoke and Charles soon emerged coughing and spluttering, to be pounced upon by the rest of us. My Army friends were flabbergasted at these goings on but they seemed to be enjoying themselves.

Next morning as we gingerly made our way to breakfast nursing thick heads, the debris of the night's jollifications could be seen everywhere. Broken glasses and damaged furniture lay all about the place. The most priceless memento, however, was a set of coal-black footprints on the ceiling of the mess lounge neatly autographed by Buster Reynolds. We never discovered how he got them there. It must have been quite an operation! My Army friends and I decided to leave before an irate Station Commander appeared. We said farewell to those of 141 who had surfaced and were soon back at Farnborough, tired, but filled with happy memories of a wonderful reunion.

I hadn't heard where I was going on my next posting after the course at Camberley so I decided to try to beat the personnel types to the gun by visiting 100 Group Headquarters in search of a job. My only wish was to fly again against the enemy. On meeting the A.O.C., I asked him what were the chances of my taking over one of his Mosquito squadrons.

He told me he wanted me on his staff where he felt my experience would be of more value. This was a great disappointment. Later that day I was discussing tactics with the Group Senior Air Staff Officer and soon found myself heartily disagreeing with the way the Mosquitoes were being employed. Although I had the greatest respect for the S.A.S.O., who was a most gallant and capable officer, it was obvious to me that I couldn't work for him without considerable disagreement on the employment of the Serrate-equipped aircraft. After friendly interviews and discussions, I declined the offer of a staff job and returned rather dejectedly to Camberley, resolved to leave my fate to an Air Ministry posting. I need only add that 100 Group got on very well without me!

Our last few weeks at Camberley were chiefly concerned with amphibious operations and their support from the air. This was natural in view of the tremendous build-up of British and American armies in Britain and their associated R.A.F. Second Tactical Air Force and U.S. Ninth Air Force. There were strong indications of the long-awaited second front to be launched across the Channel. One day I was told to report to the Commandant's Office. I called on his Adjutant and was ushered in before the Major General. With him was the familiar figure of Air Vice-Marshal Embry, who had recently taken over No. 2 Light Bomber Group, now part of the Second Tactical Air Force. Embry asked me if I would like to work on his staff and help to train the Group in the work of night interdiction.

The Group consisted of four Mitchell and two Boston Light Bomber Squadrons and six Mosquito Mk 6 Fighter Bomber Squadrons, all of which had so far been employed solely on daylight raids. My job, if I agreed, would be concerned chiefly with the Mosquito squadrons, which were to be trained so that they could make low-level night attacks on German troop movements anywhere on land or water. Embry pointed out that it was a most important task and that his Group would be the only one able to support the Allied Armies at night when the fateful D-Day arrived.

The offer was most flattering, but before accepting I said I would like to take a personal active part against the enemy. His eyes twinkled and he promised he would allow me a "ration" of combat missions. Embry then told the General he would like me to start my new job at once. The Commandant replied that it would be a pity for me not to finish the staff course, so it was agreed that I should. I was now happy in the thought that, regardless of the staff work awaiting me, I should still be able on occasion to have a go at the Hun. Embry was one of the few top Allied Air Commanders who believed that not only squadron aircrew but Station Commanders and his own staff should fly on operations. He flew on many missions despite disapproval from high authority. A great leader of men, who never asked anyone to do what he would not do himself.

The course ended on February 11, 1944, leaving me with a fair understanding of the problems of the British Army. It had also destroyed my superficial opinions of the "pongoes", among whom I could now count many friends, some of them lasting ones. Our farewell party was celebrated in fine style in the main hall at Camberley. Towards the end of the evening a combined group of R.A.F. and Army types acquired a fire-hose and as a parting gesture washed down the oil-paintings of past Commandants and other famous Army leaders on the walls.

27

I ARRIVED at 2 Group Staff Officer Night Operations with
some trepidation. It was my first staff job. However, I
was soon put at ease at Mongewell Park, a beautiful old
mansion near Wallingford, Oxford. The promise that I would
still be able to fly against the enemy kept up my spirits.

To Joan's disappointment, I still insisted that it would be
best if she and the family stayed on in Leicester. For me, war
and family life would not mix. Squadron Leader Rufus Riseley
took care of me as I settled in. He was to be my able assistant
for the next few months. I soon discovered that Embry had
gathered together a very experienced and happy staff, all of
whom were filled with the same fire and spirit as himself. The
Old Man's deputy and Senior Air Staff Officer was David
Atcherley, whom I had last seen at Debden in 1938, when he
commanded 85 Squadron. The fabulous exploits both in the
air and on the ground of David and his twin brother Dick
were legend even before the war began. It is doubtful whether
the example, leadership, and fantastic pranks of these two men
will ever again be equalled.

One of Rufus's first chores was to take me to 2 Group's
second home, Clemmie's. Mrs. Clements was the owner of
the White Hart pub in the village of Nettlebed, a few miles
from our Headquarters. During my stay with 2 Group I was
privileged to know her, and I shall always be thankful for her
unfailing cheerfulness and good nature which did so much for
morale. She lost her own son in the R.N. earlier in the war,
but her grief was kept bravely hidden. We were always

assured of a welcome at her place. Invariably when closing time came at 10.30 she would ask the R.A.F. to stay behind. However tired she was she served us the traditional bacon and eggs from her kitchen.

Remembering my promise to Sticks and Jacko when I left 141, my first task was to try to get them both transferred to the Group Staff. The personnel types were most helpful and a few days after my arrival at Mongewell my two comrades joined me. The Night Operations Staff was now complete. The influx of night boys at first caused some ribald remarks from the rest of the Air Staff, who were inordinately proud of the Group's record of daylight operations and frankly weren't too keen about a partial switch to night-flying. The major effort of 2 Group hitherto had been against enemy shipping and military installations in occupied Europe, and more recently against the growing number of V1 sites between Calais and Le Havre. Every sortie had been flown by day and required precision medium- or low-level bombing at which 2 Group was unsurpassed.

Next to "Overlord", the D-Day project, the offensive against the V sites, known as "Crossbow", stood high in the minds of the planners. Unless the majority of these sites and the supply dumps of weapons and rocket fuel were destroyed, the enemy would be able to interfere seriously with the Allied preparations for invasion. In addition, the people of London and Southern England would be subjected to very heavy attacks by the pilotless V1s, and later V2 rockets. The air attacks and defensive measures of both the R.A.F. and the U.S.A.A.F. largely defeated the enemy's V attacks, although, of course, many got through to London and the surrounding area. There was little damage to the overall war effort although nearly 10,000 people were killed and many more seriously injured by the V1 and V2 barrage. Attacks by these weapons were not completely ended until the Allies over-ran the launching sites early in 1945. But 2 Group had the honour of damaging and destroying more of the launching sites in France than any other Allied air formation.

Plans for Overlord were progressing rapidly and Embry's Group had, among other tasks, the important role of attacking German troop movements at night, once our troops had a foothold in Normandy. The job of training the squadrons for night operations had to be undertaken swiftly.

The six Mosquito squadrons divided equally between 138 and 140 Wings were the most suited for night work, so plans were drawn up to train them along the lines of the Fighter Command Night Intruder Squadrons, with the one major difference that 2 Group would carry bombs as well as guns. Our Mosquitoes were the low-level Mk 6 version, which carried no airborne radar or AI, but were fitted with 4 × 20-mm. cannons and 4 × 303 machine guns in the nose, firing forward under the control of the pilot. There was room in the bomb-bay for four 500-lb. bombs which could be fitted with various types of instantaneous or delayed-action fuses. The second crew member was a navigator. Before the Squadron went on the first night missions, Rufus and I, accompanied by either Sticks or Jacko, visited both Wings and gave a general briefing, pointing out the importance of the new task and some of the problems that might be encountered. Because of the lack of glamour that night operations seemed to offer to men who were used to day-fighting there was still resentment towards the job. We were sure that after a few missions this would disappear. We pointed out, too, that they would still be flying some daylight trips.

As a start, my little staff, with the help of the intelligence boys, planned missions against some of the airfields in Northern France. Locating these small targets while flying at 1,000 to 3,000 ft. over the blacked-out Continent, would give excellent night navigational training as well as providing something worthwhile to shoot up. If we could locate and hit the airfields, we stood a good chance of picking out German troop convoys moving along the French roads when D-Day came. On their first trips, the Mosquito crews hit the small targets and losses were negligible. So the earlier resentment began to disappear.

I began to think of Embry's promise that I should be allowed to have a go against the enemy. For some time I had been impressed by the possibilities of one or two long-range fighters roving deep into enemy territory in daylight. Intruder Squadrons 418 and 605, although normally doing night work, had demonstrated how successful such missions could be. They had achieved surprise and shot down a number of different types of enemy aircraft for light losses to themselves. If one flew at tree-top level and steered clear of heavily-defended flak areas, it was highly likely that our fighters would not be detected until they struck. Such trips were only flown when there was cloud at about 1,500–2,000 feet, covering most of the sky. There were obvious grave risks, but I felt that the probable return in enemy aircraft destroyed or damaged and the confusion we caused to the enemy more than compensated.

The Mossie 6 was an ideal aircraft for the job. At low level it was fast, manœuvrable, had an excellent radius of action and was heavily armed. I sounded out Sticks and Jacko, who were champing at the bit as I was to have another go at the enemy. They were just as enthusiastic, although Jacko felt night intruding would be the better bet since we were so much more experienced in flying when "the birds were on the ground". Having a go in daylight intrigued me and eventually my views prevailed. Now to put the request up to the Old Man. Embry seemed genuinely interested, but insisted that I should bring the plans of each of my proposed sorties to him for approval before we set off. Further, he did not like the idea of our intruding in daylight over Germany itself because of the thickness of the German defences and in particular the presence of many single-seat fighters, against which one Mosquito was no match. Occupied Western Europe, however, offered tempting targets. There were many airfields on which the enemy based bombers and multi-engined fighters such as the Me110 and JU88 with which we felt happy to deal. I pointed out to the A.O.C. that I wanted to attack aircraft in the air, not on the ground. In the air we not only put the aircraft out of action but also, more important, the crew. Past experience, both by the R.A.F. and the Luftwaffe, had shown that attacks against grounded aircraft, although spectacular in some respects, didn't write off the trained aircrew. Also, the attacking aircraft often suffered heavy losses to light A.A. fire.

Having received Embry's tacit agreement, I asked if I might have a go on the following day, February 28, 1944. I showed him a route to and from the area of Orleans, Bourges and Châteaudun in Central France, where there were a number of bomber airfields. To my joy he agreed, provided we had the requisite cloud cover. I returned to my office, where Jacko and Sticks were awaiting the result of the interview, and said we had the O.K.

Jacko was elected to accompany me. I wanted to prove to him that this sort of operation was really the answer, because I knew he still had reservations. We then consulted Group Intelligence and worked out detailed routings. We planned to clear large towns and airfields by at least five miles. Not only were they heavily defended, but if we flew over them the alarm would be raised. The coast of France was manned by many German troops. They were as capable of bringing down low-flying aircraft with rifle or machine-gun fire as were the flak batteries. So we decided to cross in and out of France at between 1,500 and 3,000 feet and then dive back down to the deck. We chanced losing the element of surprise by climbing to a height where enemy ground radar might pick us up, but it was a worthwhile risk. They would be very lucky to spot us.

Early in the morning the Met man promised us the cloud cover we needed. We had decided to start the sortie from Lasham. The obliging airfield commander there had a "Mossie" waiting for us filled to the brim with fuel, including overload tanks which could be jettisoned. If all went well the trips would take three and a half hours, but we had enough fuel for nearly six hours.

It was a cold morning so the engines were both run up to ensure oil and glycol coolant were circulating properly. Then we taxied out for take-off. With throttles wide open, we roared down the runway at Lasham. Rapidly the Mosquito gathered speed as we sped low over the Sussex countryside. Unfortunately this first trip was not a success. The weather was worse than forecast and visibility in the area of Orleans very poor. Our navigation was also faulty and for some time we were uncertain of our position. Eventually we recognized the city of Tours, on the Loire, which was well off our planned course. Jacko was obviously unhappy about the navigation and I felt it would be sensible to call it off. So we turned around and headed home. On the way back we shot up a petrol lorry just outside Le Mans. It was a Sunday. Many French civilians were out for an afternoon walk and they had a ringside seat for this piece of aggression. Most of them wisely viewed the proceedings from the ditches at the side of the road as we skimmed over their heads with guns blazing. The rest of the trip was uneventful. Later Jacko told me he would prefer to stick to night operations at which he felt more qualified. I fully understood his views, but was sorry that I hadn't been able to prove to him the value of daylight intruding.

A week later, I asked Sticks how he felt about having a go at an intruder trip. He was still keen. Again I approached the A.O.C. for permission, although after the failure of our first effort I was worried that he might say these missions were a waste of effort. When I explained why my sortie with Jacko failed Embry was quite receptive, but he forbade us to take any foolish chances. From intelligence recently gathered it appeared that the Germans had moved some of their latest heavy bombers, Heinkel 177s, into the Orleans group of airfields, the same area we had intended to look at previously. These planes were four-engined monsters, with two engines mounted in tandem on each wing, giving the aircraft the appearance of having only twin motors. It was felt they might have been moved to prepare for raids on England so an attack would be well worthwhile.

The weather looked as though it would be ideal for our trip next day, so arrangements were again made at Lasham for us to borrow a "Mossie". We set off for a second intruder mission deep into France. Sticks sat beside me in the cramped cockpit with his maps spread out on his knees. Occasionally he gave me a slight correction of course. It was a clear day with complete cloud cover at 1,500 feet and after about thirty-five minutes' flying we could make out the coastline of France. Sticks spotted our entry point and when about four miles away I pulled the "Mossie" into a steep climb into the cloud, levelling out at 3,000 feet. We maintained course for about five minutes and then dived steeply back to the deck. We were now inside the enemy stronghold heading for Orleans and hoping that we hadn't alerted the Germans to our presence.

It was exhilarating to skim just above the fields and trees of the French countryside but we had to be alert all the time, not only for signs of enemy aircraft but also to ensure that we didn't fly into a power line or a tree. This sort of flying soon had us both perspiring freely. Periodically we altered course twenty or thirty degrees one way or the other to confuse any alert German look-outs as to the direction of our flight.

Sticks was navigating confidently. Soon we were across

the Seine west of Rouen, but except for an occasional French farmer or a German soldier, who probably thought we were a Luftwaffe aircraft out on a spree, we saw nothing. The steeples of Chartres cathedral appeared in the distance. We were on course. I banked the aircraft to the right, my starboard wing nearly scraping the ground as we gave the city a wide berth. It was probably full of German soldiers and defended by flak batteries. On we sped over the Loire with its beautiful châteaux, near Orleans, but still we saw no sign of aircraft. I was beginning to feel disappointment creeping up inside me. I told Sticks my doubts. Where was the elusive Luftwaffe? We continued south for another fifty miles and seeing no aircraft around Bourges airfield set course for home via Châteaudun.

I was just making up my mind that the trip was again going to be a waste of time when Sticks called "What's that?" In the distance off my starboard wing I could see the runway of an airfield. A black blob hardly discernible as an aircraft was throwing up a trail of dust from its propellers as it took off. It was the dust that attracted Sticks's attention. For a second or so we watched, holding the "Mossie" down on the deck. Perhaps the Germans were alert to us after all and an enemy fighter was taking off to intercept. I opened the throttle wide so that we could rapidly shelter in the cloud if our suspicions were correct, for our "Mossie" would be no match for numbers of single-seat Me109s or FW190s. We could now see that the black blob was only one aircraft and a very large one at that. With a hoot of triumph which nearly deafened Sticks, I pulled our "Mossie" around in a steep turn and headed at full bore for Châteaudun.

A mile or so from the perimeter of the airfield we flew low over German flak positions and saw with amazement that the shirt-sleeved enemy gunners were waving to us thinking we were one of their aircraft. To keep them happy we waved back! Surprise was complete after all. Now we were closing rapidly on what we recognized as one of the large He177s. He was circling the airfield at 1,000 feet. We stayed on the deck until the last minute. We were approaching head on and a little to one side. When about a half a mile away I pulled up in a gentle climbing turn so that the massive fuselage of the bomber was ahead of us. A beam shot. At the last minute the enemy realized we were hostile and attempted to turn away, but it was too late. I tightened the turn a little to set the dot of my electric gunsight ahead of the bomber to allow for the correct deflection, and pressed the button. A stream of 20-mm. and 303 bullets poured from the nose of the Mossie as I tightened the turn a little more to keep my sights on the now rapidly-closing target. I had started firing at about 400 yards and now at 100 yards with the He177 looking as big as a house, a stream of flame and smoke appeared below the nose of the aircraft. It reared up like a wounded animal, then winged over on its back and dived vertically into the ground. The explosion when it hit was like an oil tank blowing up, a huge ball of red flame and clouds of thick oily smoke.

"My God," was all I could say. It happened so fast that none of the wretched crew had time to bale out. There was no time for pity. We now had our work cut out to get away. Back down to the deck we dived at 300 m.p.h., streaking triumphantly for home. A few miles from Châteaudun as we skimmed over the fields we saw a young man and girl run out of a house and wave wildly to us. They had probably seen the fight and could certainly see the funeral pall of smoke, so our victory had gladdened the hearts of two people of subjugated France.

Three and a half hours after take-off we landed at Lasham. A few hours later Sticks and I were quaffing a beer in the bar at Mongewell recounting our victory to the other members of the staff. My film from the cine-camera synchronized with our guns had been processed. Embry asked to see it, so we all trooped into one of the conference-rooms where the confirmation of our combat was shown on the screen. I now felt that I had proven the value of daylight intruding to the Boss and the Group as a whole and was looking forward to more trips in the future. It was so different from night-fighting, but I found it equally if not more satisfying and exciting.

A week later, on March 12, Sticks and I set off again. This time we intended to range farther afield, down towards Toulouse. But we ran into trouble at the start. Diving down to the deck after crossing the French coast near Bayeux, I thought I saw a flash and heard a faint ping. I asked Sticks about it but he had not seen or heard anything. Everything seemed O.K. and so for a moment I forgot it. But soon I noticed that the oil temperature of the starboard engine had risen alarmingly. As I watched, the needle climbed towards the danger point. Something was seriously wrong and I asked Sticks to work out a course for home quickly. I swung our aircraft round in the general direction of England. I switched off the faulty engine and continued on one. Our Mossie flew quite happily on the port engine alone. Forty-five minutes later we were back on the ground at Lasham. We found an oil-line had been fractured by a bullet and the dark fluid was leaking. A sharpshooting German soldier had evidently taken a pot-shot at us. Why the engine didn't catch fire I don't know, because much of the oil spilled over the hot manifold and exhaust stacks. Luck was with us again!

Two days later Jacko and I went to London to attend an investiture. We received from the King the gongs we had won some months previously, a bar to the D.F.C. for Jacko and a bar to the D.S.O. and the second bar to the D.F.C. for me. In London we met Jacko's parents and Joan and my father who had invitations to attend. There was a large throng of guests at the Palace in addition to the members of the three Services. Some civilians were also to be decorated. Our families went with the other guests into the large hall used for such occasions, while Jacko and I followed an equerry into an anteroom, where all the medallists were briefed on how to approach the King when our names were called.

Despite previous visits to Buckingham House I was nervous as I took my place in the line. A few minutes later as the band played the National Anthem, King George VI entered the crowded hall with his equerries. The recipients of the highest orders were called forward first. Slowly the line moved on. I looked among the guests for Joan and my father. I spotted them and contrived a wink! My name was called and I marched to a position in front of the King, turned left, bowed, and advanced to him. He was in the uniform of an Admiral of the Fleet. He reached behind with his left hand to a cushion held by an aide on which the decorations were laid. First he handed me the D.S.O. bar on its piece of blue and red ribbon, at the same time thanking me for what I had done and wishing me continuing success. As he quietly talked he reached back again for the D.F.C. bar, but out of the corner of my eye I could see that the cross of the decoration itself lay on the cushion. Someone had goofed! For a second he frowned. Then smiling he said there must have been a mistake. I nervously wondered what would happen. The King held a short whispered conversation with the aide, then turned to me and asked if I would wait on one side. I was to be called up again at the end of the investiture for the correct decoration. About an hour later my name was called again. By this time the King must have shaken hands with, and spoken to nearly 200 people, but he was still able to smile and make a friendly crack about the incident as he handed me the bar to the D.F.C. Apparently even in high places things sometimes go awry. Although it was a proud moment to be received by the King, I found it much harder on my nerves to stand in front of the great man in a crowded hall than fight the enemy.

28

THE hope that the Red Army with the aid of Allied air forces would be able to defeat the Germans died when the politicians decided to insist on unconditional surrender. For Hitler's gang it became a war to the death. Angry messages from Stalin pleaded for an invasion to relieve the pressure on the Eastern Front, where the fanatical Germans in stubborn retreat were inflicting terrible casualties on the Russian Army. By March, 1944, Allied plans for the invasion were nearly complete. All that was needed was the final build-up of troops and equipment and the right weather. Our air attacks on occupied Europe and Germany continued with greater emphasis on transport and communication with the aim of crippling the German defence against the Allied landings.

Work of 2 Group Staff became more demanding as D-Day drew closer and I had to reduce the number of my operational trips. New and better methods were developed to improve the efficiency of the squadrons at night strafing. The early attacks against the airfields in Northern France had shown that the crews could find the targets but that the results of low-level shooting and bombing in darkness were usually poor. The crews had to concentrate on not flying into the ground as they dived towards their targets for they could not be sure of the height of any obstacle that might be in their flight path. From a lot of thought on this problem by the staff and the squadrons, there emerged the 4.5 inch parachute flare. The idea was that once a Mossie reached the target area or spotted movement such as the dim running lights of German army road transport, the crew would release one of these flares. If dropped from 3,000 to 4,000 feet the flare would take a couple of minutes or so to float to earth, and during this time it illuminated the countryside. The Mossie crew could now see the target and had time to carry out one, and sometimes two, good attacks before the flare petered out. Stocks of these flares and suitable racks for their carriage were supplied to the Group and soon they were being used as a matter of course with much improved results. Later, to increase the illumination, clusters of these pyrotechnics were dropped.

During the remainder of March and April I flew four more day-intruder missions. I also took part in a low-level day bombing raid on the marshalling yard at Mantes Gassicourt, on the Seine west of Paris. Three of the intruder trips were with Sticks and one with the Group Navigation Officer, Squadron Leader Robertson. I also flew with Robertson on the bombing attack. The intruder flights increased my score of enemy aircraft destroyed to twenty-seven. On two of these sorties, both over Denmark, once flying with Sticks and once with Robbie, we scored double victories.

The raid on the important rail yard at Mantes Gassicourt was my first attempt at low-level bombing. Being the "sprog" (new boy at the game) I flew as "tail-end-Charlie" of a squadron of thirteen Mossies which attacked the target in pairs at intervals of a few minutes. By the time Robbie and I arrived the flak was really stirred up and there was no doubt in my mind that the dear old Hun was most displeased! It was the first time I had seen him use heavy 88-mm. A.A. guns at low level over land. The gunners were firing them almost horizontally in an effort to knock us down as we closely hugged the contours of the ground. The fact that some of their shells burst near French dwellings didn't seem to worry them. Apart from the flak, the trip was uneventful. Our bombs were delayed action so we didn't dawdle to see them burst. We left the flak-happy area in a hurry and were lucky to be unscathed. Most of the other crews taking part had run into little opposition because they had gained complete surprise. It was on number thirteen (sucker Braham) that the enemy vented his wrath!

It is worth telling the story of one of the intruder victories just mentioned, because it caused me subconsciously to become dangerously over-confident. It was in fact probably indirectly responsible for my ultimate defeat. When I started day intruding I made up my mind that if possible I would give single-seat fighters a wide berth because of their superior performance over the Mosquito and also because they usually operated in twos or larger formations. On this occasion, near Poitiers, we were cruising along looking for trouble. We spotted a German lorry on a secondary road and prepared for an attack. As we started into a shallow dive, Sticks drew my attention to a single aircraft approaching nearly head on a mile or so away. This was better meat! We pulled out of the dive, now ignoring the German vehicle, and watched the approach of the aircraft. At first I thought it was an American Thunderbolt. These fighters also ranged deep into enemy territory, but usually in large groups. This machine was alone. I was taking no chances so quickly manœuvred into the best position I could. Then I recognized the aircraft as a FW190 with a long-range underslung fuel tank. Should I run for it or fight? I didn't think I could outrun him and as the saliva in my mouth dried up with fear, I decided the only thing was to fight.

The 190 spotted me at about the same time as I recognized him. He turned sharply to get in behind me. Sticks and I knew that if he got there we were as good as finished. Pulling hard back on the control column, I found I could just keep him from getting his sights on our Mossie. Then I remembered that if the engine cooling flaps were lowered they would have the effect of tightening my turn further. For a few seconds which seemed a lifetime he chased me in an ever-tightening circle. My speed fell off from 280 m.p.h. to 250 m.p.h. Now to break the deadlock. I opened the engine cooling flaps and found that we were beginning to out-turn him. Gradually with the speed at just over 200 m.p.h. I got on to his tail. He saw the danger and suddenly flicked out of the turn and headed south on the deck at full speed. We had beaten him. At full throttle we soon reached 300 m.p.h., high-tailing it after him and wondering if we could catch him. Sticks was worried that our fuel was getting low, but to hell with it, we couldn't let the FW get away without at least a crack at him. We barely missed trees and dwellings but I could see that we were slowly ever so slowly, gaining on him. I knew that if we didn't get him in the next few minutes our petrol would run out before we got home. At 600 yards, I put my sights on the fleeing FW and fired a short, hopeful burst. No good, I could see my shells sending up fountains of earth as they hit the ground behind his tail. Curse it, I must get closer. Despite Sticks's warning about our fuel, I was now determined to get this fighter regardless of cost. Perhaps he thought he could out-run us. He was taking no evasive action. At 400 yards I fired another and much longer burst. It worked. There was a flash of flame as our shells hit his underslung tank. His port wing dropped and he cartwheeled in flames as he struck a tree and was scattered in pieces across a couple of fields. As we flashed over the crash one of his undercarriage wheels sailed through the air close by our Mossie, thrown up by the force of the impact.

Victoriously we set course for home, nursing our Mossie along to get the last drop of fuel out of her. We landed at Ford with our tanks nearly empty. We had out-fought the vaunted FW190 and at the time this was uppermost in my thoughts. The very obvious fact that the enemy pilot was inexperienced was lost to me then. I had plenty of time to realize it later.

Many of these intruder flights were flown in aircraft of 305 Polish Squadron, commanded by Wing Commander Konapaseck. One of the Flights of this squadron was completely Polish and the other partly British, with Squadron Leader Mike Herrick, a New Zealander, as Flight Commander. Flying with Sticks or Robbie I had been fortunate to score several victories in their aircraft. They celebrated our good luck with an impromptu party and presented me with the beautiful silver and enamel squadron badge, making me an honorary member of the unit. I am still proud to have this badge and its certificate, number 809.

My staff work and flights against the enemy left little time for visits to Joan in Leicester. When I wangled a day or two off I always seemed to want to rush back to my comrades and the war. The longer the war lasted, the greater my desire to take a more active part. Even though my stays at home were rarely of more than forty-eight hours I am sorry to admit that my young children and the seemingly unimportant domestic problems were an aggravation, often leading to heated arguments. Chief of these was about the bringing up of the children. My views often clashed with those of my long-suffering parents-in-law, with poor Joan many times herself in the middle trying to make the peace between us. Fortunately for me, she was full of understanding, knowing me better than I knew myself. At the time she could not convince me that my irritability and unreasonable attitude were due to fatigue. But it was fatigue which in a perverse sort of way was driving me relentlessly on to take foolish and unnecessary risks in a mad desire to get at the enemy again and again.

On one of these visits Joan showed me an article in a Leicester newspaper saying that Johnnie Johnson and I were level pegging with twenty-seven kills each and that we were the top two fighter aces in Britain actively engaged on operations. This was as amusing to me as I am sure it was to Johnnie, particularly as the local factory workers were said to be running a book on which of us would be the final victor! Much was made of the fact that Johnson hailed from near-by Melton Mowbray and that Leicester was my adopted home. The idea the public seemed to have that we were in competition to be leading fighter ace was nonsense. I could not hope to compete with Johnson even if I had wished. Our roles were completely different. He was one of the greatest day-fighter wing leaders of all time. He was seeking out the enemy FW190s and Me109s with his wing of Canadian Spitfires and winning air superiority over his area of operations. Apart from being the most experienced fighter of them all he was also the most successful individually. My success had been largely at night and only recently by day. Accompanied by various AI operators or navigators my job had been mainly lone-wolf hunting and harassing the Hun wherever we could find him. Nevertheless, I offer apologies to those carefree gamblers in Leicester who lost bets on my account. If nothing else it was most flattering.

After flying intruder missions over France and Denmark, I decided that Denmark was my happy hunting ground. The lengthy flights over the sea made navigation more demanding but the rewards were greater and more varied. Also there was less chance of being detected crossing the lightly-defended Danish coastline. In Denmark and Norway there were many Luftwaffe operational squadrons resting and refitting after fighting on the east or west fronts, and a few training aircraft. All were ideal game for the intruder. I thought of Norway as a hunting ground for the future.

During May, 1944, I could only fly two trips, both to Denmark. One was with Sticks, the other with Flight Lieutenant Don Walsh, a navigator on our staff. He had recently completed a successful tour in 2 Group's Mitchells. Like Robbie, Don had heard how interesting intruding could be and had requested to go along with me on one of these operations.

Sticks could not always get away with me without disrupting routine, so he did not object when I flew occasionally with another navigator.

On our first trip Don and I were lucky. We shot down a JU88 in flames near the beautiful cathedral city of Roskilde, west of Copenhagen. It looked as though the trip was going to be uneventful. We saw nothing on the way out, but just after we turned for home, Don spotted an aircraft flying below the cloud a few thousand feet above. We tried to approach him unseen by flying close to the lush Danish countryside until the last minute. Then with throttles wide open, we pulled up into a climbing turn to get behind him. The crew must have seen us for the 88 headed for near-by cloud cover. Just as he was disappearing into a patch of the wispy shelter, I fired a burst at a range of nearly half a mile, hoping to nail him before he vanished. I missed.

Luckily for us the cloud was patchy and it wasn't too hard to follow him through the feathery stuff as we closed in. In desperation his rear gunners fired long bursts at us. But their shooting was wild and caused no real concern. With the range closing rapidly, I fired three more short bursts each time he popped out of a patch of cloud. On the last burst, with bits flying off his aircraft, he disappeared momentarily into thicker cloud, and for a moment we thought he had got away. Suddenly, breaking into the clear again we saw him hit the ground and explode against the side of a farmhouse. Don was now thoroughly convinced that intruding was the game, but we could not know that we were to fly together only once more and that journey's end would be a prison camp in Germany.

While I was gallivanting around Europe in my Mossie, the work of the Group's night staff fell largely on Rufus Riseley. He was forbidden to fly over enemy territory because he had been shot down over France. With the help of the French Underground, he evaded capture and by devious means

231

returned to Britain with a lot of valuable information about the V1 sites. For his courage and skill in evading the enemy he was awarded the D.S.O. He was disappointed that he couldn't fly himself, but never raised objections to my frequent absences. When I did find myself behind a desk there was always plenty to do.

Use of flares on the Mosquito had improved the Group's night attack capability, but there were still serious limitations. Only a few flares could be carried and many juicy road and rail targets were left only partly destroyed or damaged because the crews ran out of illumination before they could give the *coup de grâce*. As the main role of 2 Group for D-Day and after was night interdiction, something had to be done to increase the effectiveness of our attacks. So far, the four Mitchell Squadrons had been employed entirely on medium-level daylight bombing. Many a V1 site had been blasted by these aircraft. Why not use the Mitchells with their superior carrying capacity as pathfinders for our Mosquitoes? After much deliberation this plan was agreed to by Headquarters.

It was decided to send single Mitchells to patrol at between 3,000 and 5,000 feet over areas of France where several Mosquitoes were prowling. When a Mossie crew spotted what they thought was a target they called up the Mitchell and directed the pathfinder to the position. The very accurate electronic navigation fixing aid, G.E.E., was used by both Mitchells and Mosquitoes to ensure pin-pointing of positions. The Mosquitoes circled until the Mitchell arrived to launch flares at regular intervals. These lit up the area until the Mossie crew eliminated the target or ran out of bombs and ammunition.

Some opposition to the new role of the Mitchells was expected. The job was unspectacular since they were not directly striking at the enemy. Further, there was considerable risk. The Mitchell lacked the performance of the Mosquito and was vulnerable to marauding enemy night fighters. To

232

get the importance of the job across to the Mitchell crews, members of the Group Staff visited each of these squadrons to brief the crews in detail about the new role and to offer advice on German night-fighter tactics.

It was obvious that the crews were disappointed. This was understandable. They had done so well in more satisfying operations in daylight. In general they accepted the new task with good grace. But one of the squadrons, nearly all Dutchmen, aired their views very strongly. This squadron had a fine combat record and like most of our European allies fighting for the liberation of their countries, they hated the enemy even more bitterly than we did. Since they would not be killing the enemy themselves they felt the operation was a waste of time. At one stage while Sticks and I were briefing them we were openly booed. They seemed to think we were solely responsible for allotting them this unpopular task. Their behaviour made me lose my temper, and I am afraid some harsh words passed later between the gallant Dutch Squadron Commander and myself. Later in the day things cooled down a little and we parted on reasonably friendly terms. As the fates would have it, on one of the first of these night operations, two Mitchells were lost, both from the Dutch squadron. To make matters worse our intelligence confirmed that they were shot down by an R.A.F. night-fighter. It was a tragic mistake in identification. The night-fighter mistook the Mitchells for the rather similar Dornier bombers.

29

THE A.O.C. was most insistent that his approval should be obtained for each of my intruder trips and I had always obeyed his wishes. I planned a flight to Denmark with Sticks for May 12, 1944, and I approached Embry for permission a couple of evenings before in the mess bar. Perhaps I should have known better. He was obviously in a bad mood about something that had gone wrong. His answer was pretty short but he indicated that he would think about it. This noncommittal remark was disappointing because Sticks and I felt that our enterprise promised to be most successful. Anticipating a "go ahead", I made arrangements with 107 Squadron at Lasham to borrow one of their Mossies. Next morning I went to approach the Boss again. But when I saw Meg, his W.A.A.F. personal assistant, she said he was still in an ill-humour so I decided not to approach him. As I walked back to the office pondering, I stupidly convinced myself that as he hadn't categorically said "no", it would be all right for us to proceed. I didn't worry about it any more. Sticks and I set off on the afternoon of May 11 in the communication Oxford for the short flight to Lasham. Our Mosquito awaited us. There were no messages from Headquarters recalling us so we took off for West Raynham to refuel for our flight early next morning, happy in the thought that everything must be O.K.

Shortly after breakfast we were airborne on our way across 300 miles or so of North Sea to Denmark. Any worry I might have had about not having received the Old Man's full approval slipped into the background as we concentrated on flying and navigating. As the Jutland coast loomed up, I briefly hauled back on the controls to clear the sand-dunes and then we dropped back to tree-top height, speeding along towards Aalborg at the northern tip of Denmark, where there were a couple of German airfields. The weather began to deteriorate rapidly and the clouds were nearly on the deck, so we decided to give Aalborg a miss and head towards other airfields near Copenhagen.

We seemed to have achieved complete surprise but as we skimmed over the Kattegat just north of Samos Island a small fishing boat, which I thought was Danish, opened fire on us. The gunfire was inaccurate, but it was now obvious that the alarm would be passed to the Luftwaffe. There was adequate cloud cover ahead, however, so we continued to Copenhagen. We saw no signs of the enemy in the air there so we turned west and headed towards home. Crossing back over Jutland near Aarhus, we were dismayed to see the weather was rapidly clearing. We should be lucky to have any cloud cover at all soon. I warned Sticks to watch out for enemy fighters to our rear and we continued on our way, flying as low as I dared at 260 m.p.h. People on the ground dropped to their knees in terror as we suddenly appeared from nowhere and roared a few feet over their heads. We were sorry to frighten them but these tactics offered us the best chance of survival.

Half-way across Jutland, near Herning, Sticks spotted a FW190 about a mile ahead and above us. I didn't think he had seen us, so I manoeuvred to get on his tail. He'd seen us all right, and down on the deck he dived heading at full speed northwards. It was a trick we fell for. I went after him. Sticks shouted in warning "Look out! there's another blighter coming in on the left." I saw an Me109 diving at us from behind a small tuft of cloud. At between 200 and 300 yards he fired a long burst. We turned into him to present him with a more difficult shot. There was an ominous clatter as some of his shells hit us. The Me flew close over us and pulled up into the rapidly-disintegrating cloud. I thought he was positioning, for another attack and forgot the wily FW190 for a moment. The 109 was nowhere to be seen. He had either lost us as he pulled up into the cloud or had run out of ammunition.

A quick check of our aircraft revealed no serious damage and I could still see the FW a mile or so away, fleeing towards Aalborg. "Sticks, we're going to get him," I said and turned our aircraft at full speed. "Christ, Bob, break it off and let's get out of here, we're probably running into another trap." This advice I ignored. I was determined to get the FW190. My enemy was flying as low as we were, which made it impossible for us to attack him from beneath. Gradually we gained ground as I pushed the Mossie to the limit. At 600 yards dead astern I opened fire but my shells fell short, hitting the ground behind his tail. For a second we hit his prop-wash and the Mosquito wallowed dangerously. We felt a slight thud. "Christ, that was close, Bob, we damn near hit the ground." The tension in our aircraft was terrific. We were both sweating profusely, but we were getting closer to him all the time. Near Aalborg, over the narrow waterway of Limfjorden which separates the northern tip of Jutland from the rest of the peninsula the FW pulled up into a steep climb. We followed, firing a short burst from a few hundred yards. There were flashes on the rear part of the enemy's fuselage and pieces of tail-plane fell away. The FW flicked over in a stall diving towards us. We only had time for a quick squirt and there was another flash from the nose of the enemy. This might have been flame from his guns. The FW flashed quickly past us in a steep dive and as I started to turn after him Sticks jubilantly called, "He's dived into the mud of the river, Bob." "Good, now let's get out of here." The chase had taken longer than we bargained for and our fuel was dangerously low.

Satisfied with our victory we streaked south-westward for home, nursing the faithful old Mossie along. A few miles ahead we could see the western coastline of Jutland and seconds later we were flying near a small town on our way out over the coast. Suddenly all hell broke loose and the sky was full of red balls of tracer from an enemy light flak battery we hadn't noticed. I dodged from one side to the other, but the enemy gunners were shooting well. We heard bangs and crashes as shells and fragments struck our game Mossie.

It seemed an eternity until we were out of range and well over the sea. The engines hadn't been hit but, far worse, one or more of our fuel tanks had been holed. Sticks did some rapid calculations and reckoned we should be out of petrol, at the present rate, about 100 miles short of the English coast. It was not a pleasant thought but we couldn't give up yet. To get as much range as possible I switched off one engine. As the engine stopped and the prop feathered we noticed that the tips of the metal blades were curled under. "My God, Sticks, we must have touched the ground when we hit the FW's prop-wash during the chase." A few inches lower and it would have been curtains for us.

At a much reduced speed we flew our damaged Mossie towards England. At about 100 miles from our shores with the fuel gauges barely registering anything, we climbed slowly to 3,000 feet and called "Mayday" (request for help) on the radio distress frequency. This was just about the maximum range of the radios at that height, so it was comforting to hear faintly an English voice reply, telling us to keep transmitting and to give our position as accurately as we could. A few minutes later the same voice told us the Air Sea rescue launches were racing towards us.

In spite of this encouragement, the sea looked awfully big and we weren't absolutely sure of our position. The chances of being found seemed slim indeed. These grim thoughts were running through my head when Sticks nudged me and pointed to two specks on the horizon. Ships! I turned a few degrees off course to head for them and as we approached recognized them as trawlers, heading slowly on a southerly course one behind the other. If they were this close to England in daylight they must be ours. Rather than chance meeting a small Air Sea rescue boat over the expanses of the North Sea, we decided that our salvation lay in these trawlers.

A final check of the fuel gauges showed nothing left. I told Sticks I was going to ditch and asked him to jettison the top escape hatch and to tighten up his safety-straps. In a gently gliding turn, I steered to a point about a half a mile ahead of the leading ship. The sea had only a slight swell. As we glided lower and lower there was a sudden rush of air. The top hatch whipped back out of sight. At fifty feet I warned Sticks to brace himself. Tensely I eased the Mossie as gently as I could on to the water at 125 m.p.h. With a resounding crash we hit. I threw one hand up in front of my face to protect my head as we were thrown forward against the safety-straps. The other hand pulled the stick hard back into my stomach in an endeavour to stop our aircraft from nosing into the swell. There were several more crashes and splintering noises as our wooden bird slid along the surface of the unyielding sea, rapidly slowing to a stop.

All was now quiet except for the slopping of the water against the broken fuselage, and the breathing of two frightened human beings. We scrambled through the top hatch and sat on the cockpit combing to view our surroundings. The nose of the aircraft was under water, but we were still practically dry. The Mossie had broken in half just behind the wings and the tail section was slowly drifting away. Half a mile or so away a boat was being lowered from one of the trawlers. Thinking our part of the aircraft with the engines would sink, I suggested to Sticks that we each get in our one-man dinghy. I inflated mine, hoping to climb into it without getting too wet. At that precise moment a slight swell rocked our island and we fell off our perch into the sea. My Mae West jacket was already inflated, so I swam the few feet in the surprisingly warm water to my dinghy floating near-by. Getting into the thing was harder than I bargained for and I regretted never having practised dinghy drill in the past. After much struggling I got aboard, admittedly in the wrong end of the thing, but I was too tired to care. Looking round for Sticks I saw him bobbing up and down a few yards away. Apparently he had lost his dinghy. Laboriously I hand-paddled myself over to him and dragged him across my feet. He was looking pretty green, having swallowed large amounts of the North Sea. Two of us weighed down the single dinghy and we floated exhausted, patiently waiting for the boat rowing towards us.

Willing hands pulled us on board and wrapped us in blankets. We climbed at last on board the trawler and were greeted by a middle-aged R.N.R. lieutenant, the Captain. In each hand he held a glass full to the brim with rum. Gratefully I accepted mine and swallowed it. Immediately I wished I hadn't. It was so strong, I nearly fell over the side into the water again. Sticks barely had time to say "Thanks" as he rushed to the heads to be sick.

In our gratitude to our rescuers, we gave them nearly every item of equipment we had on us as souvenirs. In return they looked after us royally, but we had to convince them that they should water down their drinks somewhat. For some time the two trawlers, or to be more exact R.N. mine-sweepers, shot up the wreckage of our aircraft with their 20-mm. oerlikons to sink the two pieces. But though hit over and over again, our proud Mossie refused to be hurried to her grave. As we steamed towards England she was still defiant to the end. We hadn't been aboard the trawler long when the flotilla

Captain approached in a fast M.T.B. to take us off so that the mine-sweepers could get on with their job. We said a fond farewell to our rescuers and were soon speeding at thirty knots towards Grimsby, seventy miles away. About half-way there, we were intercepted by an R.A.F. Air Sea rescue launch and again we transferred ships. The R.A.F. crew loaned us civilian suits and we were checked over by a doctor as we sped along at a fast clip for the harbour.

At dusk we docked at Grimsby and were met by the C.O. of a near-by bomber station who drove us back to his airfield, where we were wined and dined in fine style. But we were worn out and not in the mood for much jollification. We soon slipped off to bed. For some time I couldn't sleep. I could foresee trouble when we returned to Mongewell in the morning. Facing an irate Embry was likely to be much more formidable than battling the Hun! After breakfast next day we were flown in an Oxford back to Benson in our borrowed civilian cloths. Our uniforms were still wet. At Mongewell Park I went straight to Meg's office and asked her to tell the A.O.C. that we were back. I heard her through the open door tell Embry that the wanderers had returned, but in the most peculiar garb, and would he like to see them? Faintly I heard him tell her that he would see me when I was properly dressed in uniform. By the sound of his voice I was for the high jump.

While changing in my room I started to shake. The reaction from our six hours' flight, the battle, the crash into the drink and the lucky rescue were all added to my dread of my interview with Embry. Sticks tried to assure me that all would be well, but I wasn't convinced. Meg ushered me into the Boss's office, a long, high-ceilinged room. The A.O.C. sat at his desk at the far end with David Atcherley beside him. The entry itself was demoralizing. It meant a long walk to a position in front of the desk. All the while the A.O.C.'s unblinking steel-grey eyes were boring into mine. His first question caught me by surprise. "How did you get on?" I had expected an immediate blast. I gave him a brief account of our adventures and he congratulated me on our success. Then very quietly he told me what he thought of my flying without his express permission. At no time did he raise his voice and probably because of this the effect of his words on me were all the more devastating. I had more respect for this man than for anyone I had ever met before and this made the ordeal even worse. The strain of operations and the feeling of having let him down nearly brought me to an emotional breakdown. Seeing my embarrassment David gave me a friendly smile to cheer me up. But it didn't work. Only with great difficulty could I hold back the tears as I mumbled my abject apologies. At the end of my dressing-down, Embry said: "The matter is now forgotten. Have a beer with me at lunch-time." I hurriedly excused myself and walked into the extensive grounds of Mongewell Park. There I wept un-ashamedly alone.

Later that evening when our troubles were forgotten, Rufus, Sticks, Jacko and I drove out to Clemmie's to celebrate our safe return. Our favourite pub was crowded, mainly with R.A.F. types, but with a smattering of "brown jobs" and civilians. Much beer was drunk and many "lines were shot" but the comradeship among us was something rarely seen in peacetime.

War with all its horrors can produce some good in man. It engenders the warm fellowship such as that which per-meated Clemmie's that evening. At one stage Sticks was in a corner surrounded by a crowd of eager listeners. From time to time as I looked over at the group I became aware of pecu-liar glances cast in my direction. I suspected something fishy was going on so I walked across the smoke-filled room and was in time to hear Sticks say: "You wouldn't believe it, but when I tried to get in his dinghy he pushed me off and even threatened to smack me over the knuckles with his pistol." The expression was so serious that his audience didn't know whether to believe him or not. When I applied the toe of my shoe to his rear end he plaintively cried, "Bob I was only trying to get these so-and-sos to buy me some more free beer." What the others thought as we made our way back to the bar together I don't know. Perhaps they thought I was a cad, or that Sticks was mad. It didn't matter. We enjoyed the fun of it all.

Towards the end of May a number of us on the staff were given a general briefing on the forthcoming D-Day operations. The magnitude of the task and the intricacy of the Allied planning amazed me. We were told that on no account were any of us to fly over enemy territory until the fateful day came. No chance was being taken that someone in the know would be captured and inadvertently, or under pressure, spill the beans. Other restrictions were also imposed. Our private mail, incoming and outgoing, was censored and leave severely restricted. The restrictions, onerous at the time, were necessary and they paid dividends. The Germans were kept guessing until too late as to the exact intentions of the Allies.

It was still dark when I awoke in my room at Mongewell Park in the early hours of June 6, 1944. Overhead the continuous muffled roar of heavily-laden aircraft could be heard. It must have been this noise that shattered my sleep. Leaping out of bed and slipping on some clothes I ran down the wide staircase of the old mansion out of the front door on to the lawn. In the moonlit sky with its scudding clouds, I could faintly make out the dark silhouettes of dozens of large aircraft heading southwards. They were British and American transport planes laden with airborne troops, the advance guard of the greatest military undertaking in history—the invasion of Europe. It was warm standing there on the dew-covered grass, but my flesh was covered with goose pimples. I was tremendously proud to be a small cog in this great Allied undertaking.

From the A.O.C. downwards, many of us at Group Head-quarters had planned to fly on D-Day. The A.O.C. in his personal Mosquito under the guise of "Wing Commander Smith" intended to fly a night ground attack mission. David Atcherley, whose arm was in a cast because of an accident in North Africa some months before, convinced me that he should come along as my navigator on a similar trip. If we were hit, our chances of baling out with David's arm in the cast were virtually nil. I admired this man's courage so much that I couldn't turn him down however great the risk. I found that almost the entire top echelon of 2 Group was going to have a bash at Jerry. This again pointed up the wonderful spirit of the Group. There were few, if any, Allied air forma-tions that could equal it.

David and I took off late in the evening from Lasham in a Mosquito of 613 Squadron. In addition to our normal gun armament of cannons and machine guns, we carried four 500-lb. bombs fitted with 11-second delayed action fuses. Our patrol area for the night was the road and rail network about fifty miles behind the Allied bridgehead. In company with dozens of other Mossies of the Group we hoped to dis-rupt the flow of German Army reinforcements to their em-battled front line on the shores of Normandy.

As we flew low out over the English Channel it was soon apparent that David wasn't too familiar with G.E.E., our navi-gational device. It was a clear moonlit night which enabled us to map-read over land, but the flight over the Channel was entirely by dead reckoning. But this wasn't too difficult. The German flak from Cherbourg and the Channel Islands directed at some higher-flying aircraft helped us to locate our entry point on the French coast near St. Malo. We headed eastwards towards Granville and still farther to Argentan, searching the ground for signs of German troop movements. The enemy's night road convoy discipline was excellent. Every advantage was taken of natural cover to hide his parked vehicles and on the sound of an approaching aircraft the dim convoy running lights were doused. For some time we searched the ground for something to shoot up, both impatient to have a go at the enemy on this important day in history. Trying to pick out camouflaged vehicles from a fast, low-flying aircraft is difficult enough by day. By night it is a real problem.

Near the town of Vire, David drew my attention to fires along one of the roads. Someone had already strafed a German column. O.K., we would now finish the job. We made out several vehicles. Down we went, my thumb pressed hard on the firing button and streams of 20-mm. shells and bullets sought billets in the column of vehicles lined up in confusion below. As we pulled out of the dive, at a few hundred feet, David unloaded our bombs to create further havoc. Climbing steeply away we could see more explosions and fires but because of the smoke we couldn't be sure exactly what further damage we had done. Our patrol time was nearly up. Satisfied with our contribution to the Group's efforts for the night we headed for home.

On the way, near Granville, we saw an aircraft approaching head on only a few hundred yards away. I banked hard to the left to avoid collision and thought I recognized an Me410 (a two-seat, long-range German fighter). I quickly turned back the other way after it before it flew out of my range of vision. Then I got a broadside view and recognized it as another Mosquito. We were disappointed it wasn't a Hun, but thankful we had recognized it as friendly in time. Again the enemy flak enabled us to steer clear of hot spots as we sought a safe place to cross out over the French coast. Three hours after take-off we were back on the ground at Lasham, David apologizing for his poor navigation. Who cared? It had been a fairly successful trip. Later we found that the Mossie we at first thought was an ME410 was in fact the C.O. of Lasham. He was just starting his patrol as we were leaving. The time and place coincided. At the last minute he had also seen us and at first had thought we were hostile. Luckily, neither of us were trigger-happy.

I didn't suspect then, of course, that my active part in the war was rapidly drawing to a close. I flew on only two more trips in June, both with Robbie, before Don Walsh and I were shot down and taken prisoner. The first was a night-strafing mission and the second a day-intruder over Denmark again. On the night mission we shot up a vehicle near Granville and bombed a bridge over a river. I suppose I was never intended to be a bomber pilot because I missed the bridge! On the intruder flight we were accompanied by another Mosquito, piloted by Mike Herrick and his Polish navigator. Mike had asked me many times in the past if he could fly with me because he shared my belief that intruding was valuable. As this was Mike's first trip of the kind he was allotted a shorter and easier flight than mine. At the Jutland coast we split. Mike headed north towards the airfields at Aalborg, and Robbie and I continued eastwards to Copenhagen. We saw no enemy aircraft but shot up three army vehicles and a train with good results. Poor old Mike ran out of luck. He and his navigator fell victim to the guns of a FW190 flown, as I found out many years later, by the same pilot who eventually shot me down—Robert Spreckels. The loss of this brave New Zealander and his navigator was a severe personal blow to me. Mike and I had been friends for many years and I felt a certain responsibility for his death. My convictions about the value of intruding had influenced him to take part in the operation. His end decided me that in future I would always fly these missions alone.

A day or so after this trip, I was summoned before the

A.O.C. He jumped from behind his desk when I entered and shook my hand, telling me that I had been awarded a second bar to my D.S.O. Wonderful news for me, but what about Sticks, my navigator, who had already won the D.F.C. and bar and D.F.M. flying with me? I felt he deserved the credit for our success more than I, as he had risked his life with me for so long. When I asked Embry if Sticks had also been decorated, he said he was sorry but there was no award for him yet. Perhaps something would come through later. Months later, when I was languishing as an unwilling guest of the Germans, I learned that a well-earned D.S.O. had been awarded to Sticks.

To celebrate my new decoration I was given a few days leave and spent them with Joan in Leicester. This was the last time I saw my family until the end of the war in May, 1945. At the end of the leave as I kissed my wife and the children goodbye before returning to Mongewell Park there was no premonition of disaster in my mind.

30

Now I switch back to the beginning of my story, which was the end of the war for Don Walsh, my Aussie navigator, and me. Don and I sat dejectedly in the hut at the German radar site wondering what future we had. Soon two Luftwaffe officers arrived to escort us by car to the near-by airfield at Esbjerg. Any ideas of escape we had were quickly banished when we saw the heavily-armed and alert German soldier who was also in the car. At the airfield we were searched and briefly questioned by a Luftwaffe colonel. Then we were put in cells in the guard-house.

In the solitude the full implications of our plight dawned on me. My main worry was that Joan wouldn't know for some time that I was alive. We should be posted as missing with all the dreaded uncertainty attached to that word. It felt like a bad dream but I knew I was wide awake. I remembered the recent German atrocity—the shooting of fifty P.O.W.s at Stalag Luft 3—and began to wonder if we should ever see our homes again. Perhaps Hitler, in the last hours of Germany's struggle, would destroy us all in his mad rage. This uncertainty haunted us until the end of the war.

After a restless night we were awakened to a poor breakfast of black sausages and told to get ready to move. Two German N.C.O.s armed with Schmeisser machine pistols escorted us to a vehicle in which we drove to the station to entrain for Frankfurt-on-Main, the principal Luftwaffe interrogation centre for Allied aircrews. The long, slow journey was made miserable by the many stops due to air-raid alarms. These halts annoyed our guards who seemed to hold us personally responsible for all the bomb damage in Germany. Civilians and soldiers shouted abuse at us. We were called "Luft-gangsters" and threatened with violence. During the night some drunken German soldiers tried to enter our compartment as the rest of the train was crowded. Our guards told them they couldn't sit with us. We were English swine. The soldiers got out of hand, trying to force their way in. One of them drew his bayonet. For the first time in my life my knees were knocking and I had to grab them so that my fright wouldn't be obvious to my captors. For a moment it seemed that our choice was to sit tight and be lynched by the infuriated mob, or to jump through the carriage door and be shot in the back by our guards. Then a young S.S. soldier in black battle-dress shouldered his way into the compartment and shouted an order. The effect was miraculous. They immediately dispersed. He sat next to us, to the discomfort of our guards, and looked us up and down with disdain as though to say, "Well, Englishmen, you can thank me for saving your worthless hides." Whatever his thoughts, we were grateful for his intervention, and impressed by the authority of Hitler's *élite*.

We spent a day and night on the train and were then put in a barbed-wire encampment on the outskirts of Frankfurt—the interrogation centre. Again we were stripped and searched and locked up in separate small cells. In each there was a wooden bed and a verminous straw mattress. We were kept at this centre for about two weeks, most of the time in solitary confinement. Every third or fourth day we were brought before Hauptmann Koch for interrogation. This clever, but very correct, intelligence officer had a vast amount of general data about my Service career in a file. Apparently the Germans obtained much useful information from British newspapers, radio reports and embassy letters from such neutral countries as Ireland, Portugal and Spain. It was in Frankfurt that I first saw the official citation for the second bar to my D.S.O. Koch brought a press cutting from an English paper to my cell saying, "Wing Commander, here is something you might like to keep. Your country thinks highly of you." With a glimmer of a smile he turned away and left me to my thoughts.

An officer reputed to be one of Goering's aides, Hauptmann Kaupisch, also visited us. He was pleasant and spoke good English. Obviously he was trying to pump us for information. He told us he was shortly returning to fly JU88 bombers against England and asked us to tell him how effective the British defences were! What was the best way to avoid our night-fighters and A.A.? What he expected us to divulge I don't know, but he seemed amused when I said his best bet was to remain as Goering's aide.

At one of the interrogations a young German Air Force officer was ushered into the room and was introduced by Koch. "Wing Commander, this is the pilot who shot you down, Lieutenant Spreckels. You were his forty-fifth victim." This might be a ruse to make me talk. Neither the German pilot nor I could speak each other's language, so anything said had to be interpreted by the ever-alert Koch. The Jerry pilot wore the Knight's Cross of the Iron Cross at his throat, one of German's highest decorations for bravery. He was about 5 ft. 8 in. and good-looking with dark brown hair. He seemed friendly and shook hands, saying he was glad neither of us had been hurt. From our very limited conversation I gathered that Spreckels had lost his parents during one of the R.A.F.'s heavy raids on Hamburg. But he was quick to point out that he held no malice towards me personally. "It is the war," he said. If this was the man who shot us down—and later I confirmed that he was—his chivalry in combat was all the more praise-worthy. He could easily have killed us both in revenge for his own sad loss.

Koch sent for tea and biscuits which were most welcome. Don and I had only been allowed a piece of black bread smeared lightly with margarine three times a day and a plate of watery cabbage soup at lunch-times. The sudden lack of food after the relatively good fare I was used to in wartime England caused me to black out if I sat up too quickly on my prison bed. During tea Spreckels and I continued a guarded conversation through Koch. When I was asked how I thought the war was progressing, I said I thought that Germany's position was hopeless. The Allies were now firmly based in Europe and the Red Army was at the borders of the Reich. It could only be a short time before these massive armies with their overwhelming air support joined hands. I don't know whether my remarks impressed my captors or not.

I couldn't help admiring this man Spreckels, who seemed so frank and friendly and in many ways like so many of my friends in the R.A.F. Before leaving he said he was shortly going to the Normandy front and would be up against our Spitfires. Apparently he hadn't met these in combat and he asked my views about their capabilities. I thought it best to profess ignorance. He shrugged and finally shaking hands I wished him luck, saying I would buy him a Scotch when we had won the war. At the time I never believed that one day we should write to each other as old friends, no longer enemies.

On my final interrogation by Koch, he took me for a walk in the limited grounds of the camp while he deliberated on the world situation in general. He stressed the threat of Bolshevism and said Germany was fighting a crusade to save the world from the Red hordes. He suggested that even at this late stage, Germany and Britain should settle their differences and join forces in this bid to save the Western world. The war, he argued, was the fault of world Jewry and our two countries should never have fought one another. Goebbels had said the same things many times so I wasn't impressed. In fact, I doubt whether this very intelligent individual believed them himself. Just before I returned to the solitude of my cell, he looked at me and said, "You are fair like a German and probably have Nordic blood. How would you like to fly again, but this time for Germany against Russia?" I had difficulty in controlling my laughter. He was quick to notice it and said, "No, on second thoughts, I think if we gave you a plane you would try to get home." How right he was!

Don and I were soon on another train with other P.O.W.s on the long trip to Stalag Luft 3 at Sagan, near Breslau, not far from the Polish border. Details of prison-camp life have been so well told in many excellent books that I shall gloss over this chapter of my life in a few paragraphs.

During my ten months' imprisonment I managed like thousands of others to overcome boredom by keeping fit and studying. Escaping wasn't strongly encouraged at this late stage of the war. The risks hardly merited the effort. The enemy had shown he was prepared to commit cold-blooded murder to stop such attempts. The shooting of fifty P.O.W.s in March, 1944, was a crime by the Gestapo and the S.S. It was not condoned by the Luftwaffe, who viewed it with as much abhorrence as ourselves.

The prisoners at Luft 3 were moved twice during my stay in Germany. The first move was in January, 1945, when the Russians advancing on Breslau threatened to over-run the camp. We were taken by forced marches and in cattle-trucks (eight horses or forty men) in bitterly cold weather. The Americans went to Luckenwalde, near Berlin, and the rest of us to an old Merchant Navy camp, Marlag Milag Nord, close to Bremen. The marches and the crowded train journey devoid of any comforts were about the most unpleasant experiences I encountered. We suffered no fatal casualties but most of us were frost-bitten. The second hike was much more leisurely. It was during the warm weather of April, 1945. The Germans hoped to move us into Denmark, where, if a line could be stabilized, we could be used as a bargaining counter. By this time most of the Nazi element among our guards had left, either to hide or fight. The rest were older men and as keen as ourselves to see the end of the uneven struggle. So the prisoners set the pace of the march, which never covered more than five kilometres a day. Eventually on May 2, we were over-run by troops of the British 11th Armoured Division near Lubeck, and started back on our way to freedom.

I was flown back to England via Brussels. Now 2 Group Headquarters was in the Belgian capital and I spent a gay twenty-four hours with old comrades before continuing home. I arrived at Headquarters in the same battledress tunic I had on when I was shot down, plus a pair of American GI khaki slacks and brown GI boots—a somewhat dirty and sloppy-looking officer. Air Vice-Marshal Embry greeted me as a prodigal son. He slapped me on the back and said, "Bob, you old so-and-so, you smell. How about a bath?" There was no doubt he was right. I had slept in the same clothes for some weeks without a proper wash. While I luxuriated in that wonderful bath, washing away for the last time the stink of prison life, a new uniform was laid out for me. Group Captain (later Air Vice-Marshal) David Atcherley kindly loaned a car and driver and with friends I toured the city's bright spots. It was soon clear that the lack of alcohol in prison camp had temporarily, at least, reduced my capacity. Braham disgraced himself by passing out in the early stages of the party.

Next day I was flown back to England in a Mosquito. It was strange to be flying again after so long, even as a passenger with a hangover! But the old urge to get into the air was still there. Some hours later I was knocking on the door of my wife's parents' home in Leicester, where a wonderful reunion with Joan and my two little boys awaited me. This was broken up within minutes of my arrival by a knock at the door. The local reporters wanted a story and pictures of my homecoming. Remembering the embarrassment some of the press cuttings had caused me during interrogation in January, I am afraid I wasn't very polite. I asked the reporters to leave. They couldn't understand my attitude. After all, here was a good general interest story, so they were very persistent. In the end in exasperation I forcibly ejected them from the house. Looking back I realize this was a bit drastic. They were only trying to do their job, but prison life had made me, as it made many others, bitter and unsure of myself. Living in close contact with thousands of other men under conditions of hardship and degradation made unimportant things achieve monumental proportions. A minor argument could easily flare up into a vicious exchange or lead at times to blows. In the latter stages of the war, the news we picked up from the B.B.C. over our secret radio receiver about strikes in munition plants and industrial unrest added to our bitterness. To P.O.W.s, strikes meant a lengthening of the war and more loneliness for us and our families. The mental marks left on me by prison days made me a difficult person to live with for a time. It was many years before I fully regained my confidence and could offer my family a normal, happy life. I am ever thankful to Joan for her wonderful forbearance during this difficult time. Many a wife would have thrown me over as a thoroughly bad type.

With the end of the war I was granted a permanent commission and my future seemed assured. The R.A.F., however, was changing rapidly and thousands of wartime air and groundcrew were returned to civilian life. To many of us who had been on continuous operations during the war, the peacetime Service was dull and empty. In March, 1946, in an unsettled state of mind, I resigned my commission and decided to try Colonial Police work in Tanganyika. But even before starting the new job and while I was still on demobilization leave, I knew I had made a mistake. Air Vice-Marshal Embry, now in charge of training for the R.A.F., enabled me to rejoin the Service. From then until May, 1952, a variety of staff and flying posts came my way. Most of them were concerned with the development of night-fighters, or as they are now called, all-weather fighters.

Sticks and Jacko also stayed in the Royal Air Force, but they were older than me and there wasn't much future for them in the flying branch so they transferred to other branches. Sticks became an ace G.C.I. controller. Jacko became an air-traffic specialist, so that in his confident way he still inspired pilots as he unerringly directed them in for a landing whatever the weather. These two fine men are still my close friends. Ross, the Canadian with whom I shared my first successes using AI at night, returned to Canada early in the war and I regret I have been unable to trace him. Don Walsh returned to civilian life in Australia a disillusioned man. His wife left him while he was a prisoner. My efforts to trace Spreckels immediately after the war failed because the Luftwaffe records were in a shambles, later news about him reached me in a most interesting way.

To me, post-war England was a depressing place to live in. Its people who had fought so long and bravely became apathetic. They expected everything to be normal again at once without any more effort on their part. Nobody seemed prepared for hard work, yet there was a continuous clamour for higher wages. To me it seemed that only hard work and sacrifice could put Britain on her feet again. Even the defeated Germans in their devastated land were showing the way to eradicate the scars of war through discipline and diligence. Joan and I discussed these problems many times and worried over the future for our children. Our family had now been increased by the birth of a third son. We decided that the answer was to emigrate to Australia or Canada. After much deliberation I accepted a commission in the Royal Canadian Air Force. At the time they were looking for experienced all-weather pilots to help build up the new R.C.A.F. Air Defence Command.

With many regrets and against the advice of most of my friends who thought I was throwing up an excellent future in the R.A.F., I again resigned and accepted the Canadian offer. In May, 1952, we sailed in the *Empress of Scotland* for Canada and a new life. In the R.C.A.F. my experience in fighter operations has been of some value, and I have obtained several staff and flying appointments in Eastern Canada. Joan and the children are happy. We live well and my problem of educating the kids has largely been solved.

In 1954 I was transferred to North Bay, 200 or so miles north of Toronto, to command a unit training aircrew in flying the Canadian all-weather jet fighter, the CF100. One day I received a letter from the German consul in Bath, England. The letter had travelled first to the Air Ministry in London, then to Air Force Headquarters, Ottawa, and finally to North Bay. The consul wrote that he had worked for a Herr Spreckels in Hamburg after the war and that Spreckels, whose address was enclosed, wanted to contact me. This was great news.

Since then, Robert Spreckels and I have been regular correspondents. From the details he has supplied there is no doubt that he was the pilot who shot down Don and me on June 25, 1944. Our correspondence brought to light many things of interest. It was Spreckels, too, who vanquished Mike Herrick on the fateful trip we flew over Denmark together when Mike was killed. Spreckels spoke highly of the gallant New Zealander and his Polish navigator who put up a brave fight before crashing to their deaths. The German also told us that the FW190 which Sticks and I fought on the trip when we ended in the North Sea was from his squadron at Aalborg, northern Denmark. So it seems that our paths were close several times during the months of May and June, 1944.

Robert Spreckels is now in the shipping business in Hamburg. In spite of world tension and hatreds, my very personal ex-enemy is now counted among my company of close friends. This experience shows that airmen of different lands can get along together. As I write the last few pages of this book fifteen years after the end of what we all hope was the last war, my family and I are sailing in the motor vessel *Italia* from Montreal to Le Havre. The R.C.A.F. has posted me to Paris with an appointment at SHAPE headquarters. More important to me, this ship with its friendly crew and passengers from many lands is bringing me back to Europe and a chance to meet Spreckels again. I owe him a whisky and soda.

Library of Congress Cataloging-in-Publication Data

Braham, J. R. D. (John Randall Daniel), 1920-
[Scramble!]
Night fighter / by J.R.D. Braham.
p.   cm. — Wings of war)
Originally published: Scramble! 1st American ed. New York : Norton, 1962.
ISBN 0-8094-9637-2 (trade). — ISBN 0-8094-9638-0 (library)
1. Braham, J. R. D. (John Randall Daniel), 1920- .
2. World War, 1939-1945—Aerial operations, British.
3. World War, 1939-1945—Personal narratives, British.
4. Great Britain. Royal Air Force—Biography.
5. Fighter pilots—Great Britain—Biography.
I. Title. II. Series.
D786.B67 1992   940.54'42'092—dc20 [B]   92-22253 CIP

Published by arrangement with Joan Helen Braham.

Cover photograph © Carl Purcell
Endpapers photograph © Rene Sheret/After Image

WINGS OF WAR

We didn't know it at the time, but German intelligence operatives were so deficient before World War II that they believed P.G. Wodehouse's bumbling, fictional characters to be accurate portrayals of British secret agents, and accepted as a sign of the nation's decadence the famous Oxford Union's resolution that young Englishmen would not die for their country.

In his beautifully written book, *Night Fighter*, Wing Commander J.R.D. Braham shows how very wrong the Germans were: The young British fliers proved themselves to be fierce warriors, merciless in battle. None were more so than Braham himself, whose savage aggressiveness and utter commitment to combat were to win him twenty-nine victories in the toughest of arenas, aerial night fighting—and to almost cost him his life.

The son of a Church of England vicar, Braham won his Royal Air Force wings in August 1938, four months after his eighteenth birthday. He received the fighter assignment he requested, but in the way of peacetime service procedure, he soon found himself flying a twin-engine Bristol Blenheim, a far cry from the nimble Hurricanes and Spitfires he coveted.

Even after the War had begun, Braham's squadron, No. 29, remained largely outside of the fray. They saw little action during the Battle of France or the Battle of Britain, and his frustration grew to the flash point. Relief came in the shape of the Bristol Beaufighter, which was equipped with airborne intercept radar. It was a much more sophisticated aircraft than the Blenheim, fast, long-ranged, and heavily armed.

At the controls of the Beaufighter, Braham became a relentless hunter, each night using radar to chase an elusive enemy through the cloudy skies until he could identify the air-craft visually. "What was ahead of me? Friend or foe? At about 150 yards I could make out the exhaust pattern and wing shape. It was a Heinkel," he writes of one encounter. "The smell of cordite filled the aircraft as I fired a long burst from all guns. He started to dive, with smoke belching out astern."

TIME LIFE BOOKS

TIME-LIFE BOOKS INC., ALEXANDRIA, VIRGINIA 22314

Victory followed victory in what became for Braham an addiction to war. He married a young woman who had the great wisdom to understand that Braham was totally consumed by combat, unable to be the father and husband he would otherwise have been. When the RAF began its area bombing of Germany, Braham would insert his Beaufighter in the midst of the British bomber streams to add German night fighters to his score. He sensed that he was battle fatigued when on one raid he found a Messerschmitt 110 and fired at point-blank range. "Then as we circled I saw in the light of the moon a parachute floating gently downwards. Something made my blood boil." Not until he began maneuvering to machine-gun the helpless parachutist did Braham break off his attack, realizing that he was poised to violate the strict code of chivalry that prevailed among pilots on both sides of the conflict.

Assigned to a staff position, he persisted with combat, and on June 25, 1944, less than three weeks after the Allied landing at Normandy, he took a borrowed wooden de Havilland Mosquito on a daylight mission to the German Baltic coast. There, he made a series of fatigue-induced mistakes and was shot down by an enemy pilot. He spent the rest of the war in a prison camp where he was forced to disengage from his obsession with combat.

Braham became the RAF's most decorated fighter pilot. In addition to his recognition by the British government—including the Distinguished Service Order and the Distinguished Flying Cross—he was awarded the Belgian Order of the Crown and Croix de Guerre in recognition of his leadership of Belgian air crews attached to his squadron.

After the War he devoted himself to his family, while still enjoying a brilliant military career—first in the RAF, and then in the Royal Canadian Air Force, where he refined radar interception techniques. In 1968 he retired from the RCAF and became a historian with the Canadian Department of Indian Affairs. Ironically, after surviving all of his dangerous combat missions, he fell prey to an inoperable brain tumor and died in 1974 at the age of fifty-three.

Walter J. Boyne